Making Autocracy Work

Can meaningful representation emerge in an authoritarian setting? If so, how, when, and why? *Making Autocracy Work* identifies the tradeoffs associated with representation in authoritarian environments and then tests the theory through a detailed inquiry into the dynamics of China's National People's Congress (NPC, the country's highest formal government institution). Rory Truex argues that the Chinese Communist Party (CCP) is engineering a system of "representation within bounds" in the NPC, encouraging deputies to reflect the needs of their constituents, but only for non-sensitive issues. This allows the regime to address citizen grievances while avoiding incendiary political activism. Data on NPC deputy backgrounds and behaviors are used to explore the nature of representation and incentives in this constrained system. The book challenges existing conceptions of representation, authoritarianism, and the future of the Chinese state. Consultative institutions like the NPC are key to making autocracy work.

Rory Truex is Assistant Professor of Politics and International Affairs at Princeton University. His research focuses on Chinese politics and authoritarian systems. His work has been published in top political science journals, including the *American Political Science Review*, *Comparative Political Studies*, and *The China Quarterly*, and featured in the *Wall Street Journal* and *The New York Times*. He is the founder of the Princeton in Asia Summer of Service program, which annually sends Princeton undergraduates to rural China to run an English immersion program for local students. He currently resides in Philadelphia.

Cambridge Studies in Comparative Politics

General Editor
Margaret Levi   *University of Washington, Seattle*

Assistant General Editors
Kathleen Thelen   *Massachusetts Institute of Technology*
Erik Wibbels   *Duke University*

Associate Editors
Robert H. Bates   *Harvard University*
Stephen Hanson   *University of Washington, Seattle*
Torben Iversen   *Harvard University*
Stathis Kalyvas   *Yale University*
Peter Lange   *Duke University*
Helen Milner   *Princeton University*
Frances Rosenbluth   *Yale University*
Susan Stokes   *Yale University*
Sidney Tarrow   *Cornell University*

Other Books in the Series
Christopher Adolph, *Bankers, Bureaucrats, and Central Bank Politics: The Myth of Neutrality*
Michael Albertus, *Autocracy and Redistribution: The Politics of Land Reform*
Ben W. Ansell, *From the Ballot to the Blackboard: The Redistributive Political Economy of Education*
Ben W. Ansell, David J. Samuels, *Inequality and Democratization: An Elite-Competition Approach*
Leonardo R. Arriola, *Multi-Ethnic Coalitions in Africa: Business Financing of Opposition Election Campaigns*
David Austen-Smith, Jeffry A. Frieden, Miriam A. Golden, Karl Ove Moene, and Adam Przeworski, eds., *Selected Works of Michael Wallerstein: The Political Economy of Inequality, Unions, and Social Democracy*
Andy Baker, *The Market and the Masses in Latin America: Policy Reform and Consumption in Liberalizing Economies*

Continued after the index

Making Autocracy Work

Representation and Responsiveness in Modern China

RORY TRUEX

CAMBRIDGE UNIVERSITY PRESS

CAMBRIDGE
UNIVERSITY PRESS

One Liberty Plaza, 20th Floor, New York, NY 10006, USA

Cambridge University Press is part of the University of Cambridge.

It furthers the University's mission by disseminating knowledge in the pursuit of education, learning, and research at the highest international levels of excellence.

www.cambridge.org
Information on this title: www.cambridge.org/9781107172432

© Rory Truex 2016

First published 2016

Printed in the United States of America by Sheridan Books, Inc.

A catalog record for this publication is available from the British Library.

ISBN 978-1-107-17243-2 Hardback
ISBN 978-1-316-62370-1 Paperback

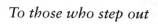

To those who step out

Contents

Figures

Tables

Acknowledgments

I have accumulated numerous intellectual debts in the process of writing this book. I am not sure I will ever be able to pay them off or pay them forward, but I suppose the best place to start is by saying thank you.

First and foremost, let me express my gratitude to my doctoral dissertation advisors – Thad Dunning, Susan Rose-Ackerman, Ken Scheve, and Lily Tsai. They were models of intellectual generosity, selflessly investing their time and energy into this project and my broader development as a scholar. I am fortunate to have benefited from their mentorship, and I think of them often as I work with my own students.

I would also like to thank my Yale professors and talented classmates, who contributed to this book on a daily basis with their insightful comments and questions. In particular, I have benefitted from the ideas of Kaeli Andersen, Peter Aronow, Erdem Aytac, Cameron Ballard-Rosa, Rob Blair, Natalia Bueno, Dan Butler, Allison Carnegie, Andres Castillo, Suparna Chaudhry, Seok-Ju Cho, Allan Dafoe, Alex Debs, Adam Dynes, Blake Emerson, German Feierherd, Nikhar Gaikwad, Adom Getachew, Petr Gocev, Joshua Goodman, Navid Hassanpour, Greg Huber, Anna Jurkeviks, Michael Kalin, Adria Lawrence, Malte Lierl, Ellen Lust, Itumeleng Makgetla, Lucy Martin, Daniel Masterson, David Mayhew, Gareth Nellis, William Nomikos, Erin Pineda, Celia Paris, Pia Raffler, Juan Rebolledo, Frances Rosenbluth, Steve Rosenzweig, Kevin Russell, Travis Pantin, Luis Schiumerini, Niloufer Siddiqui, Josh Simon, Jason Stearns, Sue Stokes, Qiuqing Tai, Dawn Teele, Guadalupe Tunon, Michael Weaver, Louis Wasser, Beth Wellman, Jessica Weiss, Steven Wilkinson, and Libby Wood. I could not have asked for a better place to grow as a scholar during those five years.

The book was finalized in my new institutional home, the Department of Politics and Woodrow Wilson School at Princeton University. I would like to thank several of my colleagues for their help with the transition to assistant professor life: Chris Achen, Mark Beissinger, Carles Boix, Brandice Canes-Wrone, Tom Christensen, Rafaela Dancygier, Christina Davis, Aaron Friedberg, Joanne Gowa, Matias Iaryczower, Kosuke Imai, Amaney Jamal, Melissa Lane, Nolan McCarty, Adam Meirowitz, Helen Milner, Andy Moravcsik, Grigo Pop-Eleches, Markus Prior, Jake Shapiro, Ali Valenzuela, Leonard Wantchekon, Omar Wasow, Jennifer Widner, Deborah Yashar, and Lynn White.

A number of scholars outside Yale and Princeton have generously offered their insights into Chinese politics and authoritarian systems. My gratitude goes out to Lisa Blaydes, Bruce Bueno de Mesquita, Eric Crahan, Bruce Dickson, Greg Distelhorst, Diana Fu, Jennifer Gandhi, Guy Grossman, Yue Hou, Kyle Jaros, Pierre Landry, Steven Levitsky, Adam Liff, Peter Lorentzen, Xiaobo Lu, Melanie Manion, Eddy Malesky, Dan Mattingly, Emerson Niou, Kevin O'Brien, Jean Oi, Steven Oliver, Jen Pan, Molly Roberts, Victor Shih, Alastair Smith, Milan Svolik, Yiqing Xu, Jeremy Wallace, Travis Warner, and Yuhua Wang for their insights in our discussions. A special thank you goes to my late friend and mentor George Downs. Katherine and I deeply miss your humor, kindness, and perspective.

Financial support for this research was provided by Yale University's Leitner Program in Political Economy, Council on East Asian Studies, and MacMillan Center for International and Area Studies, and Princeton University's general research funds. I am also fortunate to have been supported by the National Science Foundation Graduate Research Fellowship Program. I would also like to thank Robert Dreesen at Cambridge University Press for his continued support of the project and his advice throughout this process. Special thanks go to Kerry Ashford and William H. Stoddard for their excellent proofreading and general patience with my poor grasp of basic grammar.

Some debts extend to well before I began studying Chinese politics. Thank you to my parents, Richard and Sharon Truex, my father- and mother-in-law, Curtis Ensler and Kerry Ashford, my brothers and sister, Brendan, Colin, and Tessa Truex, and their spouses Eileen, Jenny, and Jorge, for all of their support. I am fortunate to come from about as strong a family as one gets, and any success I have is because of that fact. My biggest thank you goes to my wife, Katherine Ensler, who always lets me go to China when I need to, but always makes me want to come home sooner than planned. I am lucky to have her in my life.

Last, I would like to extend my gratitude to the dozens of friends and colleagues in China – who shall remain anonymous – who have taken extraordinary steps to contribute to this research project. Many of them actively step out of bounds and push for political change at great personal risk. I count those conversations as the most inspiring in my life. This book is dedicated to them.

1

Introduction

Tone Deaf?

The nearly 3,000 deputies to China's National People's Congress (NPC) are widely dismissed as little more than cronies of the Chinese Communist Party (CCP), brought to Beijing each year to warm seats and vote through the legislative initiatives of central leadership. To date, no single bill before the full NPC plenary session in March has ever been voted down, a pattern that has earned the parliament the familiar "rubber stamp" moniker among critics. Reform-minded citizens and scholars dismiss deputy policy proposals as "meaningless" and complain they never do anything "really important" (Personal Interview BJ006). National-level deputies are "elected" by provincial-level congresses, but all candidates first receive nominations from the CCP or other Party-led organizations. Strict limits on the ratio of candidates to seats effectively allow CCP leaders to pick and choose representatives (O'Brien 1988, 1990; Jiang 2003). The deputies themselves hold no campaigns, have little name recognition, and are consistently maligned as "tone-deaf" and unrepresentative of the population at large (Mu 2012). In a recent editorial, Minxin Pei puts it bluntly: "in a fundamental sense, the NPC has little connection with real Chinese society" (Pei 2010).

Conventional wisdom holds democracy to be a necessary condition for meaningful representation. Economic theories of representation assume that in the absence of elections, office holders will protect their own interests and neglect constituent preferences (Becker 1958; Barro 1973, p. 19). Manin (1997) identifies regular elections as one of his four principles of modern representative government. In designing the

U.S. House of Representatives, Madison (1788) believed biennial elections were needed for legislators to maintain "an intimate sympathy with the people." In this view, the supposed tone-deaf nature of the NPC is exactly what we should expect. Chinese representatives have little in the way of electoral accountability, and so there is no reason for them to develop meaningful constituent ties.

Many deputies work to defy their poor reputation. Shanghai deputy Zhu Guoping, for example, conducts investigations of different societal issues to inform her policy proposals. She organizes the local cadres of her area to visit hundreds of families in the neighborhood in order to be "crystal clear on changes in the needs of the people" (Xie 2009). Li Qingchang, a factory worker and deputy from Heilongjiang, established a team of three people to answer calls and pages from common citizens. He received 27,552 messages within seven years (Zhang and Wu 2008). In a recent statement to the press, deputy Wang Lin went so far as to argue that NPC deputies are more responsive than their Western counterparts:

Compared with parliamentary representatives in the West, who act on behalf of party group interest, the driving force behind the performance of our duties is the expectations of the people, it is a sacred responsibility given by the people. The expectations of the masses, this moves me, educates me, and pushes me to perform my responsibilities. (Liu 2009)

Wang's assertion is a little too bold – and reeks of Party propaganda – but it suggests we should at least pause before dismissing the possibility of authoritarian representation.

*

Many observers and citizens critique NPC deputies as tone-deaf and disconnected, but many deputies and insiders insist that they represent the interests of their constituents. This contrast yields the core questions for the book. Can meaningful representation arise in the authoritarian setting? If so, how, when, and why? What incentives do authoritarian representatives face, given the absence of true electoral accountability? And more broadly, how do representatives affect regime stability and governance outcomes?

The Purpose of a Parliament

The average authoritarian regime regularly convenes legislative meetings, at least nominally inviting other voices into the policy process

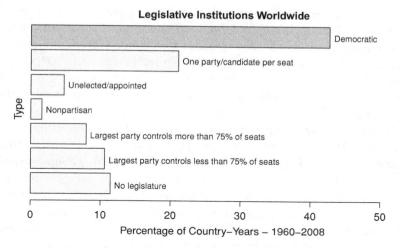

FIGURE 1.1 Variation in legislative institutions (1960–2008)

(Truex 2014). According to Svolik's (2012) recent data, depicted in Figure 1.1, around 46% of country-years worldwide since 1960 have been under authoritarian regimes with parliaments of some shape or form, compared with about 43% under democracy.[1] Historically, the modal legislator is just as likely to operate under the constraints of authoritarian rule as under the constraints of democratic accountability.

Recent empirical research suggests that authoritarian parliaments are more than just "window dressing" or "rubber stamps," as they are often maligned. Nondemocracies with nominally democratic institutions appear to be more stable than those without (Gandhi and Przeworski 2007). There is also evidence that legislatures are associated with higher levels of growth (Gandhi 2008; Wright 2008), although endogeneity concerns prevent a causal interpretation (Pepinsky 2014). Only certain types of regimes seem to need the parliamentary safety valve – those that lack natural resources, face organized opposition, and possess a weak coercive apparatus. The existence of parliaments seems to vary systematically with these factors (Gandhi and Przeworski 2007; Gandhi 2008; Magaloni 2008).

If authoritarian regimes create and manipulate parliaments to aid in their own survival (Gandhi 2008; Myerson 2008; Svolik 2009, 2012; Boix and Svolik 2013; Pepinsky 2014), we must look to their needs to

---

[1] The remaining 11% of country-years are authoritarian systems with no legislatures.

understand prospects for representation. Existing arguments identify two such needs. Proponents of the *cooptation* view argue that parliaments and accompanying elections allow regimes to identify and placate popular members of key opposition groups (Gandhi and Przeworski 2007; Gandhi 2008; Magaloni 2008; Malesky and Schuler 2010; Blaydes 2011). The *power-sharing* framework emphasizes the elite side of the story. Parliaments exist to help the dictator credibly commit to distributing resources to the rest of the ruling coalition (Myerson 2008; Svolik 2009, 2012; Blaydes 2011; Boix and Svolik 2013). This reduces monitoring costs, preserves the elite bargain and decreases the likelihood of coup attempts.

Neither the cooptation nor the power-sharing view makes strong predictions about the nature of representation, and as I explain in detail in Chapter 2, neither seems particularly well suited to the Chinese case. The CCP has proven remarkably sophisticated at the coercive side of the equation, so much so that nothing resembling an organized, unified opposition exists in Chinese society. NPC deputies are also widely considered to be regime loyalists, not malcontents (O'Brien 1994). With respect to power sharing, a number of senior leaders are members of the NPC, but most China scholars would agree that high-level CCP organs (namely the CCP Politburo and Politburo Standing Committee) are where internal bargaining really takes place.

These studies do well to draw our attention to authoritarian parliaments, but they often fail to account for the inner workings of actual parliaments. Existing micro-level research is richer in this regard and starts to reveal some interesting patterns in legislator behavior. Among other conclusions, O'Brien's seminal work on the NPC (O'Brien 1988, 1990, 1994; O'Brien and Li 1993) suggests that many deputies feel a sense of responsibility to serve as "remonstrators" for their constituents, reflecting local grievances upward to the central government. Manion's (2013, 2014) rich surveys show lower-level deputies in China speaking a new "language of representation" and engaging in pork-barrel politicking on behalf of their constituents. Similar findings are reported by Roman (2003) in his study of municipal-level representatives in Cuba. In Brazil, Desposato (2001) finds that deputies were more likely to offer dissenting votes when facing pressure from local elites and well-informed urban voters. In Vietnam, Malesky, Schuler and Tran (2012) randomly expose delegates to the Vietnamese National Assembly (VNA) to a transparency/publicity treatment by building websites that highlight their representative activities. The results suggest some "adverse effects of sunshine," as delegates receiving the treatment showed signs of conformist behavior.

Two general trends appear in this research tradition. First, despite the presence of nominal elections, delegates to authoritarian parliaments appear to feel primarily accountable to their respective regimes. Second, despite this top-down accountability, some delegates actively advocate the needs of their constituents and voice real criticism of government policies.

These studies offer a strong foundation on which to build. Theoretically, we need a framework that accounts for the incentives and trade-offs facing legislators and for the regimes and constituents they serve. Empirically, we have yet to conduct many of the core empirical analyses in the study of representation – tests of the associations between legislator behavior and policy outcomes; citizen preferences and legislator behavior; legislator behavior and career outcomes; and legislative membership and individual "returns to office." The core motivation of this book is to break new ground in all of these areas.

Representation within Bounds

My framework involves three types of actors: the Autocrat, the Deputy, and the Citizen. Chapter 2 examines the inner workings of their preferences and interactions with a formal model, but the summary in this chapter should prove sufficient for readers without an interest in the more technical derivation. The Autocrat represents the ruling regime, which I assume is trying to stay in power and has the capacity to set policy. The Citizen, which represents the population or segments within the population, has her own policy preferences, as well as the ability to engage in a protest or revolution that could potentially yield regime change. I will return to the role and preferences of the Deputy after considering some key tradeoffs facing the Autocrat.

The Information–Attention Tradeoff

In order to stay in power and avoid a costly revolution, the Autocrat must placate the Citizen and provide a minimal standard of welfare. The Autocrat's dilemma is that he has incomplete information about Citizen preferences and is uncertain how best to please the restive population. Without specific information revelation mechanisms, the Autocrat is "flying blind" and may unknowingly choose policies that endanger his own survival (Lorentzen 2011).

This is where the Deputy enters the picture and where representation can prove helpful to the regime. Parliamentary representatives reduce information uncertainty by fostering the revelation of citizen grievances, serving as "remonstrators" for the population (O'Brien 1994). I allow the Deputy to convey information about the Citizen's issue preferences using a simple message, facilitating a policy response by the Autocrat. In China, we observe this in the form of NPC deputy proposals, which annually convey thousands of policy demands to the central government, and hundreds of thousands of policy demands at lower levels in the People's Congress system. In Vietnam, the VNA's vigorous query sessions appear to play a similar informational role. In Morocco, the king has the right to create parliamentary fact-finding missions on specific issues. In Cuba, deputies to the National Assembly of People's Power (NAPP) serve on commissions that investigate societal issues (Roman 2003). These types of processes give regimes valuable insight into the needs and wants of their populations.

Representation brings informational benefits but carries certain risks. Debates in parliament have the capacity to spill over to the public discourse. In terms of the theory, I assume that conveying the message to the Autocrat also raises general Citizen interest in the issue at hand, which heightens the stakes of the policy decision. This is most problematic on issues of political reform, where the preferences of the Autocrat and the Citizen directly conflict, and where the Autocrat has little willingness to offer concessions. On these issues, loudmouth members of parliament have the potential to incite popular passions and give rise to unnecessary concessions or, worse, destabilizing collective action.

Engineering the Ideal Deputy

For authoritarian regimes trying to meet citizen demands and dampen pressures for political change, the ideal parliamentary representative exhibits a very distinct behavioral pattern. I call this concept "representation within bounds."

Concept Definition: Representation within Bounds

A behavioral pattern whereby authoritarian parliamentary representatives reflect the interests of their constituents on a broad range of issues, but remain reticent on sensitive issues core to the authoritarian state.

In terms of the theoretical framework, the ideal Deputy conveys Citizen preferences on a wide range of nonpolitical issues (what I refer to in Chapter 2 as "weak or no preference issues"), but keeps quiet about citizen demands for democratic reform ("strong preference issues"). This form of representation allows the Autocrat to learn Citizen preferences and respond accordingly, minimizing the potential for collective action.

In addition to identifying this pattern, the theory points to possible incentive structures that produce this special brand of representation. I consider two possible levers the Autocrat can manipulate to achieve the representation within bounds equilibrium. First, the Autocrat has the potential to influence the Deputy's empathy with the Citizen, the degree to which she shares the preferences of her constituents and internalizes their welfare. Everything else equal, deputies with higher levels of empathy will be more active in revealing citizen grievances. As such, the regime will devise ways to foster "selective empathy" – deputies who are politically aloof but otherwise in touch with popular sentiment. Second, the Autocrat can offer the Deputy private rents. From the perspective of the regime, rents or "returns to office" have uniformly positive effects on representative behavior, as they give the Deputy a vested interest in the survival of the political system. The theory predicts that the Deputy will enjoy substantial benefits in equilibrium, which can dampen any reformist impulses and encourage good behavior.

Theory Summary

To summarize, meaningful representation can and does arise in an authoritarian setting, in the absence of electoral accountability. It arises not from bottom-up citizen pressure, but from top-down accountability to a regime with informational needs. However, deputy activism on sensitive political issues can engender unwanted citizen attention, so regimes prefer their deputies to exhibit "representation within bounds." Engineering this behavioral pattern requires simultaneously fostering empathy with the citizenry on everyday issues, and loyalty to the regime on matters central to the nature of the authoritarian system.

This take on representation is different from other frameworks for understanding authoritarian parliaments. The quality of representation can be placed on a spectrum, shown in Figure 1.2. At the low end, deputies engage in minimal representation and do little to reflect the interests of their constituents on any issue. This appears to be the observable implication of the window-dressing view of authoritarian parliaments, as well as the power-sharing view (Myerson 2008; Svolik

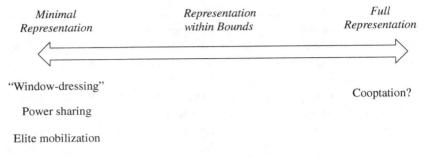

FIGURE 1.2 The spectrum of representation

2009, 2012; Blaydes 2011; Boix and Svolik 2013).[2] At the other end, deputies reflect the interests of their constituents on all issues, including political reform. This brand of full representation seems consistent with cooptation theory, which holds that parliaments are sounding boards for oppositional elements of society (Gandhi and Przeworski 2007; Gandhi 2008; Magaloni 2008; Malesky and Schuler 2010; Malesky, Schuler and Tran 2012). My theory, which focuses on the information–attention tradeoff, yields the unique representation within bounds prediction.

Research Overview

The remainder of the book is focused on testing the observable implications of the theory in the Chinese setting. Admittedly, China should not be considered a "typical case" on many dimensions (Gerring 2007; Seawright and Gerring 2008). It represents the world's largest population, second largest economy, and largest authoritarian country. Its National People's Congress and accompanying people's congresses at lower administrative levels constitute the largest legislative system in the world. There are 3,000 deputies at the national level alone.

While China's sheer size makes it generally unrepresentative of the broader population of authoritarian systems, it does possess aspects that are more typical. According to Svolik's classification (2012), the NPC can be considered a noncompetitive legislature, with "one party or candidate per seat."[3] This is the most common type of authoritarian parliament,

---

[2] A new perspective on China's People's Congress system, the "elite mobilization view" (described in Chapter 2), also suggests that deputies care little about their constituents, and simply echo the preferences of regime leadership (Lu and Liu 2015).

[3] This label is somewhat misleading, as NPC rules do require that the number of candidates exceed the number of seats, and non-Party members are permitted to run. However,

occurring in about 37% of authoritarian country-years. It is also classified as a civilian, one-party system, attributes that are found in 69% and
36% of authoritarian country-years, respectively (Svolik 2012).

My analytical goal is not to overturn the alternative theories, as this is
generally difficult to do with a single case. Instead, I will demonstrate that
my framework has more explanatory power for understanding China's
National People's Congress, a case of unusual importance. The hope is
that researchers of other authoritarian systems will find that my insights
resonate with their observations.

The empirical aspects of the project draw on a range of data gathered during several fieldwork trips in Beijing and other parts of China
from 2011 to 2015. I utilize original datasets of deputy backgrounds,
legislative behaviors, career outcomes, and financial connections; surveys
of Chinese netizens; interviews with deputies, citizens, financial experts,
and NPC insiders; and analyses of primary NPC documents. Combined,
these sources allow me to triangulate on the true dynamics of the parliament and overturn some common misconceptions about deputies and
their behavior.

There are real limitations to some of the information I have obtained.
This is an issue that confronts many China scholars, as well as other social
scientists working on sensitive issues in sensitive contexts. I will make a
point of highlighting those limitations in the interest of allowing readers
to develop their own assessments of the empirical inferences. Should the
NPC continue to liberalize, other researchers may be able to conduct better tests in the future. I try to highlight these research opportunities where
possible.

The remainder of the book is structured as follows. Chapter 2 begins
by articulating the theory more formally, using a simple extensive-form
game. The model illustrates the importance of information in authoritarian policy making, as well as the risks and rewards associated with
allowing parliamentary representation. It generates some helpful observable implications about the characteristics of a stable authoritarian representative system and the nature of the ideal deputy. These implications
are summarized in Table 1.1. I also justify the core assumptions of the
framework and define "strong preference issues" in the Chinese case.

Part of the controversy surrounding the NPC stems from the fact that
there is relatively little understanding of the nature of the institution.

China's "democratic parties" are little more than subservient organizations of the CCP,
and for this reason the NPC is categorized as having one party or candidate per seat.

TABLE 1.1 *Observable implications and empirical tests*

Observable implication	Empirical test/source
1. An authoritarian regime will incorporate deputy proposals on weak or no preference issues into policy	– Analysis of proposals/responses from Hainan province – Analysis of citizen perceptions survey – Interviews with deputies/NPC staff
2. Deputies in stable authoritarian parliaments should exhibit "representation within bounds" behavior	– Analysis of deputy proposals and constituent preferences – Case study of deputy–elite linkages in Jiangxi province
3. Regimes will devise incentives to foster selective empathy	– Analysis of deputy career paths and performance – Analysis of deputy training materials
4. Regimes will reward deputies with rents to instill loyalty	– Analysis of returns to office for NPC-affiliated companies – Interviews with financial experts

Chapters 3 and 4 describe the representational and policy-making patterns in the parliament (Observable Implications 1 and 2), which prove consistent with the concept of representation within bounds.

The theory predicts that the CCP regime actually uses the parliament for information and incorporates deputy ideas into policy making. Chapter 3 provides a short assessment of the influence of deputy proposals. I randomly select a subset of opinions from Hainan's Provincial People's Congress and trace their influence through the system. At the national level, there are no hard data released explaining what happens to any individual proposal, but Hainan's equivalent provincial process is nearly fully transparent. Although not all proposals matter, the analysis shows that roughly half appear to exert a real influence on a policy outcome. Of course, we should be concerned about possible selection issues in relying solely on a single provincial case, especially one that is an outlier on the transparency dimension. As an additional test, I present survey experiments that probe the perceived influence of different types of NPC proposals. Citizens are generally optimistic about deputy influence on many nonpolitical issues, but skeptical about its ability to bring about democratic reforms. Deputy interviews confirm that the government exhibits responsiveness to their proposals, but only for nonsensitive issues. The chapter also includes some background information on the NPC's formal institutional role and deputy channels of influence.

Chapter 4 uses new data on deputy backgrounds and behavior to investigate whether NPC deputies are really tone-deaf and disconnected, as they are commonly maligned as being (Observable Implication 2). Beginning with Miller and Stokes (1963), numerous studies of the American system have evaluated the quality of representation through the metric of "preference congruence" – the degree to which legislator behavior aligns with constituent interests. I extend this classic research design to the Chinese setting to test the citizen–representative informational linkage. I find that deputies' policy proposals show congruence with the concerns of their geographic constituents on a range of nonpolitical issues. To rule out the criticism that deputies are simply echoing provincial elites, I investigate the relationship between elite statements and deputy proposals in Jiangxi province. Although a degree of elite mobilization likely occurs in the NPC, the majority of proposals show no discernible evidence of echoing behavior.

Chapter 4 closes with a discussion of the representational limits of the NPC, the lack of activism and influence on political reforms. My database of publicly available proposals shows that very few directly challenge the regime's core political interests in any way. Interviews with NPC insiders confirm this intuition and paint the deputies as agents of the CCP, not the people.

The latter half of the book investigates the incentive structures behind these representational patterns. A functioning system of representation within bounds requires authoritarian legislators to have empathy with the citizenry, but only on issues unrelated to the regime's core interests. Chapter 5 describes the two primary mechanisms through which the CCP promotes this special brand of constituent ties (Observable Implication 3). An analysis of career paths demonstrates that deputies are rewarded for their representative activities, but punished if they transgress certain boundaries. Documents from NPC training sessions shows that the CCP encourages deputies to espouse representational norms, while simultaneously fostering loyalty to the current political system.

The framework suggests a successful authoritarian regime also motivates representatives by giving them a vested financial interest in its survival. Chapter 6 tests for the presence of rents using data on the financial ties of NPC deputies (Observable Implication 4). Approximately 500 deputies in the 11th NPC (2008–2012) can be considered chairpersons, CEOs, or leaders of various companies. Within this group, around

50 deputies were CEOs of publicly listed firms that first gained representation in the 11th NPC. A weighted fixed-effect analysis suggests that a seat in the NPC is worth an additional 1.5–2 percentage points in returns and a 3–4 percentage point boost in operating profit margin in a given year (Truex 2014).[4] A seat signals competence and connections, which in turn foster investment and new business relationships. It is likely that this reputation boost and the associated returns to office are even higher for deputies from humbler backgrounds.

Combined, these incentive structures appear to produce the representational patterns we observe in Chapters 3 and 4. Chapter 7 explains how the CCP arrived at the current equilibrium. Since its inception in 1954, the NPC has been a tool of regime leadership. Consistent with the theory, the evolution of the NPC can be understood through the lens of the CCP's informational needs. When citizens have credibly demonstrated the revolutionary threat, as during the Democracy Wall and Tiananmen Square movements of the 1980s, representation in the body has been strengthened. When deputies have stepped out of bounds, the regime has reengineered the institution to rein them in. The vibrant but bounded NPC we observe today only really emerged in the post-Tiananmen period, the result of several vacillations between openness and repression.

Chapter 8 concludes by considering the generalizability of the representation within bounds framework beyond the Chinese case. After outlining the scope conditions of the argument, I show that emerging empirical research on Vietnam and Cuba suggests the presence of some of the dynamics observed in the NPC. I close with a speculative note on the future of the CCP and China's People's Congress system.

My Contribution

Those readers familiar with political science will note that the title of this book is a play on the title of Robert Putnam's canonical work, *Making Democracy Work: Civic Traditions in Modern Italy*. There is perhaps no book more influential in the field of comparative politics. Putnam (1994) examines variation in the performance of 20 regional governments in Italy in the 1970s, using a rich multimethod design to show that citizens'

---

[4] This chapter was published in article form as Truex, R. 2014. "The returns to office in a 'rubber stamp' parliament." *American Political Science Review* 108(2): 235–51.

associational life and civic engagement improve bureaucratic responsiveness. In a phrase, social capital makes democracy work.

I have chosen the title *Making Autocracy Work* not with the intention of addressing Putnam's arguments, but to shift the discourse about the nature of authoritarian government.[5] My hope is that readers see contributions in the following areas.

First and foremost, my goal is to argue that there is such a thing as authoritarian representation. Despite Madison's assertions to the contrary, it seems that representatives can develop an "intimate sympathy with the people" in the absence of frequent elections. My analysis in Chapter 4 suggests they convey the interests of their constituents on a wide range of nonpolitical issues. Representation follows a separate logic in the authoritarian setting – it occurs without free elections and campaigns and party competition – but that does not mean it is empty.

Second, the book offers several new empirical designs and findings on authoritarian representation. I have placed a premium on gathering original data on a range of outcomes in China's legislative system, which has allowed me to investigate some core relationships in the study of representation. I have found that authoritarian legislators demonstrate congruence with their constituents; that an authoritarian government actually incorporates legislator ideas into policy making; that there are hard career incentives fostering this limited representation; and that deputies seem to accrue financial benefits from their positions. To my knowledge, all of these analyses represent firsts in the field of authoritarian politics.

Third, the book offers theoretical and conceptual ideas that likely travel beyond the NPC. The key tradeoff is that representation brings regimes informational benefits but attention costs. Regimes must learn the grievances of the population, but too much discussion of irreconcilable political sensitivities only makes things worse. These ideas may extend beyond parliamentary representation to other public arenas where information is exchanged. China scholars have already suggested that the CCP regime may only partly constrain traditional and social media, perhaps in the interest of information revelation (King, Roberts and Pan 2013; Stockmann 2013; Lorentzen 2014). Lorentzen (2013) argues that protests may even play an informational role and enable responsive governance. These

---

[5] Note that autocracy strictly refers to a government where one person rules with absolute power. Contemporary China is not an autocracy, but an authoritarian regime. I have employed this title for stylistic reasons and to have symmetry with Putnam, not to place China in the autocracy category.

types of activities appear similarly bounded, with the government cracking down on political dissent but tolerating criticism on other issues.

Finally, the broader argument suggests that democracies do not have a monopoly on responsive governance. Authoritarian regimes are often depicted as power-maximizing, rent-seeking machines that buy and coerce their way into power (Boix 2003; Bueno de Mesquita et al. 2003, 2008; Acemoglu and Robinson 2006; Svolik 2013). Yet more than a few nondemocracies, China included, gather information from their citizens, provide public goods, and strive to maintain broad public support. Consultative institutions like the NPC appear key to making autocracy work.

2

A Theory of Authoritarian Representation

Miscalculating

On February 27, 1957, CCP Chairman Mao Zedong ushered in a brief period of openness for the newly consolidated communist state. His speech, entitled "On the Correct Handling of the Contradictions among the People," urged other CCP elites to "let a hundred flowers bloom; let a hundred schools of thought contend." Months before, Premier Zhou Enlai had articulated the need for a public voice in policy making, citing unrest in Eastern Europe:

The government needs criticism from its people ... Without this criticism the government will not be able to function as the people's democratic dictatorship. Thus the basis of a healthy government is lost ... We must learn from old mistakes, take all forms of healthy criticism, and do what we can to answer these criticisms.

Zhou's reasoning gained the support of Mao, who formally announced the plan in February. The goal was to rid the government of its "three evils" – bureaucratism, sectarianism, and subjectivism – by fostering vigorous societal debate (Doolin 1961; Goldman 1962; MacFarquhar 1974). More open discussion would be good for the Party, and foster unity and loyalty among those yet to embrace its rule.

Mao's call was initially met with suspicion among would-be reformers. After some reassurance, intellectuals, students, and members of nominal democratic opposition parties began speaking their minds. University campuses became centers of reformist campaigns. A group of Peking University students created a "Democracy Wall," pasting up posters lampooning CCP authority and Mao himself (Goldman 1962). Letters of criticism overwhelmed government and Party offices.

15

NPC deputies took a prominent role in the movement. They advocated for democratic reforms and an enhanced role for the parliament. Deputy Tan Tiwu demanded Party organs be made subservient committees under the authority of the NPC (O'Brien 1990). On June 10, 1957, professor and deputy Zhang Bosheng publicly lamented NPC's stunted role in the political system:

> The NPC is nothing but a mud idol, while all power is in the hands of the Party center. The NPC merely carries out the formality of raising hands and passing resolutions. In all these years, one has seldom seen an NPCSC member put forth an important motion . . . Is this not laughable? . . . The Party must be removed from its position of superiority to the NPC and the government, the government must be placed below the NPC, and the NPC must be made an organ of genuine power. (MacFarquhar 1960, pp. 108–9)[1]

Other prominent deputies threw similar barbs at CCP authority. Members of democratic parties demanded equal status in policy debates and knowledge of meeting agendas. Many called for free elections, campaigns, transparency and controls on CCP influence (O'Brien 1990).

After several weeks of unconstrained societal debate, CCP leadership began awakening to the possibility that things might be spiraling out of control. The 1957 NPC sessions, originally scheduled for June 3, were postponed to June 20, and then again for another week. The usual preparatory meetings took on a different tone, educating deputies on the importance of Party loyalty. The long-awaited annual session began as a lively affair but quieted sharply after only a few days. As O'Brien (1990) describes, "Tension increased and deputies who made comments in the morning retracted them in the afternoon . . . Deputies increasingly attacked other deputies who had criticized the Party during the early stages of the rectification campaign." Once-vocal reformist deputies engaged in self-criticism and begged forgiveness from the Party.

In the end, forgiveness was hard to come by. Dozens of "rightist" deputies, including Zhang Bosheng and Tan Tiwu, were removed from their positions following the annual meeting (O'Brien 1990). The well of criticism on university campuses dried up within days. Shortly thereafter, Mao launched his Anti-Rightist Campaign, a two-year crackdown that saw the political persecution of an estimated 500,000 citizens. This event also signaled the demise of the NPC under his rule (O'Brien 1990).

There remains some debate among historians and China scholars as to whether the Hundred Flowers Campaign was actually a means of tricking

---

[1] I discovered this passage in O'Brien (1990), but it was originally quoted in MacFarquhar (1960).

regime opponents into outing themselves and begetting their own persecution. Mao later claimed the movement "enticed the snakes out of their
lair." Some observers contend that the events of June and July 1957 were
far from planned, and more likely represent a strategic blunder than an
elaborate ruse. "In my opinion the evidence does not suggest that by calling the flowers to bloom, the Party intended to set a trap for critics," writes
historian Rene Goldman. "Rather the Party leaders discovered that opposition was wider than they had anticipated and that therefore to allow the
criticism to continue was hazardous" (Goldman 1962, p. 153).

*

The example above illustrates some of the key tradeoffs surrounding parliamentary representation in authoritarian environments, and open discussion more broadly. In launching the Hundred Flowers Campaign, Mao
nearly triggered his own downfall, allowing calls for political reform centered in the very parliament he had created only a few years before. The
campaign was originally conceived as providing feedback on Party initiatives, but the revelation of this information quickly spilled over to sensitive political issues and nearly engendered revolution. In this instance,
Mao's blunder was not a lack of information, but that he (temporar-
ily) allowed very public agitation for regime change. He allowed activist
deputies to take their representative responsibilities too far, which further
emboldened activist citizens.

This chapter uses extensive-form games to explore the nature of these
dilemmas, why authoritarian regimes have an interest in promoting parliamentary representation, and the costs associated with doing so. Without knowledge of citizen grievances, regimes may unknowingly choose
policies that endanger their own survival (Lorentzen 2011). Representatives in parliament can serve as remonstrators for their constituents
and facilitate more responsive governance (O'Brien 1994; Manion 2014,
forthcoming). However, conveying this information raises public interest in policy issues, which can prove dangerous if opinion runs against
the political interests of the regime. Successful regimes must avoid the
twin dilemmas suggested above – they must generate information on the
citizenry, but they cannot allow their parliaments to become hotbeds of
political reform.

The remainder of the chapter is structured as follows. The next section
explains the problem of information with an extensive-form game, and
the following section presents an extension that allows for parliamentary representation. After exploring the plausibility of the key assumptions in the Chinese case, I articulate four observable implications relating
to deputy behavior and the incentive structures in a stable authoritarian

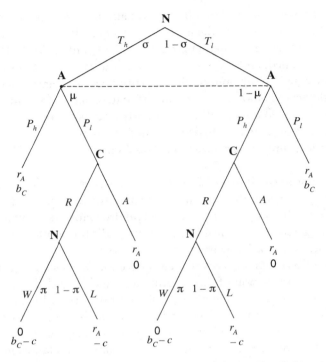

FIGURE 2.1 Authoritarian policy making with incomplete information

parliament. The chapter closes with a note on how the theory compares with existing frameworks.

The Problem of Information

A lack of information about citizen preferences can lead to suboptimal policy making, or worse, engender instability. Without firm knowledge of public opinion and other grievances, authoritarian policy making is a constant gamble. Ruling regimes must set subsidies, build roads, provide vaccinations, distribute funds, and make hundreds of other complex policy decisions, all the while hoping the net result is good enough to please an ever-changing citizenry and stay in power (Lorentzen 2011).

First, consider an idealized version of policy making under incomplete information, depicted in Figure 2.1. This extensive-form game illustrates the basic informational dilemma facing an authoritarian regime. It builds off other frameworks for understanding authoritarian politics (Boix 2003; Acemoglu and Robinson 2006; Gandhi 2008; Svolik 2012), allowing for uncertainty over citizen preferences (Gilligan and Krehbiel 1990; Krehbiel 1992) and the possibility of representation.

There are two players, the "Autocrat" A and the "Citizen" C.[2] Here I use the term "Autocrat" to capture the authoritarian regime itself, not a single leader or actor within the regime. The Autocrat's only move is to set a policy $P \in (P_h, P_l)$. There are two possible Citizen types, $T \in (T_h, T_l)$, chosen by Nature N at the beginning of the game with probability $(\sigma, 1 - \sigma)$. For simplicity, let $\sigma \geq 0.5$, meaning that T_l is never more likely than T_h. The two types correspond to Citizen preferences. If T_h is drawn, the Citizen prefers P_h, and if T_l is drawn, she prefers P_l. The Citizen receives payoff $b_C > 0$ if her favored policy is implemented, and 0 otherwise.

For now, assume the Autocrat has no policy preferences himself and is solely concerned with staying in power, which brings some rent $r_A > 0$. His main issue is uncertainty over $T \in (T_h, T_l)$ – choosing P incorrectly may engender instability. If the Citizen observes her less favored policy, she has the option of Revolution R or Acquiescing A. Acquiescing entails accepting the status quo payoff of 0. Choosing Revolution brings the Citizen a cost c but succeeds (depicted by W in the game tree) with probability π. Success allows the Citizen to implement her favored policy and enjoy the policy benefit b_C. The Autocrat is removed from office and loses his rents r_A.

We can find equilibria using the Perfect Bayesian Equilibrium solution concept.[3] Let μ correspond to the probability the Autocrat places on his leftmost decision node, the probability of the T_h type.

There are two possible pure strategy equilibria, whose proofs are relegated to the Technical Appendix for this chapter.[4] The first is the Stable Nonresponsive equilibrium, which occurs when $\pi < \frac{c}{b_C}$:

$$E1.1 = \begin{cases} s_A = P_h, & \mu = \sigma \\ s_C = (A, A). \end{cases} \qquad \text{(Stable Nonresponsive)}$$

---

[2] I adopt the convention of referring to the Autocrat as male and the Citizen as female. This is solely for the purposes of clarity and is not intended to confer gender on the actors in any way.

[3] At each stage, the relevant player's strategy should be sequentially rational given his/her beliefs and the optimal strategy of the other player, and all beliefs must be derived via Bayes' rule and the prior distribution of the state of the world, $(\sigma, 1 - \sigma)$.

[4] Mixed strategy equilibria are also possible when the Citizen's indifference condition is met, $\pi = \frac{c}{b_C}$. I will forego discussion of these equilibria in the interest of simplicity, and I will adopt the convention that the Citizen errs on the side of revolution R when indifferent between the two.

In words, this strategy set says that the Autocrat chooses policy P_h, and the Citizen chooses to Acquiesce A at both her decision nodes. This strategy only occurs when the probability of successful revolution π is so low that the Citizen would prefer to accept a payoff of 0. Intuitively, this becomes more likely when the costs of revolution c are high and the policy benefits b_C are small. This equilibrium is stable in the sense that we never observe Revolution, and it is nonresponsive in that the Autocrat never attempts to account for Citizen preferences in choosing his policy. No matter the state of the world (T_h, T_l), the Autocrat maintains power and enjoys the rent r_A.

Note that in this version of the game, it is impossible for the Autocrat to account for the Citizen's preferences because he has no way of learning them. I will relax this assumption in the next extension.

The second equilibrium is the Unstable Nonresponsive situation, which occurs when $\pi \geq \frac{c}{b_C}$:

$$E1.2 = \begin{cases} s_A = P_h, \quad \mu = \sigma \\ s_C = (R, R). \end{cases} \qquad \text{(Unstable Nonresponsive)}$$

Here, the probability π of a successful revolution is sufficiently high to make it attractive. The Autocrat would prefer just to placate the Citizen with the correct policy, but given his ignorance of her preferences, the best he can do is choose P_h, since $\sigma \geq 0.5$. If the Citizen proves to be type T_l, however, she will choose Revolution R, which will succeed W with probability π.

It is clear that the Autocrat is worse off in this situation than he was before. His expected payoff under the Unstable Nonresponsive equilibrium is $r_A(1 - \pi(1 - \sigma))$, which is strictly less than r_A, the expected payoff in the Stable Nonresponsive equilibrium. The more uncertain he is (σ close to 0.5), and the more likely revolution is to succeed (π close to 1), the worse off he gets.

The point of this exercise is straightforward. In certain circumstances, namely when the probability of successful revolution is sufficiently high, poor information on citizen grievances can destabilize a regime.

Authoritarian Policy Making with Representation

Let us now consider how parliamentary representation can potentially help the Autocrat with an extension to the basic game. My setup builds on Crawford and Sobel's (1982) classic framework and is similar to how Gilligan and Krehbiel (1990) model a legislative committee in a democratic setting, which can specialize, learn information about policy

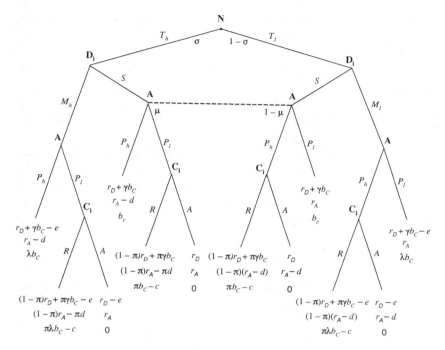

FIGURE 2.2 Authoritarian policy making with representation

efficacy, and signal that information to the broader congress. Figure 2.2 depicts a three-player game that includes a Deputy D in addition to the Autocrat A and Citizen C. As before, there are two states of the world that determine Citizen policy preferences, $T \in (T_h, T_l)$, occurring with probability $(\sigma, 1 - \sigma)$. The Citizen again has the option of Revolution R should the policy $P \in (P_h, P_l)$ not match her preferences. In the interest of space, I suppress Nature's final move to determine the success or failure of the revolution, and incorporate that information directly into the payoffs of the preceding step.

The game incorporates two key changes from that in Figure 2.1. The first is that the Deputy has knowledge of the Citizen type. If he observes T_h (T_l), he may choose to relay a Message M_h (M_l) to the Autocrat or he may remain Silent S.[5] Relaying the message has three consequences. First, it reveals information about the state of the world to the Autocrat, potentially enabling more responsive policy making. Second, it heightens

---

[5] In the interest of simplicity, I do not allow the Deputy to lie and send an incorrect message. In the Chinese case, many NPC deputy policy proposals spur the creation of study groups or fact-finding missions under the auspices of the responding office. This may prevent deputies from misrepresenting the truth or exaggerating certain grievances.

Citizen interest in the policy, which I operationalize by multiplying the policy payout b_C by some amount $\lambda > 1$. Third, it imposes a cost of effort $e > 0$ on the Deputy.

A second change is that the Autocrat now has policy preferences of his own. If the policy P_h is realized, the Autocrat experiences some disutility d, where $0 \leq d \leq r_A$. The higher the value of d, the more the Autocrat prefers P_l to P_h. If $d = 0$, the Autocrat is personally indifferent between the two policies, as in the game in Figure 2.1.

Let us assume the Deputy receives rent $r_D > 0$ for his position if the Autocrat stays in power. I also allow the Deputy to have empathy with the Citizen, receiving payoff γb_C whenever the Citizen receives her policy payoff, where $\gamma > 0$. We can think of γ as a measure of how much the two share similar policy preferences, or how much the Deputy is concerned with the well-being of his constituents. This sort of other-regarding/altruistic preferences assumption (Fehr and Fischbacher 2003), where governments/representatives care about the well-being of the population, has been used in other theories and empirical studies of policy making (Kalt and Zupan 1984; Grossman and Helpman 1994; Levitt 1996; Smith 2006).

The main purpose of this extension is to show how representation affects the equilibrium outcome, but it also yields insights into issue heterogeneity. The game utilizes a simple unidimensional policy space, but in reality, we know regimes have to set a vector of policies, and each citizen's well-being is a function of how well that vector aligns with her preferences. From the Autocrat's perspective, the ideal equilibrium outcome will be different depending on the nature of the policy issue. I examine two types of policies in turn: a "no preferences" issue and a "strong preferences" issue.

Autocrat No Policy Preferences (d = 0)
A "no preferences" issue is simply the preference situation depicted in Figure 2.1, where the Autocrat is indifferent between P_h and P_l ($d = 0$).

There are several possible equilibria in this game. As before, there is a version of the Stable Nonresponsive equilibrium that occurs when the Citizen cannot credibly commit to Revolution under any circumstances, $\pi < \frac{c}{\lambda b_C}$:

$$E2.1 = \begin{cases} s_D = (S, S) \\ s_A = (P_h, P_h, P_h) \quad \mu = \sigma \qquad \text{(Stable Nonresponsive)} \\ s_C = (A, A, A, A). \end{cases}$$

In this case, the Autocrat would never bother to placate the Citizen, and so the Deputy would prefer to stay silent S rather than expend effort e.[6]

At the other end of the spectrum, there is a Stable Responsive equilibrium where the Deputy conveys the state of the world to the Autocrat, the Autocrat chooses the policy that pleases the Citizen, and the Citizen never revolts despite having the resolve to do so:

$$E2.3 = \begin{cases} s_D = (S, M_l) \\ s_A = (P_h, P_h, P_l) \quad \mu = 1 \\ s_C = (R, R, R, R). \end{cases} \qquad \text{(Stable Responsive)}$$

This equilibrium requires two conditions. First, the Citizen must be able to commit credibly to Revolution, $\pi \geq \frac{c}{b_C}$, even when the Deputy has not heightened her policy interest. Without this commitment, the Autocrat has no need to respond, and the Deputy has no need to reveal the state of the world. Second, it must be in the Deputy's interest to go to the effort of conveying the message, which means that the cost of effort must be sufficiently low, $e \leq \pi r_D + (1 - \pi)\gamma b_C$. Intuitively, this condition is more likely to be met when the rents of office r_D are high and empathy with the citizen γ is strong. Both of these levers will prove relevant for encouraging the right kind of representation in the authoritarian context.[7]

Without these rewards, the Deputy has no real stake in the game, and he will shirk his representative responsibilities. When $e > \pi r_D + (1 - \pi)\gamma b_C$, and when the Citizen can commit to Revolution, $\pi \geq \frac{c}{b_C}$, we are left with a variant of the Unstable Nonresponsive situation from the first game:

$$E2.2 = \begin{cases} s_D = (S, S) \\ s_A = (P_h, P_h, P_l) \quad \mu = \sigma \\ s_C = (R, R, R, R). \end{cases} \qquad \text{(Unstable Nonresponsive)}$$

The Autocrat would respond to the Citizen if he knew her type, but since the Deputy remains reticent, he has no choice but to gamble on P_h and hope for the best. If he is wrong, the Citizen chooses Revolution R, and there is a real possibility of losing power.

There is also a final class of equilibria that occur at intermediate values of π, where $\frac{c}{\lambda b_C} \leq \pi \leq \frac{c}{b_C}$. In this region, the Citizen would not normally

---

[6] It is also possible that the Autocrat could play $s_A = (P_l, P_l, P_l)$, which will be preferred when he has even a weak preference for P_l.

[7] A similar equilibrium, where $s_D = (M_h, S)$ and $s_A = (P_h, P_l, P_l)$, is also possible under these conditions.

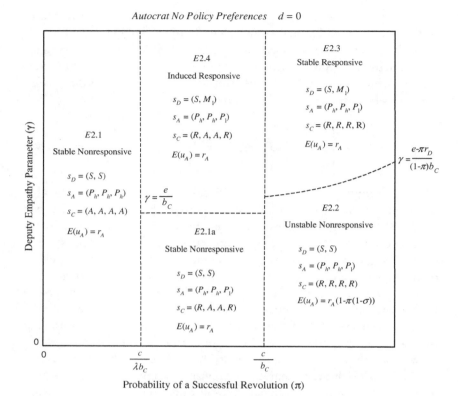

FIGURE 2.3 Representation game equilibrium outcomes – no preferences

choose Revolution, but she would choose Revolution if the Deputy conveyed a message and raised awareness of the issue (recall that $\lambda > 1$). In this instance, if the cost of effort is significantly low, $e \leq \pi \gamma b_C$, the Deputy can induce responsiveness by choosing to send the message. The Induced Responsive equilibrium is as follows:

$$E2.4 = \begin{cases} s_D = (S, M_l) \\ s_A = (P_h, P_h, P_l) \quad \mu = 1 \\ s_C = (R, A, A, R). \end{cases} \quad \text{(Induced Responsive)}$$

Note that this move by the Deputy does not actually hurt the Autocrat, who has no real policy preferences ($d = 0$). I will relax this assumption shortly.

Figure 2.3 summarizes these equilibria in a two-dimensional parameter space, the parameters being the probability of a successful revolution

(π) and the Deputy's empathy (γ).[8] The figure illustrates why Autocrats may have an interest in promoting parliamentary representation, at least on no-preference issues. Even when the probability of a successful revolution is high, the Deputy can ensure stability by relaying information to the Autocrat, who can in turn placate the Citizen. The area of Figure 2.3 in Box E2.3 is where representation is meaningful and helpful. Under the current assumptions ($0.5 \leq \sigma < 1$ and $d = 0$), the Autocrat is better off when the Deputy is more active, and so he would prefer higher values of empathy γ, lower costs of effort e, and higher rents for the position r_D.

Autocrat Strong Policy Preferences ($d > \frac{\pi\sigma r_A}{1-\pi\sigma}$)

Consider a different policy issue, one where the Autocrat strongly prefers P_l to P_h, and $d > \frac{\pi r_A}{1-\pi}$. This condition guarantees strong preferences in the sense that the Autocrat would prefer to enact his favored policy, even in the face of Revolution.

In this special case, we can quickly see how representation creates problems. If the Deputy relays his message, it exacerbates the latent conflict between the Autocrat and the type T_h Citizen. As before, there are several possible equilibria in this game, which depend on whether the Citizen is willing to risk revolution and whether the Deputy has an interest in relaying the message.

Many of the equilibria resemble those from the previous two games, so in the interest of brevity, I will focus on those that yield additional insights. In the intermediate-π region, $\frac{c}{\lambda b_C} \leq \pi \leq \frac{c}{b_C}$, the Deputy has the power to induce instability by heightening Citizen policy preferences. The Induced Unstable Nonresponsive equilibrium is as follows:

$$E2.5 = \begin{cases} s_D = (M_h, S) \\ s_A = (P_l, P_l, P_l) \qquad \text{(Induced Unstable Nonresponsive)} \\ s_C = (R, A, A, R). \end{cases}$$

Here, when observing T_h, the Deputy chooses to heighten the type T_h Citizen's awareness with the message M_h, in turn inducing Revolution. This requires γ to be sufficiently high, $\gamma \geq \frac{e+\pi r_D}{\pi b_C}$.

---

[8] The figure depicts the equilibrium space under a certain set of parameter assumptions. Note that the lines dividing the Deputy's strategy space, $\gamma = \frac{e}{b_C}$ and $\gamma = \frac{e-\pi r_D}{(1-\pi)b_C}$, do not intersect at $\pi = \frac{c}{b_C}$, with $\gamma = \frac{e-\pi r_D}{(1-\pi)b_C}$ being strictly higher. This is true only in the case where $r_D < e$, which also implies that $\gamma = \frac{e-\pi r_D}{(1-\pi)b_C}$ slopes upward with π. If $r_D > e$, this line is downward-sloping and is less than $\gamma = \frac{e}{b_C}$ at $\pi = \frac{c}{b_C}$.

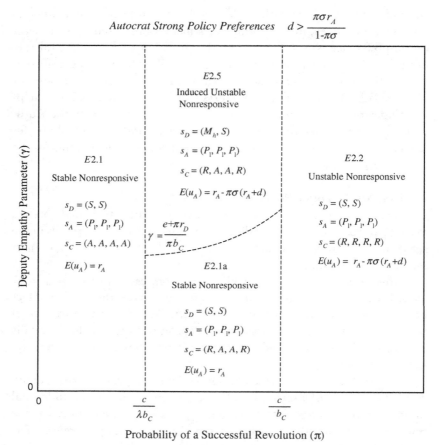

FIGURE 2.4 Representation game equilibrium outcomes – strong preferences

Note that it is precisely the Deputy's empathy that creates this difficulty. If he had simply chosen to remain Silent S when observing T_h, the Citizen would not care enough about the policy to choose Revolution R, and the Autocrat would have enjoyed his full rents r_A. When the Deputy's empathy is high enough, he prefers to heighten Citizen awareness and incite instability, in hopes of inducing concessions and the policy benefit γb_C. The Autocrat is now strictly worse off, as there is a real possibility of losing power.

The full set of equilibrium outcomes for the strong preferences parameter space are shown in Figure 2.4. This special case is meant to show a simple point: parliamentary representation is not always beneficial for an authoritarian regime. Information revelation is of little use if the regime is unwilling to respond. If representatives raise citizen attention to policies that are vital to the regime's interests, this has the potential to create instability. This is the crux of the information–attention tradeoff.

Comparative Statics and Observable Implications

The Ideal Outcome

From the Autocrat's perspective, the ideal outcome in the Representation Game is a function of the policy issue at hand. On nonsensitive policies where he has weak or no preferences, he would generally prefer the Deputy to relay the message, which allows more responsive policy making. On issues where he has strong preferences, he would prefer the Deputy to remain reticent, rather than raise public interest when he is unwilling to make concessions.[9]

The first observable implication is that the Autocrat changes his policy decision depending on the Deputy's action, albeit only for weak or no preference issues.

Proposition 1: On no or weak preference issues, the Autocrat will adjust his policy decision $P \in (P_h, P_l)$ depending on whether he observes a Deputy message $M \in (M_h, M_l)$, assuming the Citizen can credibly commit to Revolution ($\pi \geq \frac{c}{\lambda b_C}$).

Observable Implication: An authoritarian regime will incorporate deputy proposals on weak or no preference issues into policy.

If these institutions really serve an informational role, we should expect that authoritarian representatives will offer meaningful policy inputs for a wide range of nonsensitive issues.

A second observable implication is that in general, we should observe representational behavior that maximizes the informational benefits of the parliament, and minimizes its attention costs. In the Introduction, I referred to this behavioral pattern as "representation within bounds."

Proposition 2: On no or weak preference issues, the Autocrat is strictly better off when the Deputy conveys the message M. On strong preference issues, the Autocrat would prefer the Deputy remain silent S.

[9] For intermediate issues, the information benefits of representation may or may not outweigh the costs of heightened Citizen attention. The technical derivation of this is excluded in the interest of brevity but is available from the author upon request.

Observable Implication: Deputies in stable authoritarian parliaments should exhibit "representation within bounds" behavior, reflecting the interests of their constituents on the regime's weak or no preference issues, but remaining reticent on strong preference issues.

The term "representation" connotes different things to different scholars. This book will attempt to measure what political theorists would term "substantive representation" – the degree to which representatives "act in the interests of the represented, in a manner responsive to them" (Pitkin 1967). This definition leaves out other desirable elements of a representative system and other dimensions brought to mind by the term itself. Substantive representation does not include the consent of the governed and legitimacy of the representatives; the presence of free elections and accountability mechanisms; the ability of the electorate to freely express opinions; or the openness of political decisions to debate, among many other features (Manin 1997). My definition of "representation within bounds" is simply a narrower version of the substantive representation concept, a system where representatives respond to their constituents and advocate their interests, but only for a subset of issues.

Incentive Structures

Given that regimes prefer representation within bounds, we should expect that they engineer incentive structures for deputies that facilitate this special form of legislative behavior. The model includes two parameters of interest – the Deputy's rents from the position (r_D), and the degree to which he shares or internalizes the preferences of the Citizen (γ). I have left the key parameters in the Deputy calculus exogenous in the interest of simplicity. In practice, we know that authoritarian regimes exert substantial control over their legislative institutions and over the selection of the delegates who inhabit those institutions. These are not direct choice parameters for the regime, per se, but they are factors it can at least attempt to manipulate.

Figure 2.5 illustrates the Autocrat's welfare at different levels of Deputy empathy (γ), across different types of policy issues and probabilities of revolution success. Encouraging shared preferences between citizens and their representatives is not always beneficial. While rents foster loyalty to the regime, empathy aligns the Deputy with the Citizen, giving him an incentive to relay her preferences no matter what the situation. In no-policy-preference scenarios, empathy is helpful, as it encourages representation and information revelation. On strong-policy-preference issues,

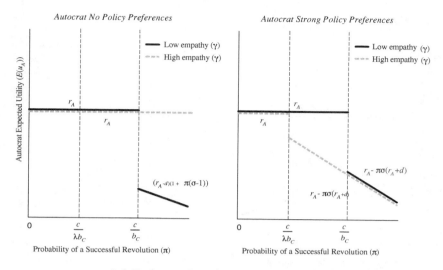

FIGURE 2.5 Understanding the role of Deputy empathy (γ)

where the Autocrat is unwilling to concede, Deputy empathy is potentially problematic.

Proposition 3: Higher Deputy empathy γ has positive effects on Autocrat welfare for no-preference issues, but negative effects for strong-preference issues. The Autocrat prefers the Deputy to have selective empathy with the Citizen that varies by issue accordingly.

Observable Implication: Regimes will devise incentives to foster selective empathy.

I use the term "selective empathy" to describe the underlying preferences that lead to representation within bounds. Representatives who exhibit selective empathy share the concerns and grievances of their constituents on no-preference issues, but they remain disconnected and distant on the regime's strong-preference issues. Regimes may rely on a rich set of mechanisms to foster this special brand of deputy–constituent ties.

Rents, in contrast, have uniformly positive effects on the Autocrat's well-being, as they give the Deputy a vested interest in the success of the regime. Figure 2.6 shows the Autocrat's expected utility across different probabilities of a successful revolution. The dark solid line shows the Autocrat's utility for a hypothetical low-rents scenario, and the lighter dashed line shows the equilibrium utility when Deputy rents r_D are higher. For no-preference issues, rents give the Deputy an incentive to do his job,

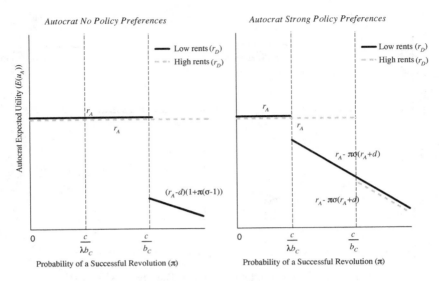

FIGURE 2.6 Understanding the role of deputy rents (r_D)

helping the Autocrat respond and avoid revolution. On strong-preference issues, rents encourage the Deputy to keep quiet and avoid heightening Citizen issue awareness (λ).

Proposition 4: Higher Deputy rents r_D have uniformly positive effects on Autocrat welfare. The Autocrat prefers the Deputy to enjoy rents to encourage loyalty and align his incentives with the regime.

Observable Implication: Regimes will reward deputies with rents to instill loyalty.

Rents are private, nondivisible benefits enjoyed by an individual or set of individuals. They come in different forms, but we typically think of rents as financial benefits, or at least offices and influence that can lead to financial benefits. Several theories of authoritarian politics hinge on the notion of strategic rent distribution. Boix and Svolik contend that parliaments are institutions of power sharing, helping autocrats credibly commit to distributing resources to the rest of the ruling clique (Svolik 2009, 2012; Boix and Svolik 2013). Selectorate theory is based on the idea that authoritarian regimes generally allocate private rents to the small group of supporters that keep them in office (Bueno de Mesquita et al. 2003, 2008). My theory predicts that deputies enjoy "returns to office"

r_D, which are necessary to foster loyalty to the regime and encourage limited representation.

If authoritarian parliaments do follow "representation within bounds" logic, they should demonstrate these two institutional properties and incentive structures.

Plausibility

The remainder of this book is dedicated to testing the dynamics of the framework above in the Chinese case. Before we move on to the empirical chapters, it is important to assess the plausibility of four assumptions that produce the core observable implications. First, deputies in China convey meaningful information about citizen preferences to the regime. Second, in the process of conveying these demands, deputies can actually heighten citizen interest in a particular issue, raising the salience of the policy decision. Third, Chinese citizens are not wholly acquiescent and can credibly commit to revolution if a baseline standard of welfare is not met. Fourth, the ruling CCP regime has strong-preference and weak-preference issues. I consider each in turn.

The Information Assumption

In the model, the logic of representation is that deputies have superior knowledge of citizen preferences and can convey that information to the regime. Many models of bureaucratic politics and delegation utilize this sort of signaling and information exchange (Crawford and Sobel 1982; Gilligan and Krehbiel 1990; Ting 2003; Bendor and Meirowitz 2004; Callander 2008; Patty 2009; Gailmard and Patty 2012). In some sense, representatives in authoritarian systems can be considered bureaucratic agents of the regime. Their policy expertise, so to speak, lies in their knowledge of public opinion and citizen grievances (Gailmard and Patty 2012).

In the Chinese case, the idea that the NPC generates information for the CCP regime is well documented by O'Brien, who has referred to the system as a "barometer of the masses" (O'Brien 1990, 1994). Manion (2011, 2013, 2014) also highlights informational themes in her analysis of lower-level congresses. The CCP draws 3,000 NPC deputies from throughout the country and, for 50 weeks of the year, tasks them with alerting the central government to regional or group based concerns. Indeed, the rule

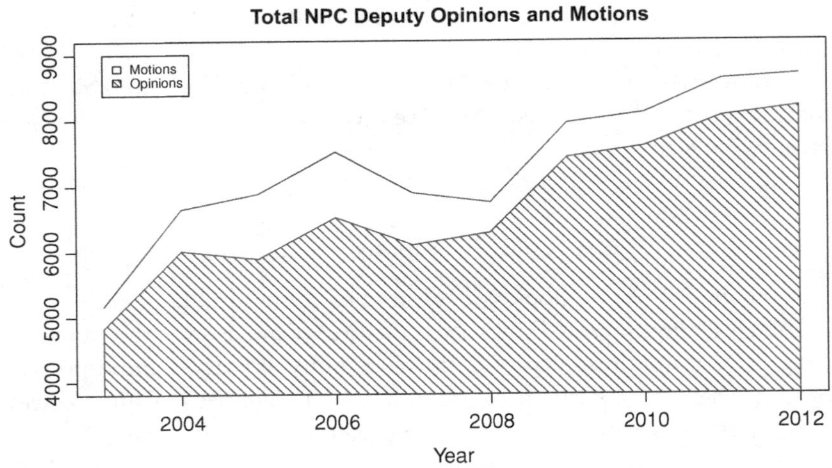

Total NPC Deputy Opinions and Motions

FIGURE 2.7 Increase in deputy participation (tenth and eleventh NPCs)

that deputies should serve on a part-time basis was designed with informational purposes in mind, as it allows them to stay closer to common citizens from their respective provinces (Jiang 2003; Shi 2007).

Of the many different forms of deputy participation, the opinions and motions process plays the most important informational role. Motions (*yian*) are short policy proposals, often calling for new legislation, that require the signatures of 30 or more deputies. Deputies may also individually file formal suggestions (*jianyi*), criticisms (*piping*) and opinions (*yijian*), which tend to be shorter and directed at specific ministries in the bureaucracy.[10] Once submitted, these proposals are referred to different NPC working committees and can eventually become bills, or they may be incorporated into policies in more informal means by various ministries and agencies. Insiders tend to believe that the proposals are given "due attention" and are considered sincerely by central officials (Jiang 2003, p. 344; Personal Interview NH001; Personal Interview NH002).

This form of interest articulation, shown in Figure 2.7, has risen dramatically over time. In 2012 alone, there were 489 motions and 8,149 opinions, representing a 67.8% increase from 2003. The proposals allow the regime to recognize and address citizen grievances before they fester

---

[10] NPC reporting standards aggregate suggestions, criticisms and opinions together, with motions broken out as a separate category. Hereafter I will use the phrase "opinions" to encompass suggestions, criticisms and opinions. These are also sometimes referred to as bill and nonbill proposals (Jiang 2003).

into broader collective action. A few examples help illustrate the nature of this exchange:

– In 2010, deputies from the Ningxia Hui Autonomous Region submitted a motion to address local water shortages. After consideration by the Ministry of Water Resources, the Ministry of Finance, the Ministry of Agriculture, and the State Council, the motion resulted in a 1.13 billion RMB public works project that gave 200,000 villagers an improved irrigation system. ("Lawmakers Satisfying" 2012)

– Deputy Yao Yiyun discovered poor working conditions at a coal mine in Hunan, and she later communicated the miners' grievances through a suggestion to the NPC plenary session. Three weeks later, the Ministry of Coal sent a task force to investigate the mine and shortly thereafter set aside a four billion RMB fund for the industry to address safety issues. (Jiang 2003, p. 346)

– In 2011, after visiting her native county of Yanling, 28-year-old deputy Tan Yan learned of local concerns over new infrastructure plans. The county had never had a train station before, and the proposed train station would not be sufficiently large to encourage tourism and business development. Along with six other deputies from Hunan, Tan proposed that the area of the station be increased from 3,500 to 6,000 square meters. This suggestion was accepted by the Ministry of Railways. (Li 2013)[11]

These examples are not to say that the central government is completely blind as to public opinion, nor that the NPC's proposal process is the only means through which the regime collects information. Public opinion polls are routinely conducted in the NPC and other institutions, and different levels of government have even experimented with deliberative polls and participatory budgeting (He and Thogersen 2010; He 2011; He and Warren 2011). The bureaucracy itself has mechanisms to transmit information upward (Merli 1998; Landry 2008). The regime also employs an extensive domestic security apparatus, headed by the Ministry of Public Security and Ministry of State Security, replete with plainclothes intelligence officers who monitor dissidents, protests and social unrest (Tanner 2004). Muckraking journalists can expose low-level corruption and improve the quality of governance (Distelhorst 2012; Lorentzen 2014). The petitions system, which has its origins in the imperial period, allows individuals or groups to offer suggestions and grievances to higher levels of government. There are millions of such complaints each year (Huang 1995; Chen 2011). Elections help convey poor governance and

---

[11] Tan commented on the success in a recent interview. "The Railway Ministry attached great importance to the suggestion and sent a team to inspect, and finally agreed to the suggestion's demands. I was so excited at that time," she said (Li 2013).

dissatisfaction at the local level, allowing central leaders to remove corrupt cadres (Chen and Zhong 2002; Landry, Davis and Wang 2010). One could also look at China's emerging social media platforms through an informational lens. Microblog chatter reveals "hot topics" and issues of broader public concern to the online population (King, Pan and Roberts 2013).

The argument here does not require that the parliament be the sole generator of information, but simply that it be a meaningful one. More information on public opinion can be beneficial for policy responsiveness, and bureaucratic redundancies abound in most political systems to reduce uncertainty and induce competition (Niskanen 1971; Miller and Moe 1983; Ting 2003). In its current form, the NPC proposal process relays high-quality information about regional and group-based grievances and citizen demands. This is a low-cost and relatively effective channel, one that generates knowledge not easily gleaned from other mechanisms in the Chinese system.

The domestic security apparatus, State Council bureaucracy, petitions system, elections, and Weibo chatter each have their own informational focus and biases. Public security agents can identify when and where dissidents are meeting, but they are not tasked or trained to identify specific governance needs. Bureaucratic reporting is vulnerable to biases induced by principal–agent problems and promotion concerns (Merli 1998; Wallace forthcoming). Weibo chatter tends to focus on government scandals or high-level issues and generally does not propose solutions to address concrete grievances. Self-censorship and preference falsification may render it an unreliable source of public opinion (Kuran 1991).

Although my theoretical framework was developed to understand the tradeoffs of authoritarian representation, it could potentially be applied to these other information revelation channels, agents of the regime, or state–society interactions. Journalists for official papers or television stations, for example, can convey information upward through investigative reporting. This type of information revelation might also come with an attention cost, which would suggest similar bounded dynamics throughout the official media space. The social media landscape offers a direct information revelation channel – no deputy intermediary is required – but carries obvious attention risks. The dynamics described in the innovative work of King, Roberts and Pan (2013) suggests that the CCP regime generally allows discussion and criticism, but censors posts on sensitive issues that heighten collective action potential. These arenas have public information revelation dynamics that are not terribly different from the legislative branch, and the model here could be applied readily with minimal adjustments.

To summarize, NPC proposals convey reliable, independent information on a broad range of social issues: where a train station should be built, how to improve cultural activities for migrant workers, or the need for irrigation projects in mountainous rural areas. The CCP regime would be less informed and less responsive without them.

The Attention Assumption

The second assumption is that the process of interest articulation in an authoritarian parliament can raise issue salience among the citizenry. In the model, this is operationalized with $\lambda > 1$, which signifies heightened stakes for the Citizen following a Deputy message. This is an important assumption. If $\lambda = 1$, meaning there was no attention effect, there would be effectively no costs to the regime of allowing representation. The regime would have no need to engineer representation within bounds, and we would observe representative activity on the full issue space. Note that this is not a standard assumption in the literature on authoritarian parliaments, mostly because existing models (Gandhi 2008; Svolik 2012) do not explicitly consider representative–citizen interactions.

To be fair, we know that not all NPC opinions and motions captivate the public interest. There are over 9,000 proposals per year, and many are never made publicly available in any form. Most Chinese citizens cannot name more than a few proposals made during the annual session, let alone the proposals put forth by their own representatives.

The spirit of the assumption is that just as certain bills before the U.S. Congress become newsworthy, certain NPC proposals attract widespread attention and become hot points in Internet forums, newspapers, and everyday discussion. This in turn makes citizens care about more about the issue and the ultimate policy decision. Technically, an alternative way to formulate this would be that when a Deputy makes a proposal, there is some probability $\phi > 0$ that it will raise citizen interest in the policy issue, which multiplies the utility b_C associated with policy congruence by the salience parameter λ. In the interest of simplicity, I removed this additional randomization and collapsed the attention effect into the single parameter λ.

A few examples help illustrate the nature of the attention effect:

– In the winter of 2011, deputy Li Dongsheng put forth a proposal to raise the exemption level of the income tax threshold from 2,000 RMB per month to

5,000 RMB per month.[12] His Weibo post detailing the income tax motion was forwarded over two million times. A first draft of an amendment was released in April that proposed raising the threshold to 3,000 RMB, in addition to decreasing the minimum tax rate from 5% to 3%. Over 230,000 public comments poured into the NPC's official online portal, nearly all expressing dissatisfaction with the new level, and many pushing for a further raise to 5,000 RMB. Members of the NPC Standing Committee met hurriedly in April, ultimately deciding to further raise the threshold to 3,500 RMB. ("China Revises" 2011; "From Little Things" 2011)

– In March 2010, a proposal for housing reform was submitted to the 11th session of the NPC annual meeting by Zong Qinghou, founder of the Hangzhou Wahaha Group, and Chi Susheng, director of a law firm in Jilin. The proposal aimed to strengthen the government's role in providing housing services and increase the supply of welfare housing. It was reported on in depth by Wangyi News, garnering nearly 20,000 comments on a discussion board. *Southern Weekly* considered it to be the most influential NPC proposal of the year 2010. ("This Year's Motions" 2010)

– In 2011, 2012, and 2013, Guangdong deputy He Youlin put forth proposals to end the One Child Policy.[13] The proposal later became the single hottest topic on Weibo's "Two Meetings" category. The key words "loosen two-child policy" rose to the top of the Baidu Two Meetings search list, with 489,866 searches during the NPC plenary session. He's efforts garnered international attention as well; *The Atlantic* ran a piece on the issue with the subheading: "the idea of abolishing the one-child policy, once taboo in China, now has a prominent backer." (Carter 2013)

We can further see the salience of the NPC through search engine statistics. Baidu now routinely publishes an annual list of hot topics and proposals during the NPC session. Searches for Two Meetings (*lianghui*) surge in March of every year, with weekly search totals reaching 100,000 on Baidu's count index. For these weeks, the NPC exceeds the societal relevance of Barack Obama (averages around 10,000 searches) and even Xi Jinping himself (averages around 60,000 searches).

These examples and statistics are simply meant to illustrate how deputy proposals can gain public relevance in Chinese society. In some instances, public attention can even force concessions from the regime, as

[12] Li became known as the first deputy to use the microblogging platform to solicit input from common citizens and turn that input into formal motions, and he broadcast this role proudly on his Weibo homepage. "As an NPC deputy, I'll bring bills about people's livelihood improvement to the upcoming NPC meetings in March, and I'd like to hear your voices through the platform of microblogging" ("Deputy Seeks" 2011).

[13] Deputy He himself commented on Weibo, "Two years ago I raised this matter, and I raised it again last year. I will raise it again this year! We must allow Chinese to have a second child. We cannot wait another minute."

in the Induced Responsive equilibrium $E2.4$. NPC deputies may be much maligned, but they do manage to pique citizen interest every year.

The Credible Threat Assumption

The four observable implications require certain assumptions about the parameter space to hold in the contemporary Chinese case. In particular, the entire notion that some representation and responsiveness occurs in the NPC requires that Chinese citizens can credibly commit to revolution. If the Citizen is too weak – i.e., the probability of successful revolution too low – the outcome is the Stable Nonresponsive Equilibrium $E2.1$. Only when the Autocrat is sufficiently concerned with mass unrest do we see representation within bounds dynamics start to emerge. As will be discussed in Chapter 7, the NPC has only recently entered into its current equilibrium, and offered little in the way of meaningful representation during the initial decades of CCP rule.

The question, then, is whether the Chinese citizenry can credibly commit to revolution, whether $\pi > \frac{c}{\lambda b_C}$. This is impossible to answer definitively, as these abstract parameter values are immeasurable, and revolution is currently an "off the path" outcome. My argument is that governance in contemporary China is characterized by a high level of policy responsiveness and citizen acquiescence. We have no way of knowing whether in the absence of this responsiveness, Chinese citizens would engage in some form of collective action aimed at regime change.

A simpler question is whether the CCP regime appears to be significantly concerned about this possibility, to the point where this concern is motivating more responsive governance. Here the answer is a definitive "yes" (Tanner 2004). The CCP itself has faced the brink of revolution multiple times since the founding of the PRC – the Hundred Flowers Movement (1957), the Democracy Wall Movement (1978), and most notably, the Tiananmen Square Protests (1989). The entire domestic security and repressive apparatus is geared toward preventing a recurrence of these contentious moments (Tanner 2004; King et al. 2013).

A few statistics illustrate the severity and perception of the revolutionary threat. The domestic security budget ($130 billion in 2013), dedicated to maintaining stability, now exceeds the military budget ($119 billion in 2013) (Blanchard and Ruwitch 2013). The Chinese government no longer releases the full domestic security budget because of the sensitivity of these figures. Contentious behavior also appears to be on the rise. In 2014, the number of labor disputes grew 29 percent, the number of land disputes grew 20 percent, and the number of general petitions grew 11 percent ("Advancing Rights Through Dialogue" 2014). According to Dui Hua, an advocacy group, there were 5,599 political or religious prisoners in China as of December 2014, 19% of whom were charged with "endangering state security" crimes ("Advancing Rights Through Dialogue" 2014, 2015).[14]

If the CCP were not concerned with the threat of revolution, it would not be investing in the repressive apparatus as much as it does. A key assertion of this book is that this concern has also led to investment in the responsive apparatus, of which the NPC is a key component.

The Policy Preferences Assumption

Thus far, the model and implications have employed abstract parameter values, classifying issues where Autocrat has weak or no preferences and strong preferences. I have argued that the CCP regime will encourage representation on the former and silence discussion on the latter. To move forward empirically, we need some way to map these values to actual policies.

The sheer number of policy issues make it impossible to devise a full classification scheme, so I proceed by trying to identify the CCP regime's strong preference issues. In fact, these policy areas were directly identified in a leaked Party communique known as "Document 9," which was authored by central leadership and disseminated in 2013 to members of major CCP committees and leadership groups. The directive identifies seven "noteworthy problems related to the current state of the ideological sphere," or "trends, positions, and activities" that should be avoided ("Document 9" 2013):

1. Promoting Western constitutional democracy (separation of powers, the multiparty system, general elections, independent judiciaries, nationalized armies)
2. Promoting "universal values" (freedom, democracy, human rights)
3. Promoting civil society
4. Promoting neoliberalism (unrestrained economic liberalization, complete privatization, total marketization)
5. Promoting the West's idea of journalism (freedom of the press, free flow of information on the Internet)

---

[14] These detentions follow predictable patterns and correspond with sensitive mobilization events, such as the anniversaries of the Tiananmen Square massacre (Truex 2015).

6. Promoting historical nihilism, undermining the history of the CCP (rejecting the revolution, rejecting conclusions of historical events, vilifying Party leaders, rejecting the Socialist path)
7. Questioning reform and opening up ("socialism with Chinese characteristics")

This list is specific to the Chinese case, though "out of bounds" lists for other regimes would contain similar elements. The issues identified are essential to authoritarian governance, and the document rejects concepts of multiparty democracy, free and fair elections, independent judiciaries, human rights, civil society, and freedom of the press/Internet. These are policies that are core to the CCP's own interests and ability to maintain political control over Chinese society, areas where the interests of the regime and the citizenry likely conflict.

Note that the list also includes some fundamental aspects of economic policy making. It warns against Western neoliberalism and also against reverting to prereform socialism. The net effect is to defend the current brand of "socialism with Chinese characteristics," which blends a predominately market economy with state-owned enterprises in key strategic sectors.

The document goes on to exhort Party members to toe the ideological line:

We must have a firm approach and clear-cut stance toward major political principles, issues of right and wrong, what to support and what to oppose... We must not permit the dissemination of opinions that oppose the Party's theory or political line, the publication of views contrary to decisions that represent the central leadership's views, or the spread of political rumors that defame the image of the Party or the nation. ("Document 9" 2013)

Here we see the Party's sensitivity to the publicity of policy ideas that go against its core interests. Representation in the NPC on any of these issue areas would be considered out of bounds and detrimental to the regime.

Though Document 9 was released in 2013, most China scholars would agree that these issues were also sensitive during the Hu-Wen administration (2003–12) and much of the earlier reform period. From here on, my references to "sensitive issues" or "strong autocrat preferences" will refer to the itemized list above.

The remaining issue space, which includes policies relating to most aspects of economic regulation, healthcare, education, environment, social policy, cultural protection, and so forth, is noticeably absent from Document 9. While certain leaders or agents within the bureaucracy might have strong preferences on specific issues within these broad categories, in general the regime should be less threatened by discourse and more willing to respond to citizen demands. I will consider these areas to be "weak or no preference" or "nonsensitive" issues.

Alternative Frameworks

How do the observable implications of the representation-within-bounds framework compare with those of other theories? As mentioned in the Introduction, the academic literature has two dominant lenses for understanding authoritarian parliaments: cooptation theory and power-sharing theory. A new framework, centered around elite mobilization and exchange, has recently been proposed in the Chinese case. There is also the popular perception that these institutions are meaningless rubber stamps or window dressing. Table 2.1 compares the observable implications of these five frameworks in terms of the nature of representation, deputy influence, deputy selection, and the presence of rents.

Cooptation theory, which holds that parliaments exist to identify and coopt members of the opposition with access to rents and policy influence, is the most prominent of the alternative frameworks (Gandhi and Przeworski 2007; Gandhi 2008; Magaloni 2008; Malesky and Schuler 2010; Malesky, Schuler and Tran 2012). The theory has similar collective action underpinnings but differs from mine in several key respects. First, proponents of the cooptation view tend to argue that parliaments and accompanying elections allow regimes to identify and placate popular members of key opposition groups (Gandhi 2008; Malesky and Schuler 2010). This suggests these institutions should contain deputies who do not share the political persuasions of the regime, deputies who are truly oppositional. We would also expect deputy representation and influence to extend to policies where the interests of the opposition and regime directly conflict. Rents are given to placate opposition leaders, who may distribute them to the rest of their opposition groups.

In the power-sharing view, parliaments exist to help the autocrat commit credibly to distribute resources to the rest of the ruling coalition, facilitating monitoring and offering a front for corruption (Myerson 2008; Svolik 2009, 2012; Blaydes 2011; Boix and Svolik 2013). As currently articulated, power-sharing theory makes fewer predictions about the nature of representation and deputy influence, but it suggests that parliaments allow members of the ruling coalition to monitor the autocrat and prevent him from further consolidating power. Selection should

TABLE 2.1 *Comparison of Alternative Frameworks*

	Representation within bounds	Cooptation	Powersharing	Elite mobilization	Rubber stamp
Function	To provide information and enable responsive policy making	To identify and coopt members of the opposition	To facilitate powersharing among the ruling coalition	To communicate preferences of elite government actors	To provide legitimacy to regime legislative initiatives
Representation	Representation of constituent interests on nonsensitive issues	Representation of opposition interests	Minimal representative activity	Representation of elite official interests	Minimal representative activity
Influence	Deputy influence limited to nonpolitical issues	High deputy influence	No clear prediction	No clear prediction	Minimal to no deputy influence
Selection	Deputies selected for quality of representation and loyalty	Deputies selected for opposition and discontent	Deputies selected for factional ties	Deputies selected for opportunistic echoing	Deputies selected for loyalty
Rents	Deputies receive rents to instill loyalty	Deputies receive rents to distribute to oppositional groups	Deputies receive rents to placate factions within regime	No clear prediction	Deputies receive minimal rents

occur with factional and power-sharing interests in mind, not to promote deputy–constituent ties, which are minimal.

The elite mobilization view has yet to appear in published research, but it remains important to consider, given that the argument is being developed in the Chinese case (Lu and Liu 2015). The basic idea is that there is little in the way of authentic representation in authoritarian parliaments. Instead, delegates are mere proxy fighters for elites in the central and provincial governments. Deputies do not learn or reveal the preferences of the citizenry, but try to echo the existing preferences of these elites to curry favor and get promoted. The observable implications of this view remain somewhat underdeveloped, but it suggests that representation and promotion patterns are driven by this elite echoing rather than by deputy–constituent ties (Shih 2008).

Finally, the rubber stamp or window dressing view embodies the idea that regimes use parliaments to provide nominal legitimacy to their legislative initiatives. Its main implications are that representation, deputy influence, and even rent distribution are all low to nonexistent, as parliaments have a minimal policy role. Deputies are selected based on loyalty, not necessarily the quality of their representative activities.

In the remainder of the book, I will test the implications of the representation within bounds framework with a combination of quantitative and qualitative evidence in the Chinese case. Where possible, I will highlight key findings as they relate to these alternative frameworks, focusing on how the observable implications differ.

To be sure, there is some truth to all five frameworks in modern China. The NPC is a multipurpose institution, and it contains elements of power sharing among CCP factions, cooptation of restive minorities, elite mobilization and proxy fighting, and the annual rubber stamping of dozens of bills, work reports, and appointments. Again, my goal is not to deny or disprove the alternative frameworks; this is impossible to do with a single case. The goal is to demonstrate that the representation within bounds framework captures the key dynamics of the National People's Congress, and therefore may have some relevance for understanding other authoritarian parliaments.

Technical Appendix

Solutions for Authoritarian Policy Making with Incomplete Information (Figure 2.1)

No matter whether $s_C = (A, A)$ or $s_C = (R, R)$, the Autocrat can do no better than choose P_h. When the Citizen plays the Acquiescence strategy

(A, A), the payoff is equivalent for both policies, $E[u_A; P_h|(A, A)] = E[u_A; P_l|(A, A)] = r_A$, and so technically the $(P_l, (A, A))$ equilibrium is possible. Under the threat of Revolution (R, R), $E[u_A; P_h|(R, R)] = r_A(1 - \pi(1 - \sigma))$, while $E[u_A; P_l|(R, R)] = r_A(1 - \pi\sigma)$. Since $\sigma \geq 0.5$, P_h is always preferable.

The key condition in this game is that which governs the Citizen's decision between Revolution R or Acquiescence A. For the type T_l, note that $E[u_C; A|P_h] = 0$, while Revolution brings an expected payoff $E[u_C; R|P_h] = \pi b_C - c$. R becomes more attractive than A if and only if $\pi \geq \frac{c}{b_C}$. An equivalent condition holds for the type T_h. Thus, $s_C = (A, A)$ if $\pi < \frac{c}{b_C}$, and (R, R) if $\pi \geq \frac{c}{b_C}$, yielding $E1.1$ and $E1.2$.

Solutions for Authoritarian Policy Making with Representation (Figure 2.2) Autocrat No Policy Preferences ($d = 0$)

This game is governed by two conditions: whether the Citizen can credibly commit to Revolution R, and whether the Deputy has an interest in conveying the Message M. Recall from the previous game that when $\pi \geq \frac{c}{b_C}$, R becomes more attractive than A. This holds true for the Citizen in this game at her second and third decision nodes. When the Deputy has relayed a message, as at the Citizen's first and fourth decision nodes, the threshold of π that makes Revolution R attractive is lower, because the payoff from the policy b_C is now λb_C. The condition becomes $\pi \geq \frac{c}{\lambda b_C}$. Thus, whenever $\pi < \frac{c}{\lambda b_C}$, $s_C = (A, A, A, A)$, and whenever $\pi \geq \frac{c}{b_C}$, $s_C = (R, R, R, R)$. In-between values yield $s_C = (R, A, A, R)$.

The Deputy must decide when and where to relay information to the Autocrat at the cost e. This decision will depend the equilibrium strategies of the other two players. Under the stable nonresponsive equilibrium, $E2.1$, $s_A = (P_h, P_h, P_h)$ and $s_C = (A, A, A, A)$. At his first decision node, $E[u_D; M_h|s_A, s_C] = r_D + \gamma b_C - e$, while $E[u_D; S|s_A, s_C] = r_D + \gamma b_C$, so S is the more attractive option. The equivalent relationship holds at the Deputy's second decision node, and so $s_D = (S, S)$, yielding the equilibrium in $E2.1$.

At the opposite end of the spectrum is the situation where $s_C = (R, R, R, R)$ and $s_A = (P_h, P_h, P_l)$, meaning that the Citizen can credibly commit to Revolution and the Autocrat will placate if he can. Consider the Deputy's calculus at his second node. If he relays the message M_l, the Autocrat will choose P_l, and he will receive a payoff of $r_D + \gamma b_C - e$. If he withholds this information, the Autocrat will mistakenly choose P_h despite the Citizen being type T_l, and $E[u_D; S|s_A, s_C] = (1 - \pi)r_D + \pi\gamma b_C$. That is, with probability $1 - \pi$ the Autocrat will win and the Deputy will keep his rent r_D, and with probability π the Citizen will win and the Deputy will get the policy benefit γb_C. The Deputy will choose M_l at his second decision node only when $e \leq \pi r_D + (1 - \pi)\gamma b_C$, $E[u_D; M_l|s_A, s_C] > E[u_D; S|s_A, s_C]$. This condition can be rewritten in terms of the empathy parameter, $\gamma \geq \frac{e - \pi r_D}{(1-\pi)b_C}$. Intuitively, the Deputy is more likely to fulfill his representative responsibilities when the costs of effort are lower, his empathy with the citizen is higher, and the policy benefit and rents of the position are greater.

Note that at his first decision node, the Deputy would never choose to send the message M_h. Recall that at all equilibria, $s_A = (P_h, P_h, P_h)$ or (P_h, P_h, P_l). At his second decision node, the Autocrat would always choose P_h since $\sigma \geq .5$. If the Deputy observes T_h, sending the message M_h would never change the policy outcome, making S preferable. Given $s_C = (R, R, R, R)$ and $s_A = (P_h, P_h, P_l)$, the Deputy will choose to play (S, M_l) if $\gamma \geq \frac{e - \pi r_D}{(1-\pi)b_C}$, and (S, S) if not. This yields E2.3 and E2.2, respectively.

There is a similar cut point for the Deputy at intermediate values of π, where $s_C = (R, A, A, R)$ and $s_A = (P_h, P_h, P_l)$. Here, if the Deputy remains Silent S at his second decision node, the Autocrat will implement P_h, and the Citizen will Acquiesce, giving a payoff of r_D to the Deputy. If he chooses M_l, the Autocrat will respond with the correct policy P_l to stave off Revolution from the Citizen. This gives the Deputy a payoff of $r_D + \gamma b_C - e$, and so $E[u_D; M_l|s_A, s_C] > [u_D; S|s_A, s_C]$ only when $e < \gamma b_C$, or $\gamma > \frac{e}{b_C}$. Therefore, given that $s_C = (R, R, R, R)$ and $s_A = (P_h, P_h, P_l)$, the Deputy's strategy $s_D = (S, M_l)$ if $\gamma > \frac{e}{b_C}$ and (S, S) if not. This yields E2.4 and E2.1a.

Autocrat Strong Policy Preferences ($d > \frac{\pi \sigma r_A}{1-\pi\sigma}$)

The solution space to this game is governed by conditions similar to those for the previous two. Again, we are concerned with when the Citizen will be willing to choose Revolution R, and when the Deputy would choose to relay a message M_h. The difference here is that the Autocrat has a strong enough preference for P_l that he would never choose to placate the Citizen with P_h under any circumstances, even when he knows revolution is imminent.

The Citizen's Revolution condition is effectively the same as before. Whenever $\pi < \frac{c}{\lambda b_C}$, $s_C = (A, A, A, A)$, and whenever $\pi \geq \frac{c}{b_C}$, $s_C = (R, R, R, R)$. Values in between yield $s_C = (R, A, A, R)$.

The restrictive condition of this case, that $d > \frac{\pi r_A}{1-\pi}$), guarantees that the Autocrat will always play (P_l, P_l, P_l), regardless of the Citizen or Deputy strategy. Suppose the Citizen is playing $s_C = (R, R, R, R)$. In playing $s_A = (P_l, P_l, P_l)$, the Autocrat is deliberately risking Revolution rather than make a policy concession. This yields an expected payoff of $r_A - \pi\sigma(r_A + d)$. If the Autocrat deviates to P_h at his first decision node, his payoff is $r_A - d$, which is strictly less than $r_A - \pi\sigma(r_A + d)$ when d is sufficiently large, $d > \frac{\pi\sigma r_A}{1 - \pi\sigma}$.

The Deputy must decide whether it is worth the effort to relay the message. Note that if $s_C = (A, A, A, A)$ or (R, R, R, R), the Deputy's message has no potential to change the outcome, and so $s_D = (S, S)$. This yields the outcomes E2.1 and E2.2, respectively. When $s_C = (R, A, A, R)$, and $s_A = (P_l, P_l, P_l)$, the Deputy has the ability to induce instability by heightening Citizen preferences. If he relays message M_h at his first node, he will induce a Revolution outcome, yielding $E[u_D; M_h | s_A, s_C] = (1 - \pi)r_D + \pi\gamma b_C - e$. If he remains silent, he will maintain his rent r_D. Thus, relaying the message M_h becomes attractive if $\gamma > \frac{e + \pi r_D}{\pi b_C}$. This yields the Induced Unstable Nonresponsive equilibrium E2.5. If γ is not sufficiently high, the Deputy will choose S at his first node, yielding the Stable Nonresponsive equilibrium E2.1a. The Autocrat prefers this latter situation.

3

Does the NPC Matter?

Supported, Concerned, Submitted, Best Wishes

Lei Chuang looks the part of an activist. When we met, he was 26 years old and enrolled in an engineering graduate program at Shanghai Jiaotong University. He wore long hair and thin-framed glasses. He spoke about Chinese politics and society without reservation.

Lei's issue was discrimination, specifically discrimination against carriers of Hepatitis B. The virus is transmitted through blood and other bodily fluids and can cause cirrhosis of the liver and other life-threatening conditions. In China, vaccination programs remain underdeveloped, and recent estimates suggest the country may have as many as 130 million carriers (Niu 2011). The disease is particularly widespread in rural areas, where doctors have a tendency to reuse syringes, and citizens are less aware of the risk of transmission.

Hepatitis B carriers in China are a stigmatized group, both socially and professionally. Most citizens lack basic knowledge about how the virus is spread, and many wrongly believe that sharing food or chopsticks with carriers brings risk of infection. A 2005 survey by the Chinese Foundation for Hepatitis Prevention and Control (CFHPC) shows that 37.5% of respondents from Sichuan and Guangzhou said they would not want to work or eat at a table with carriers of the virus (Lu 2006). Employers are not legally permitted to inquire about a prospective employee's carrier status, but many do so anyway. Carriers are routinely denied employment once traces of the virus are discovered in their blood samples during mandatory physicals. Another survey found that 35% of state-owned enterprises publicly stated that they would not employ

Hepatitis B carriers. Over 60% screen their employees for the virus, paying a trivial fine for doing so ("Hepatitis B Carriers" 2012).

Lei is a Hepatitis B carrier himself and has some personal experience with discrimination. In 2007, his brother signed an employment contract with a company in Wuhan, but was later refused employment because of his condition. In August of that year, Lei began his first of many awareness campaigns, walking around city streets holding a sign reading, "I am a Hepatitis B carrier" (Zheng and Sun 2012). In 2011, he started writing letters to Premier Wen Jiabao – one new letter every day – asking him to dinner as a representative of the Hepatitis B community. The dinner would publicly demonstrate that there is no risk of infection from sharing a meal. Lei began growing out his hair, refusing to cut it until Wen accepted the invitation (Personal Interview BJ4213).

In 2012, Lei took his campaigns one step further. He drafted a set of policy proposals directed at fighting discrimination against Hepatitis B carriers (Lei 2012). The first called for increased penalties for employers that used carrier status as an employment criterion, and another aimed to strengthen personal privacy by removing carrier status from health records. Lei's third proposal demanded a ban on "liver disease" advertisements, which spread misinformation about the disease and dupe citizens into paying for phony medical treatments (Zheng and Sun 2012).

Lei posted these proposals, which resemble well-written formal NPC opinions, on his personal blog. He used Weibo to forward them to NPC and CPPCC deputies just prior to the annual meetings in March (Lei 2012).[1] His messages were always polite:

Respected representatives, hello, my name is Lei Chuang, graduate student at Shanghai Jiaotong University, and a Hepatitis B carrier. I have long paid attention to China's Hepatitis B discrimination problem. I hope you can work to eliminate Hepatitis B discrimination and liver disease advertisements through your opinions at the two meetings. (Zheng and Sun 2012)

He also posted a picture of himself with a sign reading, "Representatives at the two meetings, please pay attention to the Hepatitis B problem. – Lei Chuang, Hepatitis B virus carrier."

Lei's Weibo posts proved effective. Shortly after starting the Weibo campaign, Lei received a message from deputy Chang Kejun, a representative from Jiangsu province. Chang had seen Lei's policy proposals and turned them into three official opinions, which he put forth at the annual

---

[1] The full text of Lei's proposals is available in Chinese on his personal blog, http://blog.sina.com.cn/s/blog5b359b300100yma7.html.

sessions days later. Chang's message, which was only eight characters in Chinese, nevertheless conveyed a deep meaning: "Support, Concerned, Submitted, Best wishes" (Zheng and Sun 2012).

Public opinion surrounding Hepatitis B discrimination is slowly changing, as is the government's handling of the issue, in part because of NPC activism. In January 2013, the State Committee on Films and Broadcast Media announced that liver treatment commercials could no longer be aired, in line with Lei's suggestion and the formal opinions submitted by Deputy Chang ("State Committee on Films and Broadcast Media" 2013). Carriers of the virus are beginning to fight and win employment discrimination suits (Personal Interview BJ20213b). Lei is optimistic that the situation will continue to improve (Personal Interview BJ4213).

As for Lei himself, he planned on earning his master's degree the coming May, delayed one year because of his activist efforts. His hair is now pulled back in a pony tail, and he continues to write letters to the new premier, Li Keqiang. When asked whether he would ever cut his hair again, he said he planned to once he reached 1,000 days of letters (Personal Interview BJ4213). When asked whether he would be seeking formal employment after graduation, Lei smiled.

"Not yet," he said. "I still have some things to do."

Partial Responsiveness

A citizen facing personal discrimination, and realizing widespread discrimination against others, launches a publicity campaign and contacts his representatives for help. Some respond and submit formal policy proposals on his behalf. New policies are adopted that begin to address the problem.

This storyline sounds familiar, but the authoritarian setting is somewhat new. According to the theoretical framework, an authoritarian regime facing a threatening population has an incentive to account for citizen preferences in policy making. On issues where the regime has no strong preferences of its own, it may seek to respond to citizen demands, and create mechanisms to learn about those demands. Recall the theory's Proposition 1 and its observable implication:

Proposition 1: On no or weak preference issues, the Autocrat will adjust his policy decision $P \in (P_h, P_l)$ depending on whether he observes a Deputy message $M \in (M_h, M_l)$, assuming the Citizen can credibly commit to Revolution ($\pi \geq \frac{c}{\lambda b_C}$).

Observable Implication: An authoritarian regime will incorporate deputy proposals on weak or no preference issues into policy.

Lei's story resembles that of the Stable Responsive Equilibrium E2.3 from the Authoritarian Policy Making with Representation game in Figure 2.2. The Deputy conveys the Citizen's preferences on a weak/no preference issue, and the Autocrat selects the congruent policy. This is the responsive side of the NPC.

Note that the theory restricts responsiveness to a subset of issues, which is one of the key characteristics of the system of representation within bounds. Lei's story is moving, but it likely would have had a different ending if his policy goal had been to institute free and fair elections for People's Congress deputies, not simply to curb discrimination against carriers of Hepatitis B. The former issue is core to regime survival – explicitly mentioned in Document No. 9 – while the latter is relatively innocuous. If the theoretical framework is correct, deputy influence will be limited to these types of nonsensitive policy areas.

The purpose of this chapter is to test the observable implication above and get an objective read on the influence of NPC deputy policy proposals. Proponents of the rubber stamp view tend to dismiss the entire institution as meaningless. One prominent legal scholar observed, "These motions and opinions, they do not matter. They do not matter at all" (Personal Interview BJ006). This sentiment has been echoed by some of the representatives themselves. Hu Xiaoyan, an NPC deputy and migrant worker from Guangdong, famously commented, "As a parliamentary representative, I don't have any real power" (Bristow 2009).

Part of the controversy may stem from ambiguity. The NPC's proposal process remains largely opaque, and the skeptical observer may conclude that the proposals are pointless just because it is difficult to see their direct influence. There is also ambiguity in the language that surrounds the institution. In calling herself powerless, Hu Xiaoyan may be saying that she has no influence at all, or she may be referring to the fact that her influence on political issues and processes is minimal. Words like "meaningless" and "powerless" obscure important nuances.

My goal is to provide a test of the partial responsiveness idea in Observable Implication 1. Throughout the book, I take the approach of trying to solidify my inferences and understanding through triangulation, using different methods and sources to ascertain the true nature of representation and policy making in China's people's congress system. In this chapter, I will report findings from three research activities. The story that emerges is consistent. People's Congress deputies are not the most powerful actors in China's political system, but they are definitely not powerless. The evidence suggests that proposals that touch on sensitive political reforms generally fall flat, but proposals in other areas can be influential.

The remainder of the chapter is structured as follows. The next section provides some general background on the nature of the contemporary NPC and channels for deputy influence. More information on the historical evolution of the NPC is available in Chapter 7. The following section offers a detailed analysis of policy proposals from Hainan, which releases the full text of all deputy opinions and government responses. These documents offer an insider's glimpse into the nature of deputy–government exchange. I then present insights from interviews with several deputies at different levels of the People's Congress system, focusing specifically on the influence of their proposals. These first-hand accounts offer additional insights into the inner workings of the policy process. Last, I assess citizen perceptions of deputy influence through an original online survey. Citizens typically do not have a deep understanding of NPC processes, but their attitudes toward the institution demonstrate an awareness of its limitations.

NPC 101

As stated previously, the National People's Congress is formally the "highest organ of state power." Article 62 of the 1982 constitution gives the NPC the following powers, among others:

(1) to amend the Constitution;
(2) to supervise the enforcement of the Constitution;
(3) to enact and amend basic laws governing criminal offences, civil affairs, the State organs and other matters;
(4) to elect the President and the Vice-President of the People's Republic of China;
(9) to examine and approve the plan for national economic and social development and the report on its implementation;
(10) to examine and approve the State budget and the report on its implementation;
(14) to decide on questions of war and peace; and
(15) to exercise such other functions and powers as the highest organ of state power should exercise.

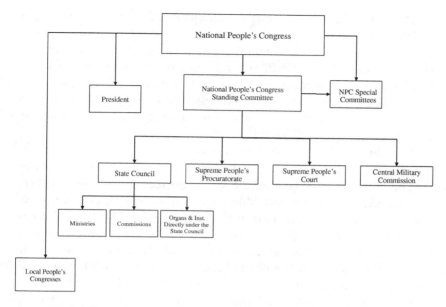

FIGURE 3.1 Formal institutional structure of the People's Republic of China

On paper, the NPC is the most powerful institution in the Chinese political system. It has the sole power to amend the Constitution, to enact laws, to elect the President and other key officials, to approve the State budget and economic plans, and to make war.

The NPC's appointment and supervisory powers grant it authority over the other major institutions in the Chinese government. This hierarchy is shown in Figure 3.1. Arrows indicate directions of *de jure* control.

The full plenary session of the 3,000-deputy NPC meets only once per year in March, as part of the annual "two meetings" (*lianghui*), the other of which is the Chinese People's Political Consultative Conference (CCPCC), an advisory representative body. During the rest of the year, authority is delegated to the NPC Standing Committee (NPCSC), which has about 175 members and meets regularly throughout the year. The NPCSC is endowed with nearly the same lawmaking powers as the NPC itself, although all constitutional amendments and high-level personnel appointments must flow through the full congress. The Standing Committee is the closest thing China has to a professional legislative body, and it is responsible for the day-to-day business of lawmaking (Jiang 2003).[2]

---

[2] Of the 37 laws or decisions promulgated in 2009 or 2010, the NPCSC passed 35, and the broader NPC only 2 (Law InfoChina Database).

The NPC also has "Special Committees" (*zhuanmen weiyuanhui*), which meet regularly to draft and discuss laws and policy proposals in different issue areas.[3] These committees are under the formal institutional control of the NPC and NPCSC and much of the government's actual legislative work is delegated to them (Chien-Min 2005). Each has its own staff, which works full time throughout the year (Jiang 2003). Their emergence in the reform period reflects a growing specialization and institutionalization of the NPC itself.

The NPC has formal authority over the other major institutions in the Chinese government, including the State Council (the executive branch), the Supreme People's Procuratorate (public prosecutor), the Supreme People's Court, and the Central Military Commission (the armed forces). These institutions in turn have their own subunits. The NPC also sits above the rest of the legislative system, the local people's congresses that replicate this basic structure at the provincial, prefectural, county, and township levels. The office of the President itself requires formal NPC appointment and is considered subservient to the legislative branch.

This formal organizational chart, and the constitution itself, grossly overstate the authority and importance of the NPC. While all institutions are subject to NPC supervision, in practice, they operate quite independently. The State Council is widely held to be the more powerful institution, as it effectively controls the entire bureaucracy, including ministries, commissions, and dozens of other organs. Combined, these institutions cover nearly all of the administrative and policy tasks of modern government, including tax collection, economic regulation, transportation, education and cultural management, and even the banking and media environments. The jurisdictional purview of the NPC is limited to the lawmaking process ("China's State Organizational Structure" 2014).

And of course, the authority of the NPC is curbed by the authority of the CCP, which has *de facto* control over the Congress and the entire government. This control – which is a major theme of this book – is exerted primarily through personnel appointments. As described in Chapter 6, the CCP tightly controls the nomination and election processes at every level in the people's congress system, ensuring that around 70% of deputies

---

[3] The committees are currently as follows: the Ethnic Affairs Committee; Law Committee; Committee for Internal and Judicial Affairs; Financial and Economic Committee; Education, Science, Culture and Health Committee; Foreign Affairs Committee; Overseas Chinese Affairs Committee; Environment and Resources Protection Committee; and Agriculture and Rural Affairs Committee. Additional committees or small working groups may also be convened to address specific policy issues.

are Party members. Leadership positions in the People's Congress system are also granted to senior Party leaders. The position of Chairman of the NPCSC is generally given to the second or third highest ranked member of the seven-person CCP Politburo Standing Committee. Wu Bangguo, NPCSC Chairman for the 11th NPC, was formally the second most powerful person in China during the Hu Jintao era. Zhang Dejiang, the new NPCSC Chairman under Xi, is currently the third most powerful. Other high-ranking Party members occupy the dozen or so Vice Chairman positions. In this way, the NPC and local people's congresses cannot diverge too far from the CCP, as they are led by and composed of the Party itself.

Deputy Mechanisms of Influence

For their part, NPC deputies have three main channels through which they can attempt to influence policy: voting, draft meeting participation and policy proposals.

Voting

The constitution requires majority approval for standard laws, and a two-thirds majority for constitutional amendments. Given CCP dominance of the institution, votes are never really contentious. There is little in the way of the vote counting or trading that we observe in a democratic context. To date, no single bill, work report, budget or appointment before the full NPC plenary session has ever been voted down.[4] Recent years have seen a rise in dissenting votes and abstentions, but these are largely symbolic oppositional acts and do not signal any real policy influence.[5] In fact, many deputies do not know the meeting agenda until right before the sessions begin, leaving them insufficient time to even read through the final pieces of legislation they are voting on (Personal Interview NH002). Appointments to high-level offices – such as the President and Premier – are decided behind closed doors at CCP meetings months in advance, and NPC deputies have effectively no input into these decisions. Vote counts are not publicized and are often not publicly available. These patterns fuel perceptions of the NPC as a meaningless rubber stamp institution.

[4] As Tanner (1995, 1998)) documents, the NPCSC has rejected a few contentious bills in its history, but the vast majority pass through without much in the way of opposition.

[5] At present, voting occurs through a secret ballot, although many deputies insist their voting patterns are known by Party authorities (Personal Interview BJ33113; Personal Interview BJ4413).

Draft Meeting Participation

Though voting is largely symbolic, deputies attempt to influence draft laws and policy in other ways, which are often overlooked. The voting process is uneventful in part because much of the consensus building occurs beforehand. The 2000 Legislation Law dictates that all draft laws must go through a relatively lengthy process of NPC review and debate before going to a vote – at least three separate draft discussions – which typically occur in the NPCSC or the associated NPC Special Committees (Paler 2005). Nonmember deputies frequently attend to offer their ideas and expertise. Over the five-year period of the 11th NPC (2008–12), more than 1,000 deputies attended draft meetings of the NPCSC as nonvoting members, and another 3,800 deputies participated in NPC Special Committee meetings.

Deputies suggest points of improvement and review the merits of the legislation. They often invoke their specific credentials to give weight to their opinions. Consider the comment by NPCSC member Xu Zhihong during a draft meeting for the Food Safety Law, which was passed in response to the Sanlu milk powder scandal.[6]

Different departments and administrative structures lack internal communication, and a few sectors lack supervision altogether, so when a situation emerges they cannot respond in a timely manner, which leads to serious problems. For example, the breeding of milk cows is overseen by the Department of Agriculture, the quality of milk products is overseen by the General Administration of Quality Supervision, Inspection, and Quarantine, while the sale and distribution of milk has no monitoring whatsoever. (*China National People's Congress Yearbook* 2009)

Xu goes on to describe provisions in the bill that would strengthen oversight and communication. This sort of contribution typifies this process. Many deputy comments focus on the bureaucracy and the appropriate delegation of responsibility between different departments.

As several China scholars have documented, the NPC has increased its role in the legislative drafting process in recent years. Draft discussions and specific deputy comments sometimes alter the language and content of a bill substantially (Tanner 1995; Jiang 2003; Paler 2005). This is a meaningful channel for information revelation that allows deputies to convey their knowledge to the regime.

---

[6] In 2008, an estimated 300,000 Chinese citizens fell ill after consuming milk or milk products tainted with melamine. Government investigations focused primarily on the Shijiazhuang-based Sanlu Group, whose milk powder was linked to the deaths of several infants.

Policy Proposals

The strongest channel for deputy influence is the opinions and motions process – sometimes referred to as the bill and nonbill papers process (Jiang 2003). Much of the existing work on representation in the People's Congress system has rightly focused on these proposals (O'Brien 1994; Manion 2011, 2013; Kamo and Takeuchi 2013; Li 2015). As discussed in Chapters 1 and 2, deputies are encouraged to convey citizen grievances and public opinion in the form of short policy recommendations. At the national level, deputies now propose over 9,000 opinions and motions each year, with hundreds of thousands more submitted to the provincial-, prefectural-, county-, and township-level congresses.

The proposal process has three general stages: submission, classification, and response. In the submission phase, deputies draft their policy ideas, which are often informed by direct contact with their constituents. The submission period occurs once per year and falls during the annual session in March. Motions (*yian*) call for new legislation or amendments to existing legislation and require the signatures of at least thirty other deputies. Opinions (*jianyi, yijian, piping*) are less formalized policy ideas that do not require additional signatures, although many deputies do seek out their colleagues to demonstrate support for their initiatives. Most of the signatures are exchanged during training sessions or delegation meetings just prior to the full session. Occasionally, opinions and motions receive the support of a full delegation.

Once the proposals are submitted to the NPC Presidium – the administrative committee of the full plenary session – they are formally classified into motions and different types of opinions, as well as by issue area. Some proposals are rejected if they do not meet the basic formatting and processing requirements, and some would-be motions are reclassified as opinions for similar reasons. When the classification is complete, the opinions and motions are sent to the appropriate government departments for processing. Motions remain in the formal legislative system and are usually sent to one of the NPC Special Committees or the NPC Standing Committee. Opinions are sent to the different ministries, administrative offices, institutions, and organizations under the State Council and generally do not reenter the legislative system (Jiang 2003; Liu 2014).

By law, all opinions must receive a formal response from a government office within six months. In their responses, the various ministries and agencies typically describe the contents of the proposal as they relate to the current policy environment, as well as any additional policy measures that will be taken as a result. The responding parties will also give the proposals an additional classification at this stage based on the intended response. For proposals given an "A" classification, the problem raised in the opinion has already been resolved. "B" opinions will be placed in a government work plan and gradually be resolved, and "C" and "D" proposals raise criticisms that the office cannot immediately address.[7] At this stage, deputies have the option of seeking additional clarification or reprocessing of their proposals, should they prove unsatisfied with the initial outcome.

For motions, the process is slightly different. NPC Special Committees determine whether the bill will be placed on the formal legislative agenda, incorporated into existing legislation, or dismissed. NPC deputies are kept informed of the processing outcome, although there is no legal six-month requirement for motion proposals (Jiang 2003; Liu 2014).

There remains some debate over whether these opinions and motions have any policy influence, in part because the process itself remains quite opaque at the national level. Most opinions and motions are not publicly available on the NPC website, and the government responses also remain confidential. One citizen expressed her frustration with the lack of transparency; "Every year, we hear about some opinion that we like, but we do not know what happens to it" (Personal Interview BJ003).

Official statistics and reports suggest that the opinions and motions have some influence. In the annual NPC Standing Committee work report, Chairman Wu Bangguo describes the efforts to incorporate deputy input during the past five years:

> We conscientiously implemented the Law on Deputies to People's Congresses, maintained an attitude of serving deputies, improved our services for them, and supported them in exercising their duties in accordance with the law. We handled 2,541 motions introduced by deputies, deliberated and passed 38 laws introduced in 227 of them; and are deliberating 8 legislative items introduced in 136 of them. We dealt with 37,527 deputy proposals; we have already resolved or made plans to resolve 76% of the issues raised in them, and over 90% of deputies are fully or somewhat satisfied with our work in this regard. (Wu 2013)

This seems like a positive sign for responsiveness – deputy opinions and motions are resolved, and deputies seem satisfied with the final outcomes. Still, we might be worried that these figures overstate the importance of the opinions and motions, or that the regime is painting a particularly rosy picture. In the remainder of the chapter, I try to get an independent read on the nature of this process.

---

[7] This classification is not necessarily indicative of a proposal's influence.

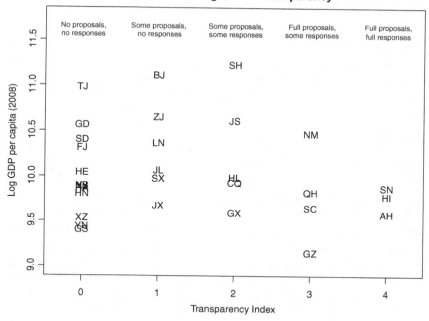

FIGURE 3.2 Economic development and legislative transparency
Note: The figure shows availability of information on provincial people's congress websites. Data collected in the summer of 2015.

Hainan Case Study

Hainan is a subtropical island, just off the southern coast of neighboring Guangdong. The whole province comprises an area of 13,100 square miles, about the size of Connecticut and Massachusetts combined. Recent government policies have focused on cultivating the image of "Hainan International Tourism Island," and the local economy largely revolves around the tourist industry.

The 385 deputies to the Hainan Provincial People's Congress (HPPC) meet once per year in February, just prior to the National People's Congress meeting in March. The HPPC case is particularly interesting because it represents the most transparent provincial legislative system in all of China (see Figure 3.2). Nearly all the opinions and motions, as well as the written responses from the relevant offices, are posted on the Hainan government website. This allows a glimpse of the opinions and motions process at the provincial level – who proposed what, who responded, and whether the proposals affected any policy change.[8]

HPPC Analysis

Like the proposals at the national level, the provincial-level opinions and motions in Hainan cover a broad range of topics. Among the 195 opinions proffered in 2012, 183 have full information available on the site. According to the official classification scheme, the most common topic is Transportation and Construction (50 proposals), followed by Science and Education (46 proposals); Agriculture, Forestry, and Water (40 proposals); Finance (21 proposals); Civil Affairs (8 proposals); Ecology and Environment (2 proposals); and Safety and Justice (1 proposal). Fifteen proposals fall into the residual "Other" category. Different government offices receive and respond to the proposals according to their content. The most common respondent is the provincial Department of Transportation (35 proposals), followed by the Departments of Education (19 proposals), Water Services (13 proposals), Finance (12 proposals), and Health (12 proposals), among many others.

To assess the influence of deputy proposals, I randomly selected ten opinions from 2012 for analysis. For each selected opinion, I conducted a close reading of the proposal and the response from the relevant office, attempting to discern if the opinion had any tangible policy influence. The randomness of the draw ensures that in expectation, the ten opinions are representative of the full population of proposals. We should feel relatively comfortable extending the insights learned from the analysis to the rest of the provincial-level proposals from Hainan. Extending the inferences to other provinces and the national level is another matter, which I return to later.

Tables 3.1 and 3.2 provide short summaries of the ten proposals, as well as summaries of the official responses.[9] Each proposal was also assigned a crude influence rating of high, medium, low, or unknown. These ratings are subjective, but in essence, high-impact proposals had an obvious and substantial effect on policy; low-impact proposals had no tangible effects; and medium-impact proposals seemed to contribute to

---

[8] As of the original writing of the manuscript in 2012 and 2013, the HPPC was the first congress with the full set of proposals and responses available. As of 2015, Anhui and Shaanxi also post the full set of proposals and responses.

[9] The full Chinese text of the opinions and responses is available on the Hainan provincial government website, www.hainan.gov.cn/code/V3/tian/. The proposals are fully searchable by proposal number, year, and topic.

TABLE 3.1 *HPPC opinion analysis – high/medium influence proposals*

Name	Proposal summary	Response summary	Influence
#2079: On the Construction of the Fire Escape Route for Jianfengling National Forest Park	*Deputy Huang Jiaqi:* The current fire escape/prevention roads for Jianfengling National Forest Park are inadequate. Proposal calls for an 280 million RMB investment to construct 46.6 KM of roads.	*Provincial Forestry Bureau:* Response recommends the project be included in the annual provincial key projects. The Forestry Bureau will expedite the approval process. The project will get the total investment of 280 million.	High
#2006: On the Enrichment of Migrant Workers' Cultural and Spiritual Lives	*Deputy Yun Weicun:* Proposal calls for a number of measures to improve the quality of life of migrant workers: specialized libraries, museums, performances; a fund to promote cultural enrichment opportunities; special training schools and weekend campuses; and personal counseling sessions.	*Provincial Department of Culture, Radio, Television, Publication, and Sports:* The response details a new plan including free public cultural facilities that cater to migrant workers; special mobile libraries for migrant workers; public library reading rooms; and special funds for migrant worker cultural activities.	High
#2115: On Supporting Construction to Increase Small Scale Irrigation and Drinking Water Safety in Qiongzhong County	*Qiongzhong Delegation:* Proposal calls for the relevant departments to increase investment in Qiongzhong county's small-scale irrigation and safe drinking water projects.	*Department of Water Services:* Response expresses agreement with the severity of the irrigation problem in Qiongzhong. The office will fight for small-scale irrigation projects and will allocate 12.65 million RMB for projects in Qiongzhong.	Medium

(*cont.*)

TABLE 3.1 (cont.)

Name	Proposal summary	Response summary	Influence
#2120: On the Establishment of My County's First Public Cemetery	*Deputy Wang Guangye:* Proposal calls for the establishment of a 500 acre public cemetery in Qiongzhong County, including financial support of 30 million RMB.	*Provincial Department of Civil Affairs:* Response discusses that the financial burden for burial reform rests on city/county governments, but given Qiongzhong's impoverished situation, the department recommends it receive additional support.	Medium
#2144: On the Correction of the Bridges and Viaducts of the East Central Railway	*Deputy Lin Xu:* Proposal describes problems with construction standards for Hainan's East Central Railway and calls for the government to rectify the situation – widening the bridge pavement, strengthening fences, and constructing sidewalks.	*Department of Transportation:* The office plans to organize a meeting in July of members of the Hainan East Railway Company and the relevant government offices to carry out on-site research into the problems raised in the proposal.	Medium

TABLE 3.2 *HPPC opinion analysis – low influence proposals*

Name	Proposal summary	Response summary	Influence
#2155: On the Widening of Rural Highway Construction Standards to Meet the Needs of Rural Public Transportation	*Deputy Cai Yangsheng:* Roads in certain rural areas are not up to standard. The proposal calls for the widening of rural road pavement standards to 4 or 4.5 meters, as well as financial support.	*Department of Transportation:* Existing regulations state that general oversight for road construction fall under the purview of city/county governments.	Low
#2158: On Strengthening the Planning and Supervision of Urban–Rural Architectural Style	*Deputy Yang Sitao:* Proposal calls for better supervision of the construction process, including: clearer standards on construction, more complete approval processes and supervision, and more public participation.	*Department of Housing:* The office has already created a guide to construction in Hainan, which includes many concerns outlined in the proposal. It will continue to work on preserving historical areas and creating public participation mechanisms.	Low
#2119: On the Construction of Minority Folk Museums	*Deputy Wang Guangye:* Proposal calls for construction of folk museums to protect Li and Miao heritage. The folk museums could include training, research, and foreign exchange centers. Each project requires 100 million RMB investment.	*Provincial Ethnic and Religious Affairs Commission:* Response agrees with the need to strengthen the protection of minority heritage but states that the financial obligation for public cultural facilities falls under the purview with city/county governments.	Low

(cont.)

TABLE 3.2 (cont.)

Name	Proposal summary	Response summary	Influence
#2114: On Increasing Education Investment in Qiongzhong County	*Qiongzhong Delegation*: Proposal asks the provincial government for additional funding of 173 million RMB to support two local education projects in Qiongzhong County, an impoverished area.	*Department of Education*: The response describes recent efforts by the provincial government to support education projects in Qiongzhong, including support for the two projects described in the proposal. The department recommends that Qiongzhong County find alternative means of funding.	Low
#2193: On the Four Districts of Haikou City Entering into the Provincial Transfer Payment System	*Deputy Tian Lixia*: Currently the four districts of Haikou City are excluded from the transfer payment system from the provincial government to cities and counties. The proposal calls for their inclusion.	*Department of Finance*: Not available.	Unknown

policy making in a limited way. One proposal, which concerned extending provincial transfer payments to districts within Haikou city, did not have a publicly available response.

Of the ten proposals, two can be classified as high-impact, three as medium-impact, four as low-impact, and one as unknown. I estimate that roughly half of the proposals appear to have some form of policy influence.

Deputy Yun Weicun's opinion, titled "On the Enrichment of Migrant Workers' Cultural and Spiritual Lives," seems to have been the most influential. It was also the most convincing in its argumentation and evidence. The first part of the proposal cites the results of a survey of 3,336 migrant workers in Haikou to show the hardships facing this disadvantaged group:

Cultural life is monotonous, and entertainment is solitary. The main source of cultural activities for migrant workers is self-entertainment or attending the activities organized by their work unit. Self-entertainment includes reading magazines and newspapers, surfing the internet, watching television, and playing cards, which comprise 25%, 19%, 15%, and 15% participation, respectively. In the survey, the migrant workers responded that the public cultural facilities in the city are relatively few, and the programs organized by the unit are few and uninteresting. They also expressed excitement about watching movies, listening to concerts, and going to the library, but the current expenses for these cultural activities make it difficult for them to attend due to their low incomes.

The proposal goes on to use the survey evidence to describe additional migrant woes, including difficulties finding suitable marriage partners and stress from financial problems.

The second half of the opinion contains a series of policy ideas, stemming from the survey findings, to directly improve the living conditions of migrant workers. Deputy Yun calls for the improvement of public cultural services such as libraries, museums, and concerts directly targeting migrant workers. He also demands the creation of new funds to provide migrant workers with a subsidy for their cultural activities and the establishment of special schools that can provide technical training and counseling sessions.

The response by the Provincial Department of Culture, Radio, Television, Publication, and Sports was equally thorough, and demonstrated a sincere commitment to Yun's recommendations. On April 6, 2012, the office coordinated a meeting of several government departments that resulted in a new policy program, described in the "Opinion on the Further Strengthening of the Migrant Workers' Cultural Work." The response details a series of policies that will be enacted in the coming years, many of which are directly taken from the original proposal. The province will create rural public movie screenings; establish cultural and athletic programs for migrant workers; promote migrant worker access to museums and libraries; establish mobile book stations; create literary clubs; send books and movies to migrant worker factories and mines; provide psychological and financial counseling; and create opportunities for the integration of migrant workers into city life. The provincial government will set aside special funds to maintain these programs.

Not all proposals had this level of impact, nor should we expect them to. Some proposals, such as deputy Wang Guangye's opinion on the construction of minority folk museums, have little success because their requests are targeted at the wrong level of government. Wang's proposal outlines concerns over the disappearing heritage of the Li and Miao minorities and calls for the construction of museums and other cultural centers, each requiring an investment of around 100 million RMB. The response from the Provincial Ethnic and Religious Affairs Commission agreed with the general importance of cultural preservation, but noted cooly, "In accordance with the current financial management system, construction of public cultural facilities at the city and county level are under the purview of city and county governments." The provincial-level congresses are tasked with handling provincial-level issues, and proposals with scope outside the authority of the provincial government are usually dismissed.[10]

Many opinions make similar financial requests, and their success or failure seems to depend on the budgeting decisions of the various provincial-level departments and the severity of the issue at hand. Deputies from the Qiongzhong delegation, representing an impoverished mountainous county in central Hainan, came together to propose an opinion to raise investment in small-scale irrigation projects. In its response, the Department of Water Services agreed to continue fighting for irrigation in the county and committed to allocating 12.65 million RMB over the following four years. A similar proposal from the Qiongzhong delegation, requesting 173 million RMB in additional funding for two school projects, was met bluntly with the recommendation to "find alternative sources of funds."

---

[10] Deputies report that this type of jurisdiction issue is a common reason that their proposals are rejected (Personal Interview HN41113; Personal Interview HN42313).

None of these ten proposals are particularly threatening to the regime, nor central to its own political interests. These are weak or no preference issues where the Autocrat has no strong inclinations of its own, but is seeking to adjudicate different policies to placate the Citizen as well as possible. It is no coincidence that in choosing ten random proposals, I have not turned up any that advocate political reforms of any importance. In fact, a closer look reveals that out of the 183 proposals with public information, not a single one touches on anything inimical to the regime's direct interests. There are no proposals on political reforms of any sort. This is to be expected and is characteristic of the system of "representation within bounds." As we will see in the next chapter, deputies at the national level rarely advocate for meaningful political change, either.[11]

Limitations and Alternative Perspectives

This look at the provincial-level opinions process in Hainan produces a few tentative conclusions. First, it appears that at least some proposals, although certainly not all, have a tangible policy influence. Collectively, the ten opinions in the close analysis initiated a systematic cultural enrichment initiative for migrant workers; reallocated 12.65 million RMB for small-scale irrigation projects; raised funding for the construction of a 500 acre public cemetery; spurred a task force to address construction deficiencies and safety concerns on a central railway line; and raised 280 million RMB in investment for the construction of a fire prevention road in a national forest.

Second, the bureaucratic units do appear to take the deputies' proposals quite seriously, even proposals that do not ultimately achieve tangible influence. In response to deputy Yang Sitao's opinion, "On Strengthening the Planning and Supervision of Urban–Rural Architectural Style," the Department of Housing produced a several page comment that offered a detailed three-point description of existing policy measures to improve supervision of construction, as well as a five-point plan of future initiatives. It is unclear whether Yang's ideas really shifted the department's

---

[11] Recall that according to official press statements, there were actually 195 opinions made in 2012 in the HPPC, which means that we are missing information on 12 proposals. It is possible that some of these proposals are missing precisely because they touch on political issues. My impression is that it is more likely that the proposals were not released either because of laziness and bureaucratic mismanagement, or because they were of such poor quality as to be embarrassing to the government. Interviews with NPC staffers suggest that these two issues are quite common (Personal Interview NH001), and so we should not assume that the omitted proposals call for sensitive political reforms.

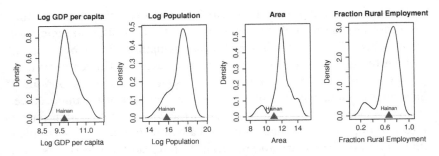

FIGURE 3.3 Representativeness of the Hainan case
Note: The figure shows densities of provincial variables for 2008. Hainan is depicted with a gray triangle.

thinking, but it is clear that the department is attentive to the issue and his proposal's contents.

Third, the idea of partial responsiveness does seem to have some empirical truth, although it is difficult to know for sure because proposals on the regime's "strong preference issues" are so few and far between. It is telling that we do not observe any on the publicly available website. Either such proposals are rarely made, or when they are, they are buried out of public view. This is not a parliament where opposition is actively voiced, as is described in the cooptation view.

There are two core limitations of this Hainan case study. The first is that we simply do not know counterfactually whether the high-influence policies would have been enacted even in the absence of deputy activity. The analysis is based on the official record – proposals and responses – but we might be concerned that this record distorts the true nature of the proposal process. Perhaps deputies know that some kinds of proposals are likely to be implemented, and so they propose them simply to get formal legislative recognition. Perhaps bureaucratic or provincial leaders "ghost write" deputy proposals that they would like to implement, and the deputies themselves are meaningless pawns in this process.

A second concern relates to the representativeness of the Hainan case, and whether we can infer from the HPPC to other provincial people's congresses or the NPC. Figure 3.3 shows the distributions of several covariates for China's provincial-level units. Hainan, while slightly smaller than most provinces, is at around the median level of economic development and urban–rural divide.

Still, we might be worried that Hainan's transparency is precisely what makes it responsive, and less progressive congresses might not actually incorporate deputy ideas into policy making. The theory rests on the idea that public attention drives government responsiveness, so to the extent that transparency drives public attention, the Hainan provincial government may be more attentive to deputy requests. Even worse, perhaps the authorities in Hainan have increased legislative transparency precisely because the information revealed makes them look good. If the transparency in Hainan is causally determined by responsive governance itself, we cannot generalize very far from this case.

Together, these concerns suggest that the method and case employed in this section offer a "most likely" or "disconfirmatory crucial case" for the theory (Gerring 2007). If we cannot find evidence of partial responsiveness using this method in the HPPC – which may have preconditions for responsiveness – it is unlikely that we would find the relationship in other cases. The fact that we have found partial responsiveness does not mean that we have fully confirmed the theory, but simply that the test has failed to disconfirm the theory. This a is weaker form of evidence than a "least likely case" or "typical case," but it is the best evidence that can be mustered at this point in time.

I will leave it up to the reader to judge whether this finding from Hainan teaches us anything about the proposal process elsewhere in the People's Congress system. My personal opinion is that while Hainan is unique in terms of some of its economic characteristics, its legislative processes are effectively the same as those in other provinces, as well as in the National People's Congress. Just like NPC deputies, representatives in the HPPC draft opinions and motions, which are referred to relevant government offices and responded to in kind. The only difference is that these proposals and responses are published on line. I suspect that many of the patterns and tendencies from the HPPC can telescope upward to the national level and generalize to other provinces, although Hainan may prove to be at the more responsive end of the spectrum.

As an additional check on partial responsiveness, the next two sections consider how deputies think about their own influence, and how citizens view things from the outside.

Deputy Perceptions

How do deputies and NPC insiders view the opinions and motions process? My limited interviews reveal two findings, both consistent with the "representation within bounds" framework. First, deputies in general are satisfied with the responses from the handling government agencies.

Second, deputies with a reformist bent – those who tend to push the boundaries with their proposals – are more skeptical and report instances where their opinions were disregarded or dismissed.

One deputy, newly elected to a municipal-level congress in Hunan, eagerly described her first formal opinion, which helped improve waste management in the city. Before attending the annual meeting, she called some of the other professors and students from her school and asked if there were any specific concerns. One dean said that a lot of people had complained about the garbage compactor located outside of the university's main gate. Residents dumped trash in and around the compactor, and it would sometimes accumulate for days before being removed. The compactor was also located next to some food stands and attracted swarms of mosquitoes in the summer months. This gave a terrible first impression of the school, which was in the process of trying to improve its image (Personal Interview HN42313).

She wrote an opinion on this issue, using food safety and sanitation as justification, and submitted it in 2013. Shortly thereafter, she ran into the mayor of her city, who was aware of her proposal, and he informed her that the compactors would be relocated to less populated areas. The deputy felt moved that her voice had been heard (Personal Interview HN42313).

Another deputy from Beijing reports a similar experience. In her local neighborhood, a pedestrian walkway was obstructed from the view of oncoming motorists, and nine people had been hit and killed in the previous few years. After learning about the numerous traffic accidents, the deputy relayed the problem to the municipal government in the form of a formal opinion. The opinion was referred to the Beijing Municipal Committee of Transportation, which invested 3.6 million RMB to construct a pedestrian underpass (Personal Interview BJ4413).

Interestingly, that same deputy – who was not affiliated with the CCP or any of the several "democratic" parties – reported much different feelings on how some of her edgier political proposals had been treated.

> But then to me, being a people's deputy, I have to change the rules, to make sure officials know what they can and can't do. They need to know that they too must follow the Constitution . . . But they only let you bring up certain things. Even if you have discussed at the sessions, they would say, "No, do not discuss it any more." You are controlled . . . It has the potential to arouse people.

She went on to describe how her dedication to promoting human rights and the rule of law ultimately cost her the deputy seat (Personal Interview

BJ4413). We will return to the relationship between deputy actions and career outcomes in Chapter 5.

Recall that according to official government statistics, 90% of NPC deputies report feeling satisfied with how their proposals were handled by the responding organizations. My limited interviews suggest that deputies in general do indeed feel that their voices are being heard (Personal Interview BJ32713b; Personal Interview HN41113; Personal Interview HN42313; Personal Interview HN42413), but that certain reformist deputies are less satisfied with their level of influence (Personal Interview BJ33113; Personal Interview BJ4413). This finding accords with the idea of partial responsiveness.

Other academic treatments of the NPC describe a similar pattern of deputy influence. In his comprehensive description of NPC processes, Chinese legal scholar Jiang Mingan describes numerous instances of deputy influence through the introduction of opinions and motions. In 2001, Deputy Hu Pingping introduced a motion demanding more investment in compulsory education. The bill was assigned to the NPC Education, Science, Culture, and Public Health Committee. The committee determined that although the motion did not merit additional legislation, it did reveal shortcomings in implementation. It ultimately resulted in a "major adjustment in compulsory education for rural areas," and Hu was satisfied with the outcome (Jiang 2003, p. 345).

In another example, Jiang describes a set of twenty-one motions jointly introduced by 700 deputies in the 9th NPC (1998–2002), calling for improvements to campus safety for students and teachers. The State Council appointed a special task force to address the issue, which collected additional insights from the Public Security Bureau, the Ministry of Education, and the Legal Office of the State Council. The task force lead to the introduction of more comprehensive measures to promote campus safety (Jiang 2003, p. 345).

In his many examples of deputy influence, Jiang – who is a former NPC staff member – does not cite a single one that seems to touch on meaningful political reform. His analysis categorizes 495 proposals by issue area from the 9th NPC. Only two concern "political system reform." Very few national-level proposals seem to address these issues, let alone have a major influence.

Perhaps the best evidence for partial responsiveness is the nature of deputy activism. Recall that the model suggests that the Deputy will tend to be more active when the Autocrat is willing to respond, and that conveying Citizen preferences comes at some cost in effort. In the NPC, we observe deputies taking time out of their normal lives to propose thousands of opinions and motions. As I will further show in Chapter 4, they tend to focus their efforts on nonpolitical issues. If the opinions–motions process were really just a meaningless exercise, it is hard to imagine that deputies would expend the amount of energy they do. And if the regime were equally responsive to political and nonpolitical proposals alike, it is hard to imagine we would observe deputy efforts being focused almost exclusively on the latter.

The View from Outside

A final method of gauging the influence of the NPC's proposal process is to ask normal citizens how they view the institution. Most Chinese citizens do not have intimate knowledge of the inner workings of the People's Congress system. Their lack of interest may stem from the relatively closed nature of the system and the lack of electoral accountability (Shi and Kong 2006). Still, from interviews and casual conversations, it seems that many citizens grasp the partial responsiveness inherent in the opinions and motions process.

To assess citizen perceptions more comprehensively, I conducted an original online survey of Chinese netizens. The China Policy Attitudes Survey (CPAS), done in partnership with a local marketing firm, elicited attitudes on politics and policy making in China. In total, 10,000 survey solicitation links were sent out, yielding a sample of 2,270 responses.[12] More information on sample quality is available in Truex (forthcoming).

Respondents were exposed to series of hypothetical NPC deputy opinions and asked to give their level of support for the policy, as well as their perceptions on whether it would ultimately be adopted. The text below shows the wording for this set of questions.

> M1. Suppose there is a new policy idea to require all senior government officials to publicly report their family's annual earnings. This policy was proposed by an NPC deputy.

---

[12] Data from this survey have already passed through the peer-review process (Truex forthcoming). It should be emphasized that the CPAS sample is by no means representative of the Chinese population – only 39.9% of citizens (538 million) had Internet access as of June 2012 – but it can be considered loosely representative of the online population. These citizens tend to be younger, wealthier, better educated, and more likely to live in urban areas.

a. How much do you support this policy idea?
 1. Do not support at all (*genbenbuzhichi*)
 2. Do not support (*buzhichi*)
 3. Neutral (*hennanshuo*)
 4. Support (*zhichi*)
 5. Completely support (*wanquanzhichi*)
b. In your opinion, how likely is it that this policy will be adopted?
 1. Completely unlikely (*wanquanbukeneng*)
 2. Unlikely (*bukeneng*)
 3. Somewhat likely (*youxiekeneng*)
 4. Likely (*keneng*)
 5. Very likely (*feichangkeneng*)

The hypothetical opinions covered a range of issues. In addition to the asset disclosure system in question M1 above, the respondents provided their assessments for policy proposals with the following aims: to fund a one billion RMB irrigation project for a rural county; to lower the legal marriage age to 18 for both men and women; to institute direct elections of deputies to the provincial people's congress; and to provide 5% more funding to build special hospitals for Hui Muslims.

Some of these proposals run against core regime interests. An asset disclosure system would undermine rent distribution among the CCP elite and could even bring about damaging scandals. Direct elections for the provincial people's congress would inhibit the ability of the Party to manipulate the people's congress system and could potentially beget calls for further elections at higher levels of government. In terms of the model, these policies are "strong preference issues" where the regime has its own policy preferences that contradict those of the citizenry, or at least a portion of the citizenry.

The other three policies are relatively innocuous. Irrigation projects, special hospitals for minority groups, and the marriage age are not core to regime survival, so there is no inherent conflict between the Autocrat and the Citizen. These are "no preference" or "weak preference" issues, in the parlance of the theory.

Based on the CPAS data, citizens do seem to systematically perceive partial responsiveness to NPC opinions and motions. Figure 3.4 shows "heat maps" of assessments toward the five different proposals. The proposals on the top with light gray dots are the three noncore issues, while the two on the bottom with dark gray dots are more central to regime

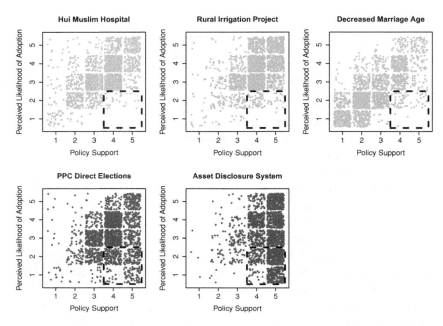

FIGURE 3.4 Citizen perceptions of the proposal process
Note: The figure shows heat maps of citizens' support for different hypothetical deputy opinions against their perceived likelihood of adoption. Each dot represents one individual response. Responses jittered to better show the distribution. Dotted boxes indicate citizens with unmet expectations. All data drawn from the China Policy Attitudes Survey.

survival. Each dot represents a single survey question response, jittered to better show the distribution. The plot shows responses in two dimensions – the individual's support for the policy and the perceived likelihood of adoption.

For the three nonsensitive issues, we see real congruence between public opinion and the perceived likelihood of adoption. The Hui Muslim hospital and rural irrigation project proposals receive high levels of support, and most citizens believe this type of policy will ultimately be adopted. This is evidenced by the clusters of responses falling in the upper right quadrant. The marriage age proposal also shows this alignment of expectations, but in the opposite direction. Most respondents do not support lowering the marriage age to eighteen, but they also feel that this proposal is unlikely to be successful.

The two more sensitive issues tell a different story. The asset disclosure system is almost uniformly supported, as is the policy calling for direct election of provincial people's congress deputies. Almost all of the points fall on the right side of the plots. Despite this support, citizens remain skeptical that these proposals will ultimately have any influence.

The dotted boxes indicate respondents with unmet expectations, those who support a policy but feel that it is unlikely to be adopted. For the two sensitive issues, a large number of respondents fall into this region, while almost none do so for the innocuous issues.

It is also worth noting that more educated, politically savvy citizens seem less enamored with the NPC in general. In related research, I use the CPAS data to show that citizens exposed to images of an NPC public participation portal express greater satisfaction with the regime and feelings of political efficacy, but this finding is limited to less educated citizens (Truex forthcoming). Education in China proves strongly associated with more liberal political attitudes, and the partial responsiveness in the NPC may not be enough to placate citizens who yearn for political reform.

"Small Things"

To summarize, there is evidence that the CCP regime exhibits partial responsiveness to demands proffered by People's Congress deputies. Opinions and motions on sensitive political reforms seem to be silenced and discarded, but those conveying other grievances can actually make a difference. The representation afforded by the people's congress system does have a meaningful informational role in Chinese policy making.

Many observers become frustrated with NPC deputies for not utilizing their authority to push for political reform. There is a tendency to dismiss their influence. One young professional describes her impressions:

Those deputies, whatever they do is very restricted. They will not be able to actually change much. If they wanted to put something forth that really changed things, the government would not let them. They would say, "why do you not support the Party?" They change some things, but mostly small things. (Personal Interview BJ003)

She believes deputies can change "small things," but also laments that they are tightly controlled by the CCP and may be powerless on political matters.

I agree with this citizen's general assessment, but I have come to dislike this language, after learning a hard lesson on dismissing deputy activism. In the analysis above, I described one deputy's efforts to relocate the garbage compactor outside of the local university (Personal Interview

HN42313). I had seen the garbage compactor upon entering the campus, but it had just been emptied, so it did not strike me as a particularly serious issue. During the interview, as the deputy told her story, I remember thinking that she was missing the mark on what really mattered. The deputy was passionate about waste management reform, but there had to be more important issues – even nonpolitical issues – that needed attention.

Later that week, I went out to lunch with a good friend from the neighborhood, and asked him the same question I had asked the deputy. What exactly was the most pressing issue that needed fixing in this city?

"Garbage," he said. "The garbage problem is very serious."

Before dismissing deputy influence as insignificant, it is important to remember that significance lies in the eye of the constituent. Deputies can get roads built, hospitals funded, regulations changed. These are not small things. This chapter has shown that the proposal process is a meaningful input into nonsensitive policies. The next will test whether deputies are really tone-deaf to constituent demands.

4

Testing Representation

Hongyu Online

NPC deputy Zhou Hongyu counts his constituent emails daily. Zhou's personal website – www.hongyu-online.com – was the first of its kind, providing detailed information on his legislative activities. Constituents can read the full text of Zhou's latest opinions and motions, brush up on the details of his personal story, and even contact him with their own ideas. "The Website is receiving an increasing amount of mail from netizens, especially during the annual session of the National People's Congress," he explains. "This morning when I logged on it, I received 18 mails. At noon, I had another dozen. Just now, I received four more. And it's not over yet" ("NPC Deputy Zhou Hongyu" 2007).

Zhou's website, combined with his passion for the job, has made him something of a super-legislator. In his first two terms in office (2003–12), Zhou singlehandedly proposed 212 different opinions and motions, addressing issues ranging from the antiquated petition system to rampant employment discrimination. He frequently turns constituent emails into formal proposals, but his personal pet issue is education reform. In 2003, Zhou's first year as a deputy, he put forward a suggestion for instituting free compulsory education in rural areas, but his proposal was later denied by the Ministry of Finance on the grounds of financial unfeasibility. Zhou redoubled his efforts, working with other experts to calculate the cost of the free education program ("Prof a Student" 2011). He raised the proposal again in 2004, this time including a more complete sustainability calculation, and reportedly slipped it into Premier Wen Jiabao's hands during a brief exchange ("NPC Deputy Zhou Hongyu" 2007). Two years later, Zhou's opinion became reality in the 2006 Amendment to the

Compulsory Education Law, which guaranteed nine years of free compulsory education for children in the countryside.

This diligence has earned Zhou a reputation as one of China's top legislators, and he has quickly risen up the People's Congress hierarchy. He was recently reselected to serve his third NPC term, and he now concurrently serves as deputy director of the Hubei Provincial People's Congress Standing Committee. The state media frequently celebrate his accomplishments with lengthy interviews. Some have fondly labeled him "cannon mouth Zhou" or "the crowing rooster" because he loudly alerts the government to citizen demands. *The Global Times*, a pseudo-CCP mouthpiece, recently praised Zhou's efforts ("Deputies' Bite" 2012):

The ongoing reform in China calls for more persistent "crowing roosters" like Zhou. Our reform is going through a critical period where we need to clear things up. NPC deputies should be loyal to their obligations by crowing, "It is dawn. Time to get up!"

Zhou Hongyu continues to crow. Most recently, he has been working on ensuring educational equality for migrant workers, improving school bus safety, reforming the college entrance examination system, and increasing vocational education opportunities (Rui 2012). Despite his legislative success, Zhou retains a modest public persona and is quick to attribute his accomplishments to the responsiveness of Party leadership. "Since 2003, when this government came into operation, there has been an obvious change in its concept of administration," he says. "It is a pragmatic government that's close to people" ("NPC Deputy Zhou Hongyu" 2007).

How to Be a Deputy

For an authoritarian regime trying to respond to rising citizen demands, Zhou Hongyu might be the ideal parliamentary representative. His website portal and other investigations give him insight into the problems of his constituents, and he dutifully conveys these insights in dozens of policy proposals each year. Zhou is careful, though, in that he constantly reaffirms his loyalty to the regime. His motions and opinions do not call for sensitive political reforms, and they do not touch on issues that are core to the CCP's own interests. This is the nature of "representation within bounds."

According to the theoretical framework, the Autocrat would generally like the Deputy to convey her knowledge of the Citizen's preferences with message M. This facilitates the sort of responsive policy making we saw in Chapter 3. At the same time, he would prefer the Deputy to remain reticent S on issues where he is unwilling to make concessions, issues where the Citizen has contrarian preferences. Recall Proposition 2 and its observable implication:

Proposition 2: On no or weak preference issues, the Autocrat is strictly better off when the Deputy conveys the message M. On strong preference issues, the Autocrat would prefer the Deputy to remain silent S.

Observable Implication: Deputies in stable authoritarian parliaments should exhibit "representation within bounds" behavior, reflecting the interests of their constituents on the regime's weak or no preference issues, but remaining reticent on strong preference issues.

Successful regimes will try to walk this middle line, promoting representation on certain issues and curbing representation on others.

The previous chapter was dedicated to exploring the opinions and motions process and testing responsiveness to deputy ideas in China's policy-making apparatus. This chapter is dedicated to exploring the nature of representation and testing whether deputy proposals display any systematic connection with the demands of the population.

This chapter presents some of the first research to compare the actions of authoritarian legislators with the concerns of their geographic constituencies. Using a nationally representative survey from 2008, I derive public opinion estimates on various policy issues at the provincial level (Gelman and Little 1997; Park, Gelman and Bafumi 2004; Warshaw and Rodden 2012). I pair these with new data on the backgrounds and behavior of all 2,978 NPC deputies. Across three of the four issues with public opinion data, the NPC deputies display congruence with their provincial-level constituents. We also see congruence using demographic or group density measures – such as rural, business, minority or migrant worker interests. The data also show temporal increases in deputy activity in response to various governance shocks – the 2008 Sichuan earthquake, the 2008 Sanlu milk powder scandal, the 2011 Wenzhou train accident, and the 2013 Beijing "Airpocalypse." As before, though, activism proves limited to nonpolitical issues. Deputies rarely advocate meaningful political reform and appear largely tone-deaf on this front.

Empirically, one key concern is the influence of regime leadership on deputy activism (Shih 2008; Lu and Liu 2015). Recall that according to the "elite mobilization" view, NPC deputies simply echo the preferences of Party elites in order to curry favor and get promoted, what Shih (2008) has called "nauseating displays of loyalty." The fact that we observe congruence might be because Party elites have already learned the preferences of the citizenry through other means, not through information revelation in the people's congress system. To address this issue, I collected information on the public statements of the governor and Party secretary of Jiangxi province and tested whether and how they were related to deputy activism. This analysis suggests that the vast majority of deputy statements cannot be mapped to publicly expressed leader preferences, and that leaders often lag deputy attention to an issue. This is consistent with the information revelation mechanism of the theory.

In short, something resembling representation can and does arise in the authoritarian context, although it appears limited to a subset of the issue space. The remainder of the chapter tries to establish the truth of this claim empirically. The next sections describe the basic research design and data collection. I then turn to conducting tests of congruence, using direct public opinion data and demographic proxies as measures of constituent preferences. I also explore temporal shifts in deputy activism as they relate to known public opinion shocks. The chapter closes with a discussion of alternative perspectives and limitations, focusing on the elite mobilization argument.

Data and Research Design

Beginning with Miller and Stokes' (1963) seminal work, scholars of American politics have evaluated the strength of representation in the U.S. Congress through the lens of "preference congruence" – the link between public opinion and legislator activity.[1] Congressmen from liberal districts display more liberal voting behavior, and those from conservative districts prove farther right. More recent inquiries now take this general congruence as given and focus on teasing out the conditions leading to "ideological shirking" (Hurley and Hill 2003; Lax and Phillips 2009a).

These studies are most helpful from a research design standpoint. Generally the first step is to construct a measure of constituency preferences or public opinion. Early studies of the United States relied on demographic proxies such as race or religion (Kalt and Zupan 1984; Krehbiel 1993;

---

[1] See Miller and Stokes (1963), Erikson (1978), Kalt and Zupan (1984), Peltzman (1984), Jackson and King (1989), McDonagh (1993), Levitt (1996), Hurley and Hill (2003), Brace, Sims-Butler, Arcenaux and Johnson (2002), Ardoin and Garand (2003), Clinton (2006), and Percival, Johnson and Neiman (2009).

Levitt 1996), party vote shares in presidential elections (Ansolabehere, Snyder and Stewart 2001; Canes-Wrone, Brady and Cogan 2002) and referenda outcomes (Kuklinski 1978; McCrone and Kuklinski 1979; McDonagh 1993). Others have employed direct survey measures of public attitudes, constructing district-level attitudes by aggregating individual survey responses (Miller and Stokes 1963; Gelman and Hill 2007; Lax and Phillips 2009a; Warshaw and Rodden 2012).[2] Miller and Stokes's (1963) original study, for example, uses survey responses on constituents' attitudes toward civil rights, foreign involvement, and social welfare. More recently, Lax and Phillips (2009a) investigate policy responsiveness on gay rights, utilizing a survey that measures attitudes toward gay marriage, sodomy laws, hate crimes, and protection against discrimination.

The second step in the analysis is to determine whether the constituent preference measures are systematically related to legislator behavior. In the U.S. setting, scholars frequently employ roll call data (Poole and Rosenthal 1984; Poole and Rosenthal 1985; Levitt 1996), placing individual legislators on a unidimensional liberal–conservative spectrum using thousands of different votes. Simple regressions of legislator ideology on constituent ideology allow a test of congruence, with positive relationships indicative of substantive representation (Miller and Stokes 1963; Ansolabehere, Snyder and Stewart 2001; Clinton 2006; Bafumi and Herron 2010).

The analysis in this chapter will benefit from this well-forged methodological path. Data availability will prevent me from replicating some state-of-the-art techniques, but the Chinese legislative system has grown transparent enough in recent years to allow for an extension of this basic research design. I will use public opinion and demographic data, as well as a measure of legislator behavior, to investigate whether NPC deputies aim to address the issues most pressing to their geographic constituents. If we observe congruence, this will be evidence that there is a degree of representation in the body, at least on nonsensitive issues.[3]

The analysis involves the use of two primary datasets: the NPC Deputy Database (NPCDD) and the China Survey. The NPCDD was compiled

---

[2] See also Wright, Erikson and McIver (1985), McCrone and Stone (1986), Gibson (1992), Brace, Sims-Butler, Arceneaux and Johnson (2002), Hurley and Hill (2003), Park, Gelman and Bafumi (2004), Selb and Munzert (2011).

[3] It is important to emphasize that when I assert that the NPC affords a degree of representation, I am referring solely to substantive representation (Pitkin 1967). I am by no means claiming that Chinese citizens can hold their representatives accountable, or view them as legitimate. The NPC largely fails on these other dimensions of representation.

by the author from publicly available sources in Chinese in the summer of 2011, spring of 2012, and summer of 2015. I also employ basic demographic and economic data to aid in the measurement of constituent interests.

Measuring Legislator Backgrounds and Activity

The NPC Deputy Database contains personal background information for all 2,987 NPC members in the 11th Congress (2008–12). While the official Chinese version of the NPC website contains some basic information on the deputies (age, gender, party membership, etc.), a richer set of variables was collected using Baidu Encyclopedia, China's version of Wikipedia. Like Wikipedia, Baidu contains short profiles of noteworthy individuals, and roughly 80% of members had detailed information on the site. In instances where the information was not detailed enough, additional Internet searches of newspapers and other websites were conducted until the missing information could be filled in. Government lists were also used to create indicators for key positions (membership in NPC committees, party leadership positions, previous legislative experience, etc.). In total, 2,683 members (90%) have full data, and those without are missing only a few variables. In addition to providing information on the demographic profile of the NPC, the data will allow me to incorporate personal background characteristics into the analysis.

This background information was augmented with detailed records of all publicly available proposals and informal policy-relevant press comments put forth by the deputies from 2008 through 2012, 3,104 statements in all. The full text of the motions and opinions is not available at the national level, but newspapers frequently provide short three- to five-sentence summaries of the policy content.[4] An example motion summary from an article on deputy Zheng Xinsui is shown below:

> To ensure good water quality of the Danjiangkou Reservoir, NPC Deputy Zheng Xinsui raised two or three regulatory measures to strengthen water pollution control. First, to block all excessive sewage source. Second, to do the local soil and water conservation work. Third, to establish unified and coordinated supervisory bodies. (Zhang 2008)

The popular Latent Dirichlet Allocation (LDA) model was used to place the proposals into different issue categories (Blei 2012; Grimmer

---

[4] The data management company Oriprobe aggregates newspaper articles mentioning NPC deputies. Any articles mentioning opinions, motions, or other policy ideas were selected and included in the topic model. A limited number of opinions and motions are posted directly on the NPC website, and these were also included in the database.

and Stewart 2013; Lucas et al. 2015; Roberts, Stewart and Tingley 2015). LDA is a form of unsupervised machine learning where an algorithm identifies various topics contained in pieces of text without conceptual restrictions from the analyst. Topics are simply distributions of words, and documents are modeled as mixtures of different topics. In comparison with standard hand-coding procedures, the core advantages of the topic modeling approach are that it is scalable, replicable, transparent, and less vulnerable to biases from coder error or researcher manipulation. On the part of the researcher, the effort shifts from developing and implementing a coding scheme to adjusting and interpreting the topic model output (Lucas et al. 2015).[5]

The topic model estimated places the 3,104 comments in the 25 categories shown in Table 4.1.[6] The table shows the proportion of comments in the sample most closely associated with the different topics, as well as the most common four words associated with each topic. Deputies discussed a range of issues over the five-year period, including healthcare (Topic 3, 4.6% of proposals), environmental protection and energy conservation (Topics 8 and 25, 5.6% of proposals), housing (Topic 11, 2.6% of proposals), food safety (Topic 20, 4.2% of proposals), rural interests (Topic 22, 4.3% of proposals), and business regulation (Topic 23, 4.4% of proposals).

With these topics in hand, each document was coded into its "most likely" category and then merged with the NPC Deputy Database. This yields a count variable for every topic, giving the total number of proposals/policy-relevant comments on each issue for each deputy. These measures will compose the main dependent variables for the analysis.[7]

Measuring Constituent Interests

Data for public opinion comes from the China Survey, conducted under the auspices of Texas A&M and Peking University's Research Center on

---

[5] Earlier versions of this analysis used a predefined coding scheme (Truex 2014). The core results on preference congruence remain the same when either a coding scheme or an unsupervised machine learning approach is used. The shift to the latter was done in the interest of transparency and replicability.

[6] For this analysis, I set the number of topics $K = 25$, as this produced a manageable and interpretable set of topics.

[7] Note that the LDA model actually represents each document as a mixture of different topics. Creating variables off of the most likely topic actually loses some information from the model, and an alternative approach would be to create more granular dependent variables that utilize this mixture information. I eschewed this approach in the interest of simplicity and interpretability, and because it is more consistent with previous circulated versions of the analysis.

TABLE 4.1 *Proposals and comments in the 11th NPC (2008–12)*

#	Topic name	n	%	Highest probability words
1	NPC session	137	4.4	peopl, year, congress, nation
2	Legal system/lawmaking	114	3.7	law, system, legal, right
3	Healthcare	144	4.6	medic, health, hospit, insur
4	Cultural protection/ minority issues	113	3.6	cultur, chines, nation, heritag
5	Education	207	6.7	educ, school, student, univers
6	Water conservation/ irrigation	79	2.5	water, river, conserv, construct
7	Development	302	9.7	develop, industri, econom, promot
8	Energy/emissions	104	3.4	energi, power, develop, industri
9	Taxation	115	3.7	incom, tax, increas, fund
10	Crime, order, and punishment	128	4.1	court, case, crimin, peopl
11	Housing	81	2.6	hous, afford, citi, price
12	Economic integration	118	3.8	develop, region, cooper, taiwan
13	Pharmaceutical industry	61	2.0	drug, medicin, price, chines
14	Government/social stability	195	6.3	peopl, social, govern, public
15	Coal/steel industry	105	3.4	coal, industri, product, steel
16	Disaster prevention	108	3.5	year, disast, tourism, will
17	Internet management	102	3.3	inform, network, internet, children
18	Technology/innovation	135	4.3	technolog, innov, research, develop
19	Regional development	117	3.8	area, develop, region, forest
20	Agriculture/food safety	129	4.2	agricultur, food, product, safeti
21	Migrant workers/labor	117	3.8	worker, employ, migrant, labor
22	Rural interests	133	4.3	rural, farmer, villag, urban
23	Business environment	137	4.4	enterpris, market, financi, develop
24	National security/interests	56	1.8	servic, beij, said, olymp
25	Environmental protection	67	2.2	protect, environment, environ, pollut
	Total proposals and comments	3,104		

Notes: The table shows the motions, opinions, and informal policy opinions that are publicly available from 2008 to 2012. The data are drawn from the NPC Opinion Deputy Database, which was gathered by the author using Chinese newspaper sources in summer of 2011, spring of 2012, and summer of 2015. The topics were produced by a topic model with $K = 25$ using the STM R package (Roberts, Stewart and Tingley 2015).

Contemporary China (RCCC) in 2008. The survey used multistage probability sampling to obtain a nationally representative sample of 3,989 adults.

While certain issues are still too politically sensitive for nationwide survey research, the questionnaire did ask respondents to rate the seriousness of several societal issues on an increasing scale from 0 to 10. For the analysis here, we will focus on how respondents rated four issues: environment, housing, healthcare, and public order. These questions map closely to the topics identified in Table 4.1, allowing us to assess whether deputies are more likely to propose policies relating to the issues deemed most serious by their geographic constituents. The question wording for the "issue seriousness" variables is shown below, along with the relevant topics from the NPCDD:

> Q902. Now we would like you to consider a few problems that many countries face. On a scale from 0 to 10, with 0 indicating this is not a problem at all in China and 10 indicating this is an extremely serious problem, how serious do you think these problems are in China today?

> Environmental protection (*huanjing baohu*) (Topics 8 and 25)
> Public order (*shehui zhian*) (Topics 2 and 10)
> Housing (*zhufang*) (Topic 11)
> Healthcare (*yinliao fuwu*) (Topic 3)

The task is to take the full sample of individual responses from the China Survey and construct provincial-level measures of issue seriousness. The simplest method is to disaggregate the data down to the provincial level, perhaps weighting them to account for the China Survey's sampling design. The main issue with this approach is that without a substantial number of survey observations, the estimates can become imprecise (Miller and Stokes 1963; McCrone and Stone 1986; Hurley and Hill 2003), especially at low levels of disaggregation (Warshaw and Rodden 2012).[8] Simple disaggregation of the China Survey appears problematic, as some of the provincial units have as few as 54 respondents.[9]

---

[8] It is possible to improve precision by pooling multiple surveys (Wright, Erikson and McIver 1985; Gibson 1992; Brace, Sims-Butler, Arceneaux and Johnson 2002), but this approach assumes that preferences are temporally stable over time, an assumption that can prove tenuous if the gap between surveys is substantial. For our purposes, relatively few national-level surveys have been conducted in China, and those that have typically do not ask the same battery of questions.

[9] For areas with few observations, these unpooled preference estimates will have a tendency to be more extreme (Gelman and Hill 2007, p. 256).

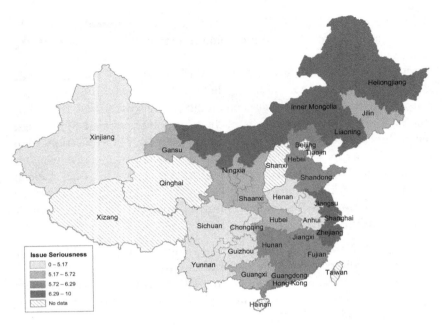

FIGURE 4.1 Perceived seriousness of the environmental issue
Note: The figure shows environmental "issue seriousness" scores. All estimates derive from the 2008 China Survey using the MRP model described in the Technical Appendix.

In response to these perceived issues, scholars of representation have moved toward estimating constituency-level preferences with a technique called multilevel regression and poststratification (MRP). MRP utilizes census information and places respondents in their geographic context with a multilevel model (Park, Gelman and Bafumi 2004; Gelman and Hill 2007; Lax and Phillips 2009b; Selb and Munzert 2011; Warshaw and Rodden 2012).[10] The basic idea is to get more precise measures of public opinion by bringing geographic information to bear.

I use this MRP procedure to derive estimates of the mean issue seriousness scores for each province from the 2008 China Survey. Interested readers are encouraged to look at the Technical Appendix of this chapter for specific details on the estimation process. Figure 4.1 illustrates the

---

[10] In a systematic comparison of simple disaggregation and MRP using public opinion data on gay rights, Lax and Phillips (2009a) find that MRP yields smaller predictive errors and more reliable estimates. MRP proves particularly effective when data are scarce, and it can be employed successfully with a single national-level poll.

scores for the environmental issue. The map is shaded by quartile, with darker regions corresponding to areas where citizens express greater concern for environmental issues. As would be expected, citizens in the more densely populated coastal areas seem to care more about the environment, and those in the interior provinces less so. There is also considerable variance in "issue seriousness" across the other three issues.

Note that there are a large number of proposals that do not map well to specific questions on the China Survey. As an additional assessment of the quality of representation, we can employ demographic data instead of public opinion measures (Kalt and Zupan 1984; Krehbiel 1993; Levitt 1996) to see whether the presence of certain groups is systematically related to deputy activity. This sort of analysis is not a direct test of congruence between public opinion and legislative activity, but positive relationships would give further evidence that deputies are attentive to the needs of their geographic constituents.

The analysis will consider proposals focused on the four groups with a reasonable number of group-focused proposals: farmer/rural citizens (topics 20 and 22), the business community (topic 23), minority groups (topic 4), and migrant workers (topic 21). To measure farmer/rural interests, I use the share of the provincial economy composed of agriculture (*farming*), which ranges from 0.01 in Shanghai to 0.30 in Hainan. To measure the minority community, I measure the fraction of the population that is non-Han (*nonhanpop*), which ranges from 0.00 in Jiangxi to 0.95 in Tibet. To measure the business community, I use the fraction of the population employed by "Top 500" companies (*businessemp*). This measure ranges from 0.00 in Ningxia and Tibet to 0.10 in Shanghai. For migrant workers, I use abs[1 − actual population/registered population], the absolute value of 1 minus the ratio of the province's actual population to its registered population (*migrantexp*). This measure is high for provinces that either (a) have a large migrant population (such as Beijing, *migrantexp* = 0.38) or (b) have had a lot of migrants leave the province (such as Henan, *migrantexp* = 0.09). All measures are constructed from official government statistics and reports from 2008.

Testing Representation

The next step is to determine whether the constituent measures are systematically related to deputy behavior. The simplest analysis is to investigate the bivariate relationships with aggregated data at the provincial level. I will avoid reducing the four issue seriousness measures to a

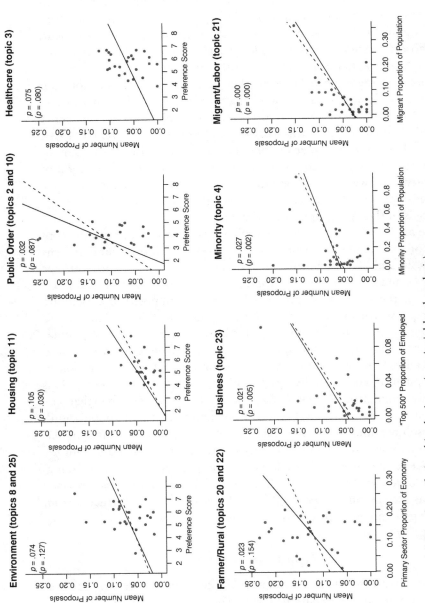

FIGURE 4.2 Bivariate relationships by issue (provincial-level analysis)

Notes: The figure shows scatterplots of the mean number of issue proposals per deputy (Y_p) against the provincial issue seriousness or group density variable (P_p) for the 25 provinces with full data. The plots also include visual estimates of the linear model $Y_p = \alpha + \gamma P_p + \epsilon_p$ for the eight different issues. The dotted lines and *p*-values in parentheses are from a robust regression that accounts for outliers. All *p*-values reflect one-sided hypothesis tests.

single liberal–conservative spectrum (Poole and Rosenthal 1984, 1985; Levitt 1996; Pan and Xu 2015).[11] Figure 4.2 shows scatterplots of the mean number of issue proposals per deputy (Y_p) against the provincial issue seriousness or group density variable (P_p) for the 25 provinces with full data. The plots also include visual estimates of the linear model $Y_p = \alpha + \gamma P_p + \epsilon_p$ for the eight different issues. The coefficient of interest is γ. Congruence would require $\gamma > 0$, while $\gamma \leq 0$ would suggest that deputies' proposals do not map well to the concerns of their geographic constituents. The p-values from a formal one-sided hypothesis test are shown in the upper left corner of each plot, and the dotted lines reflect the results of a robust regression that accounts for outliers.

Despite the small number of observations, the analysis shows strong positive relationships between preference scores and deputy behavior in the NPC. The estimate of γ is positive and reaches conventional levels of significance in seven of the eight regressions, and six of eight once outliers are accounted for.

The provincial-level estimates are suggestive of congruence, but to better capture the data-generating process, I also estimate a count model at the deputy level:

$$Y_i \sim \mathrm{NB}\Big(y_i\big|\; e^{(\alpha + \gamma P_{p[i]} + \beta X_{[i]} + \epsilon_{p[i]})}, \sigma^2\Big). \qquad \text{(NBREG)}$$

Here, each deputy's total number of proposals on a given issue Y is modeled as drawn from a negative binomial distribution with dispersion parameter σ^2.[12] The issue seriousness or group density variable (P_p) is the same for all deputies within a provincial delegation. The model also includes a constant α and a vector of deputy-level covariates X that are related to preferences and participation.[13] Standard errors are

---

[11] Pan and Xu (2015) do find evidence that ideology in China can be measured on a unidimensional scale, but note that I am measuring issue seriousness assessments, not ideology.

[12] The data exhibit overdispersion, which suggests that a negative binomial specification is more appropriate than a Poisson model. It is also possible to estimate a simple probit/logit model with a binary dependent variable, but I prefer the count variable and negative binomial specification are preferable in that they capture more information.

[13] The demographic variables include indicators for gender (*female*), not attending university (*lowed*), non-Han (*minority*), and a continuous measure for age (*age*). The professional variables include indicators for CCP membership (*ccp*), democratic party membership (*demparty*), legal training or experience (*legal*), being a hero/athlete/celebrity (*sociaelite*), being a member of the CCPCC (*partyelite*), being a CEO of a publicly listed company (*economicelite*), and being a professor or researcher (*researcher*), and a continuous indicator for the number of previous NPC terms (*npcexp*).

TABLE 4.2 *Issue seriousness coefficient estimates* $(\hat{\gamma})$

	(1) Environment (Topics 8 and 25)	(2) Housing (Topic 11)	(3) Health (Topic 3)	(4) Order (Topics 2 and 10)
Issue seriousness (P_p) –	0.136	0.426***	0.096	0.466***
Full MRP	(0.116)	(0.102)	(0.138)	(0.162)
Excl. professional	0.129*	0.409***	0.118	0.253*
covariates	(0.086)	(0.102)	(0.139)	(0.163)
Excl. demographic	0.175*	0.437***	0.079	0.464***
covariates	(0.113)	(0.102)	(0.134)	(0.169)
Excl. all individual	0.166*	0.418***	0.098	0.264*
covariates	(0.106)	(0.102)	(0.130)	(0.164)
Issue seriousness (P_p) –	0.124	0.456***	0.110	0.439***
Trim MRP	(0.120)	(0.106)	(0.147)	(0.167)
Issue seriousness (P_p) –	0.142*	0.348***	0.120	0.478***
No Types MRP	(0.111)	(0.112)	(0.138)	(0.165)
Issue seriousness (P_p) –	0.121	0.269***	0.113	0.439***
Disaggregated	(0.117)	(0.123)	(0.136)	(0.158)

Notes: The table shows results of negative binomial regressions of deputy proposals on provincial issue seriousness (P_p) and deputy-level covariates. The primary associations prove robust across four different methods for estimating issue seriousness: the full MRP model (Full MRP); the MRP model without provincial-level covariates or the regional effect (Trim MRP); the MRP model without individual-level covariates (No Types MRP); and the estimates from simple disaggregation (Disaggregated). Standard errors are clustered at the provincial level and reported in parentheses. The p-value indicators correspond to tests of the one-sided null hypothesis $H_N : \gamma \le 0$. * $p < 0.10$, ** $p < 0.05$, *** $p < 0.01$.

clustered at the provincial level to account for the grouped structure of the data.[14]

Tables 4.2 and 4.3 shows the regression results and robustness across different covariate sets, as well as four public opinion estimation procedures (Full MRP, Trim MRP, No Types MRP, and Disaggregated).[15] The estimate for the coefficient γ is positive for all eight issue areas, and it reaches conventional levels of significance in 30 of the 44 regressions.

To get a sense of the magnitude of these effects, we can consider how the probability of offering a proposal changes for different levels of constituency density/preferences. I simulate the probability of offering a

---

[14] More formally, clustered standard errors account for the possibility that for two deputies i and j from the same province p, $\mathrm{cov}(\epsilon_{p[i]}, \epsilon_{p[j]}) \ne 0$.

[15] The estimation procedures are detailed in the Technical Appendix to this chapter.

TABLE 4.3 *Group density coefficient estimates* ($\hat{\gamma}$)

	(1) Farmer/rural (Topics 20 and 22)	(2) Business (Topic 23)	(3) Minority (Topic 4)	(4) Migrant/labor (Topic 21)
Group density (P_p)	1.814*	9.135**	0.653	3.399***
	(1.390)	(4.397)	(0.718)	(1.106)
Excl. professional covariates	2.162*	9.526**	0.636	3.259***
	(1.338)	(4.505)	(0.713)	(1.141)
Excl. demographic covariates	1.959*	9.813***	0.921	4.732***
	(1.322)	(4.048)	(0.642)	(1.213)
Excl. all individual covariates	2.192**	10.434***	0.944	4.622***
	(1.301)	(3.880)	(0.627)	(1.138)

Notes: The table shows results of negative binomial regressions of deputy proposals on provincial group density measures (P_p) (*farming, businessemp, nonhanpop, migrantexp*) and deputy-level covariates. Standard errors are clustered at the provincial level and reported in parentheses. The *p*-value indicators correspond to tests of the one-sided null hypothesis $H_N : \gamma \leq 0$. * $p < 0.10$, ** $p < 0.05$, *** $p < 0.01$.

proposal as a function of the issue seriousness or group density variable (P_p) in the province, holding the individual-level covariates constant at their median values.

Residents of Guangxi prove least concerned with the housing issue (issue seriousness = 4.03), in sharp contrast to residents of Shanghai (score = 7.90). According to the estimates, this level of change in perceived issue seriousness raises the likelihood of a housing proposal for this "median deputy" from 0.005 to 0.091, an eighteenfold increase.[16] On minority and cultural preservation issues, moving from Jiangxi (*nonhanpop* = 0.00) to Tibet (*nonhanpop* = 0.95) would increase the "median deputy's" likelihood of a minority-related proposal from 0.053 to 0.146, nearly a three-fold increase. The congruence on business issues is also striking. A deputy from Shanghai (*busemp* = 0.10) is about five

[16] Note that these probabilities are low by the nature of the data collection. As mentioned before, the NPCDD contains only 3,014 motions, opinions, and informal policy statements from 2008–12. The true number of proposals is much greater – there were nearly 9,000 in 2010 alone. The analysis here does not purport to estimate a deputy's true probability of making a proposal, but simply to show that the probability for the data we can observe seems to be systematically related to perceived issue seriousness at the provincial level.

times more likely to comment on the business environment and regulations than a deputy from Ningxia (*busemp* = 0.00).[17]

The congruence analysis above suggests that there is a connection between deputies' activities and the interests of their constituents. As an additional test, I investigate whether deputies respond to shocks in public concern over various governance issues, exploiting the temporal nature of the data.

In the analysis period, several societal events heightened citizen demands for reform:

> *Pollution* – In January of 2013, air pollution in Beijing reached record levels, with the U.S. Embassy's air pollution index reading 755, beyond the scale maximum. The event became dubbed the "Airpocalypse."
>
> *Disaster preparedness* – On May 18, 2008, an earthquake struck Wenchuan County, Sichuan, resulting in the deaths of nearly 70,000 people, many of them children trapped in the rubble of poorly constructed schools.
>
> *Food safety* – In the summer of 2008, milk powder adulterated with melamine – a compound used in countertops and dry-erase boards – was distributed throughout China, resulting in the hospitalization of over 50,000 infants.
>
> *Railway management and transportation* – On July 23, 2011, two high-speed trains collided in Wenzhou, Zhejiang, killing 40 people.

Each of these events created widespread societal discussion and government criticism. They relate to issues that can be considered weak or no preference policies, as they are not core to the nature of the one-party state.

Figure 4.3 shows a simple temporal congruence test. Using publicly available proposals and comments from 2003 to 2015, I identified the proportion in each year that contained keywords relating to the four governance shocks above: earthquake, food safety, railway, and pollution.

We can see visually that these topics increased in salience in the NPC shortly after they increased in salience in Chinese society. For example,

---

[17] When asked to discuss variance in the nature of deputy proposals, one NPC staff member remarked, "Deputies from poorer western provinces propose different types of motions than deputies in the richer eastern areas. A lot of their proposals are about helping out farmers, strengthening the social safety net. Deputies from the eastern provinces talk more about the business climate and investment. This reflects divisions in society" (Personal Interview NH001).

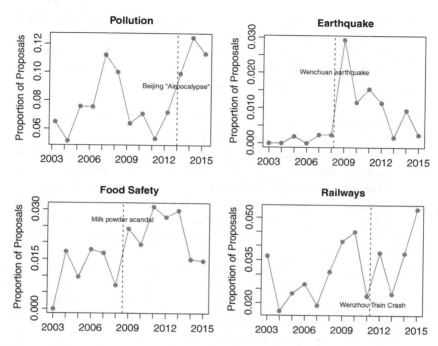

FIGURE 4.3 Exploring temporal variation – weak preference issues
Notes: The figure shows the proportion of proposals in each year that contain keywords relating to four governance shocks. All comments are drawn from the Oriprobe deputy database.

following the Beijing "Airpocalypse" of January 2013, comments on pollution among NPC deputies increased 35%, making up nearly 10% of all proposals. This proportion increased further to 12.4% of proposals in 2014. The food safety issue similarly took off in the NPC following the milk powder scandal, with discussion of the issue increasing over 200% between 2008 and 2009. Proposals on railway safety and earthquake preparedness similarly spiked following the governance shocks, with proposals increasing 67% and 1,100%, respectively.

This temporal look illustrates the crisis-based responsiveness of the Chinese system. In addition to the deputy reaction, we also observe a strong policy response shortly following each scandal. In December 2008, the government amended the Law on Protecting Against and Mitigating Disasters from Earthquakes. In 2009, it introduced a new comprehensive Food Safety Law. In 2013, it disbanded the Ministry of Railways. And following the pollution crisis, governments at various levels have taken measures to improve air quality, with a new nationwide Environmental Protection Law taking effect in 2015.

In other instances, scandals in Chinese society potentially heightened citizen demand for reform on an issue, but the issue itself was too sensitive or too core to the nature of the one-party state:

Corruption/abuse of power – On October 6th, 2010, 22-year-old Li Qiming hit two other university students with his car. When confronted by the police, he yelled, "My father is Li Gang!" – the deputy director of the local public security bureau. The phrase later became an Internet meme, signifying corruption and the abuse of power.

Village elections and governance – In December of 2011, villagers in Wukan expelled CCP officials because of land disputes and corruption. The event later came to symbolize the inadequacy of the village elections system.

Domestic security – On July 17th, 2013, fruit vendor Deng Zhengjia was killed in public by urban management officials (*chengguan*) after an altercation. News of his death brought widespread public criticism of the urban law enforcement system. In January 2008, citizen Wei Wenhua was killed by similar officials after filming a confrontation between villagers and officials.

Although not specifically identified in Document No. 9, issues of corruption, village elections and domestic security are touchy subjects for the regime. While the CCP leadership does openly discuss corruption, it does not need deputies to draw attention to embarrassing corruption scandals. The corruption discourse must occur on its terms, as evidenced by Xi Jinping's recent crackdown on anticorruption dissidents. Similarly, the government routinely amends the Electoral Law and invites deputy input, but it does not want to highlight that the tightly controlled elections have failed to produce adequate governance at the lowest levels. The domestic security apparatus is essential to the repressive authoritarian state. The CCP does not want societal discussion of its repressive nature, let alone discussion in the NPC.

Figure 4.4 shows NPC activity on these strong preference issues. Comments on corruption actually decreased sharply following the Li Gang incident, and rebounded only after Xi Jinping formally launched his anticorruption campaign and reopened the issue space. Discussion of village elections was muted following the Wukan incident in 2011. Discussion of the *chengguan* and other domestic security forces is a nonissue in the

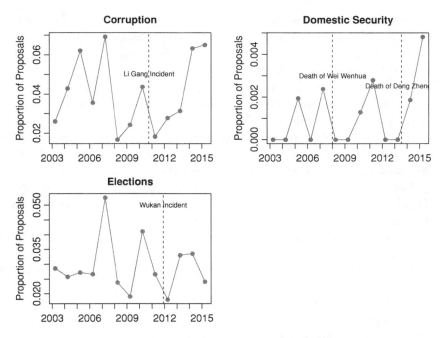

FIGURE 4.4 Exploring temporal variation – strong preference issues
Notes: The figure shows the proportion of proposals in each year that contain keywords relating to three governance shocks. All comments are drawn from the Oriprobe deputy database.

NPC, even following highly publicized deaths. There were only eight or so comments on the urban police force in a twelve-year period.

Limitations and Alternative Perspectives

While many observers paint deputies to China's National People's Congress as tone-deaf and disconnected (Pei 2010; Mu 2012), the new data gathered and analyzed here show something different. At a broad level, deputies' proposals seem to address the issues deemed most serious by the people they claim to represent. Shocks in public opinion seem to be met with a legislative response, but only for nonsensitive issues.

Before we proceed to the next chapter, it is important to be forthright about the three major limitations of this representation analysis. First, it is possible that my sample of publicly available proposals might not be representative of the full population of proposals. This is an issue for any dataset drawn from newspaper sources and official websites, to an extent, but it may be particularly worrisome in the authoritarian context. Certain comments may be purposely omitted from official websites or managed out of the media space.

There is no way to objectively assess the representativeness of the data. Personal conversations with NPC staffers would suggest that the "publicly available bias" might not be terribly severe. When asked why only a subset of proposals appear on the official website, one staffer replied bluntly, "It's because we are too lazy" (Personal Interview NH002). From her perspective, the primary reason why some proposals are not made public is a lack of institutional resources. Of course, this opinion should be taken with some skepticism, but it gives at least some justification for relying on newspapers and official government websites.

Second, the analysis can be criticized on the grounds that the independent (issue seriousness scores/group density) and dependent (deputy policy proposals) are not measured on the same scale. Thus, it is impossible to tell just how responsive deputies are to their constituents, only the general direction of the relationship (Bafumi and Herron 2010). Scholars of representation in the United States have devised ways around this issue. Levitt (1996) uses vote scores compiled by Americans for Democratic Action (ADA) to develop same-scale preference measures for senators and their constituents. Bafumi and Herron (2010) ask participants to rate their support for specific bills, in turn placing them on the same roll call based scale as their representatives. Unfortunately, closed NPC voting procedures make it impossible to employ either of these two methods, and the voting process itself is not really the main forum for representative activity anyway.

The NPC has grown more transparent over time, and those close to the institution assert that there are plans to release even more information in the coming years (Personal Interview BJ009). My analysis offers an initial assessment of the quality of representation in the NPC, but I hope that other scholars will be able to replicate and extend the inquiry, as happened with Miller and Stokes' (1963) initial study of representation in the U.S. House of Representatives. With better data, future research may be able to overcome the limitations I have encountered here.

The third criticism is that some of these findings may be considered observationally equivalent to the elite mobilization view. Perhaps deputies do not really convey the preferences of the citizenry, but simply echo the concerns of provincial or central leaders, who have learned these preferences through other means. In this view, there is not much in the way of representation in the NPC, and the institution is characterized by an empty exchange between leaders and deputies.

My interviews with those close to the People's Congress have never suggested this dynamic (Personal Interview NH001; Personal Interview NH002; Personal Interview BJ21513; Personal Interview BJ32713b; Personal Interview BJ4413; Personal Interview HN41113; Personal Interview HN42313), and most deputies would likely insist that they receive their inspiration from below, not above (Manion 2014, forthcoming). Still, to rule out this criticism more rigorously, we must consider the temporal interplay between elite policy priorities and deputy statements.

To this end, I compiled 88 public statements from Jiangxi governor Wu Xinxiong and party secretary Su Rong from 2008 to 2010, which gives us a sense of elite policy preferences over time for this province. Jiangxi is chosen because it is a relatively representative province in several basic attributes (size, income levels, rural–urban divide, etc.), and it had consistent leadership throughout the 11th NPC. At the time of the analysis period, both Wu Xinxiong and Su Rong were both considered rising stars in the political system, and they would occupy their positions for the duration of the 11th NPC. Both would eventually be promoted, Su Rong to vice-chairperson of the Chinese People's Political Consultative Conference, and Wu to director of the National Energy Administration.[18] Both leaders voiced distinct policy positions during their early tenure in office, allowing us to see whether their ideas were indeed echoed by deputies in the Jiangxi delegation.

This analysis is summarized in Figure 4.5. It shows provincial leadership statements and the publicly available deputy proposals, grouped by year. Any possible "echoing" relationships, defined as a topical match between a deputy proposal and a prior leadership statement, are depicted with solid rightward black arrows. Any possible leader responses to deputy statements, topical matches that occur in opposite temporal order, are shown with dotted leftward arrows.

Su Rong was officially appointed Secretary of the CCP provincial committee in November of 2007. He had previously served in the same role in Qinghai and Gansu, earning recognition for being tough on the Falungong religious sect. He did not immediately articulate strong policy goals

---

[18] Su Rong ultimately lost out in the power struggle following Xi Jinping's ascension. A close ally of security head Zhou Yongkang, Su Rong was himself investigated for corruption and expelled from the Party. For this reason, I limit the analysis to Su's early tenure as Jiangxi Party Secretary, as he was still considered quite powerful and influential at this time.

Provincial Leader Statements (2007–8)

- Development/Rural Interests (grain production): Wu Xinxiong, 21-Mar-08, 13-Jun-07
- Energy and Emissions (water/air): Wu Xinxiong, 1-Aug-07
- Housing (affordable housing): Wu Xinxiong, 1-Nov-07
- Business Environment (finance and insurance): Wu Xinxiong, 14-Jan-08
- Disaster prevention (snow): Su Rong, 29-Jan-08; Wu Xinxiong, 5-Feb-08

Provincial Leader Statements (2008–9)

- Disaster Prevention (flood): Su Rong, 10-Jun-08
- Regional Development (Poyang Lake Ecological Zone): Su Rong, 5-May-08, 2-Jan-09; Wu Xinxiong, 8-Mar-08, 17-Feb-09
- Education (university administration reform): Su Rong, 19-Jun-08, 9-Jul-09, 21-Jul-08
- Energy/Emissions (nuclear power): Wu Xinxiong, 17-Mar-08
- Economic Integration (Hong Kong): Wu Xinxiong, 28-Aug-08, 13-May-08
- Development (railway construction) Wu Xinxiong, 10-May-08, 12-Aug-08, 30-Dec-08, 13-Feb-09, 4-Mar-09
- Development (tourism): Su Rong, 18-Aug-08
- Technology/Innovation: Su Rong, 5-Nov-08; Wu Xinxiong, 5-Nov-08
- Migrant Workers/Rural Interests (employment, income, pension, training): Su Rong, 15-Dec-08, 5-Jan-09, 7-Jan-09, 11-Jan-09, 17-Feb-09, 12-Mar-09; Wu Xinxiong, 22-Dec-08, 19-Feb-09
- Housing (affordable housing): Wu Xinxiong, 25-Aug-08

Provincial Leader Statements (2009–2010)

- Migrant Workers/Rural Interests (employment, income, pension, training): Su Rong, 14-Apr-09, 22-Apr-09
- Energy/Emissions (nuclear and solar power): Su Rong, 8-July-09; Wu Xinxiong, 30-Mar-09, 26-May-09
- Crime, Order, and Punishment (organized crime): Su Rong, 18-Aug-09
- Business Environment (SOE reform): Su Rong, 5-Jan-09; Wu Xinxiong, 9-Oct-09
- Regional Development (Poyang Lake Ecological Zone): Su Rong, 1-Feb-10, Wu Xinxiong, 30-Mar-09, 27-May-09, 27-Jan-10
- Development/Rural Interests (grain production): Wu Xinxiong, 25-Dec-09
- Government/Social Stability (petitions): Su Rong, 25-Feb-10
- Development (tourism): Wu Xinxiong, 16-Oct-09

Deputy Proposals (2008)

- Rural Interests/Healthcare (medical cooperatives): Liao Liping
- Rural Interests/Energy and Emissions (biogas): Xie Mulan
- Migrant Workers (household registration,education, labor protection): Long Guoying, Xu Guifen
- Rural Interests (rural microcredit): Gao Xiaoqiong
- Development (tourism): Zhou Meng
- Cultural Protection (dance): Long Hong
- Regional Development/Environmental Protection (Nanchang): Hu Xian

Deputy Proposals (2009)

- Regional Development (Poyang Lake Ecological Zone): Zeng Qinghong
- Crime, Order, and Punishment (criminal law): Zhang Zhonghou
- Development (tourism): Li Yuying
- Education (rural education): Cai Xiaoming, Liu Yanqiong
- Technology/Innovation: Zhou Meng, Wang Hai, Business Environment: Gong Jianhua
- Government/Social Stability (social management): Wan Kai
- Regional Development (Western China): Wan Kai
- Education (university administration reform): Liao Jinqiu
- National Security/Interests (oil reserve): Chen Liguo
- Migrant Workers/Rural Interests (employment, household registration): Hu Xian, Wan Kai
- Rural Interests/Healthcare (rural medical cooperatives): Li Li, Liao Liping

Deputy Proposals (2010)

- Regional Development (Poyang Lake Ecological Zone): Liu Lizu, Zeng Qinghong
- Water Conservation/Irrigation (irrigation): Sun Xiaoshan
- Rural Interests (insurance system): Lu Bing
- Government/Social Stability: Liu Heping
- Environmental Protection: Zhou Meng
- Education ("red education"): Zhou Meng, Li Yuying
- Rural Interests (pension): Lan Nianying
- Migrant Workers/Education (education): Liu Yanqiong
- Migrant Workers (occupational protection, lungs): Li Li
- Energy/Emissions (low carbon): Wang Hai, Hu Xian
- Rural Interests (political representation): Sun Xiaoshan
- Culture preservation (instruction): Long Hong
- Development (railway construction): Shao Liping
- Pharmaceutical Industry: Gong Jianhua
- Housing (affordable housing): Cai Xiaoming, Liu Sanqiu

Possible Deputy Echoes

Possible Leader Responses

FIGURE 4.5 Testing the elite echoing criticism

for the province. His lone speech of note occurred shortly before Chinese New Year in January 2008, and it concerned disaster relief, as parts of the province were engulfed in snow and ice storms ("Pay Attention to Snow Disaster" 2008). Wu Xinxiong, who had taken over as governor of Jiangxi months before, made several statements prior to the 2008 NPC meeting that began to capture his policy goals. He repeatedly discussed grain targets and actively promoted "efficient agriculture" ("Both Gold" 2007). In November 2007, he asked other officials to improve the implementation of "livelihood projects," and specifically to increase affordable housing construction. In concert with Su Rong, Wu also made comments to improve disaster preparedness in the wake of the early 2008 ice storms ("Ice and Snow" 2008).

None of these policy issues appear to have been echoed by NPC deputies in the 2008 session of the 11th NPC. Many were distinctly rural issues, though nothing to do with grain production. Deputy Liao Liping raised ideas on how to improve the rural cooperative medical system; Xie Mulan highlighted the importance of the biofuel industry for farmers' incomes; and Gao Xiaoqiong discussed how to increase access to microcredit in rural areas. Two deputies brought up the plight of migrant workers and demanded reform of the household registration system and increased access to education. Deputy Zhou Meng highlighted ways to advance tourism in the region (NPC Deputy Database).

Su Rong's policy preferences for Jiangxi began to emerge more strongly in 2008 and 2009. On a series of university visits, he repeatedly talked of the need to reform the higher education system, specifically to introduce more meritocratic processes into the recruitment of university administrators ("Jiangxi Opens" 2008). Later in the year, he began to highlight the need to improve employment prospects for migrant workers and farmers. In several speeches in December 2008 and January 2009, he discussed the effects of the global financial crisis on Jiangxi's migrant population, noting that millions of migrant workers were being forced to return home and lacked adequate income-generating prospects. In one speech, he commented simply, "What I am most worried about is increasing the income of farmers next year" ("Jiangxi Province" 2008).

Several other policy priorities emerged in 2008 and 2009. Many of Wu Xinxiong's statements revolved around ways to improve economic development in the province, and he highlighted the need for more railway construction ("Ministry of Railways" 2008), economic integration, and technological innovation ("Jiangxi High-End Talent" 2008). Both leaders made several statements about the ongoing development of the "Poyang

Lake Ecological Zone," an infrastructure project designed to promote investment in the region ("Su Rong: Play" 2008). Su Rong once commented on how best to use tourism to create industrial advantages ("Su Rong: Accelerate" 2008).

In 2009, a few deputy comments and proposals from the Jiangxi delegation could potentially be construed as "echoing," although it is difficult to know the internal motivation of the deputies in raising these issues. Deputy Li Yuying commented on the need to improve tourism; Zhou Meng and Wang Hai highlighted technology and innovation; and Liao Jinqiu discussed higher education reform. Deputies also commented on the plight of migrant workers, though mostly on the need for reform of the household registration system.

Following the 2009 NPC session, Su Rong and Wu Xinxiong continued to discuss many of the same issues: tourism, migrant worker employment and income ("Jiangxi: Strong Support" 2009), general development, and the Poyang Lake Ecological Zone. Their statements also indicate an increased focus on sustainable energy and reducing emissions ("Jiangxi Provincial Government and CNNC" 2009), as well as the need to increase efficiency in state-owned enterprises ("Analysis Report" 2010).

In the 2010 NPC, we again see a few statements from deputies suggestive of echoing behavior. Deputies Wan Hai and Hu Xian discussed energy efficiency and carbon emissions, for example. Deputies Li Li and Liu Yanqiong discussed the issues facing migrant workers, calling for increased access to education and better protection from occupational hazards. Deputies Cai Xiaoming and Liu Sanqiu made proposals related to affordable housing, an issue that had been raised in two speeches by governor Wu Xinxiong two years prior.

Despite these examples, some general patterns emerge that suggest the limits of the elite echoing narrative and buttress the arguments made throughout this book. First, although some deputies do author proposals that address the pet issues of provincial leaders, the majority do not. Even if we adopt the most conservative criterion – that any proposal that remotely relates to a leadership statement is simply echoing – at most only about 20 to 25% do. The other 75–80% offer real initiatives that diverge substantially from leader priorities. Among Jiangxi deputies, we saw proposals on rural medical cooperatives, the national oil reserve, biogas, traditional dance, cultural instruction, microcredit, household registration reform, "red education," occupational protection, and irrigation, among many others. None of these can be mapped to publicly observable statements by provincial leaders. Even for those comments that do have a topical mapping, the substantive arguments are often quite distinct. On the migrant worker issue, deputies repeatedly discussed education provision and the need for household registration reform. Su Rong, in contrast, focused primarily on job training, employment and income generation opportunities.

Second, there is evidence that deputies lead provincial leadership on several issues, rather than simply lag behind. For example, comments from the Jiangxi delegation on tourism and migrant workers preceded Su Rong's own comments. It is possible that Su Rong's focus on migrant workers was partially a result of deputy activism. Similarly, Wu Xinxiong's comments on the need to improve healthcare in rural areas only came after deputy Liao Liping's proposal to the 2008 NPC. The issue then reverberated back and forth between leaders and deputies for the remainder of the analysis period.

To summarize, the analysis suggests that while some echoing may occur in the NPC, the value of this lens for understanding the NPC is limited. The vast majority of NPC proposals diverge substantially from leadership initiatives, and may even be the source of inspiration for those initiatives.

What about Political Reform?

This chapter has focused on establishing a descriptive inference about congruence in the NPC for nonpolitical issues. I should close by noting the other half of the story, the nature of representation on strong preference issues where the interests of the regime and its citizens directly conflict. On these matters, deputies prove deserving of their bad reputation.

As discussed in Chapter 3, very few proposals ever touch on political reform. In his analysis of the 9th NPC, Jiang (2003) classifies exactly two proposals – out of 495 – as relating to "political system reform." In the complete Hainan proposal set from Chapter 3, I observed exactly zero, although it may be possible that a few did but were not publicly disclosed – which is telling in itself. Figure 4.4 shows that in the wake of political scandals, deputies remain largely mute. In my NPC Deputy Database, words relating to issues in Document No. 9 were few and far between. Only 45 proposals in the 11th NPC – out of over 3,000 in the dataset – even mentioned the word "democracy," and the word itself carries a different connotation in the Chinese political system. Another 23 mentioned "human rights," 14 mentioned "transparency" and access to information, and 29 mentioned "freedom." Most of these proposals were not inherently sensitive.[19] There are no proposals on instituting free and fair multiparty elections, relaxed Internet controls, media protection, freedom of speech and expression, or anything else that would jeopardize the core nature of the one-party state.

It remains an open question whether or not Chinese citizens actually want a fully democratic system – a possibility I consider in the conclusion of the book. The CPAS survey data from Chapter 3 would suggest they seem to prefer a more transparent and participatory political system, at the very least. And by and large, NPC deputies fail to deliver in this regard. The next chapters consider the incentive structures that produce this bounded representative behavior.

Technical Appendix

The MRP procedure was used to derive estimates of the average issue seriousness scores for each province from the 2008 China Survey. Recall that each respondent rated several issues in terms of perceived seriousness on an increasing scale of 0–10. The MRP procedure allows us to combine these responses with geographic and census information to create an issue seriousness score (*score*) at the provincial level.

The first step is to develop a model of perceived issue seriousness at the individual level using geographic and demographic covariates. For each respondent in the China Survey, we have information on the individual's age, gender, industry and employment status, and province/region of residence. Government statistics also provide basic information on the provinces themselves, including their region, average income level, fraction of output from different sectors, and population density.[20]

I estimate the following varying-intercept multilevel linear model of individual preferences Y_i, with indices d, s, p, r standing for the individual's demographic (age-gender) category, sector, province, and region,

---

[19] Many of the comments concerned small suggestions and word changes to an amendment to the Electoral Law, which gave rural and urban citizens equal representation in the People's Congress system. Others concerned changes to procedures in village elections.

[20] In comparison with other uses of MRP, my model includes relatively few individual-level covariates (age, gender, and sector). This is because the individual microdata from China's 2005 1% census are not publicly available, and the published cross-tabs include at most three variables. The post-stratification procedure requires us to know the exact number of individuals of each demographic–geographic type, so the data availability issue puts a binding constraint on the specificity of the model. Still, existing work has proven even relatively simple MRP models quite accurate (Lax and Phillips 2009b).

respectively:

$$Y_i = \gamma + \alpha_{d[i]}^{\text{dem}} + \alpha_{s[i]}^{\text{sec}} + \alpha_{p[i]}^{\text{prov}}. \tag{MRP}$$

Here,

$$\alpha_d^{\text{dem}} \sim N(0, \sigma_{\text{dem}}^2), \quad \text{for} \quad d = 1, \dots, 10;$$

$$\alpha_s^{\text{sec}} \sim N(0, \sigma_{\text{sec}}^2), \quad \text{for} \quad s = 1, \dots, 13.$$

The model includes varying intercepts for the individual's demographic type and sector. The demographic variable has ten age–gender categories, and the sector variable contains indicators for thirteen industry types.[21] The two individual-level variables are modeled as drawn from a normal distribution with mean zero and some variance to be estimated. This means that each sector and demographic type is given its own intercept; the term $\alpha_{s[i]}^{\text{sec}}$ in the equation above actually represents thirteen different intercepts, one for each sector. In line with existing work using MRP (Warshaw and Rodden 2012), the effects of the individual-level variables are not allowed to vary geographically (Gelman and Hill 2007, pp. 301–10).

Geography enters into the model through the provincial indicators $\alpha_{p[i]}^{\text{prov}}$:

$$\alpha_{p[i]}^{\text{prov}} \sim N(\rho_{r[p]}^{\text{reg}} + \beta X_{[p]}, \sigma_{\text{prov}}^2), \quad \text{for} \quad p = 1, \dots, 25.$$

The twenty-five province intercepts are themselves modeled as a function of the region and a vector of provincial-level covariates X that includes population density; income per capita; ratio of permanent to registered population; fraction of output from manufacturing; proportion Han; health institutions per capita; percentage of environmentally protected land; and the intensity of air pollutants.

The region variable is its own modeled effect, with different intercepts for the four regions of China:

$$\rho_r^{\text{reg}} \sim N(0, \sigma_{\text{reg}}^2), \quad \text{for} \quad r = 1, \dots, 4.$$

The model is estimated using R's GLMER function. In the interest of simplicity and transparency, the model is kept the same for all of the issue

---

[21] For the demographic variable, five age categories (≤ 29, 30–39, 40–49, 50–59, 60+) were interacted with gender to create ten distinct types. The sector indicators include construction; education, health, culture and research; energy; farming and animal husbandry; finance; government and social services; manufacturing; mining; real estate; retail and restaurants; transport and telecommunications; other; and unemployed.

seriousness variables. The replication files and full results of the models are available from the author by request.

With the coefficients in hand, we can then generate predicted values $\hat{Y}_t$ of issue seriousness for the 3,250 types (25 provinces with census data, 10 demographic categories, and 13 sector categories). For each province, every type's predicted value is then weighted by its proportion in the population based on the 2005 1% census, the post-stratification step. The final average issue seriousness scores (*score*) are simply the sums of the weighted predicted values for all types.

Despite its benefits, the MRP approach relies on a series of assumptions – most notably the functional form of the preference model – and should be viewed with some skepticism. In the case of this analysis, however, it appears that the main substantive results do not rely heavily on specific MRP assumptions. In addition to the "Full MRP" model estimated above, I also constructed MRP estimates that excluded the individual-level variables for demographics and sector ("No Types MRP") and the vector of provincial level covariates ("Trim MRP"). I also estimated scores using simple disaggregation at the provincial level. The final scores are very similar, with correlations ranging from 0.953 to 0.993 across the four issues. Table 4.2 shows that the substantive conclusions of the chapter are not particularly sensitive to the use of these different estimation procedures.

5

Getting Ahead

Xu Zhiyong Is Missing

Xu Zhiyong went missing sometime in the morning on July 29, 2009. At the time, Xu was the prominent head of the Open Constitution Initiative (*gongmeng*), a research and advocacy group dedicated to promoting the rule of law in China. Heightened media attention brought about Xu's release about four weeks later, but only after his organization was charged with tax evasion and saddled with 1.4 million RMB in fines and back taxes (Canavas 2009).

Six years before, Xu was emerging as a star in the people's congress system. In 2003, he was elected as an independent candidate to a lower-level people's congress in Haidian, a district of Beijing. Xu quickly earned a reputation as an activist deputy eager to address the needs of the people. In 2004, he worked with deputies at the national level to propose an amendment – which was subsequently adopted – to include the words "human rights" in the country's constitution. Other motions aimed to improve education for children of migrant workers and to ensure fair compensation for displaced residents.

Xu's activism made him something of a cult hero among proponents of democratic reform. One *TIME* reporter described Xu as "probably the person most committed to public service that I've met in China, and possibly in my whole life" (Osnos 2009). In 2009, the magazine *Mr. Fashion* – China's version of *Esquire* – ran a feature that asked sixty prominent individuals to explain their vision of a "Chinese Dream."[1] Xu Zhiyong was featured on the cover.

[1] This use of the term predated Xi Jinping's introduction of the "Chinese Dream" slogan.

At the time of his first detention in 2009, Xu had started pushing the boundaries a little too far. In 2009, his Open Constitution Initiative issued reports condemning oppression of minorities in Tibet and advocating greater transparency in government expenditures. Xu also personally worked to provide legal assistance to citizens illegally detained in black jails, which sadly probably contributed to his own detention months later.

Shortly after the charges of tax evasion – a common pretense for political purges – Xu's organization and its website were banned. Xu himself was prohibited from teaching law, which he had been doing at the Beijing University of Post and Telecommunications for many years. He lost his deputy seat in Haidian in the following election.

After his fall from Party grace, Xu remained vibrant and vocal. He founded a new organization, Citizen (*gongmin*), with the purpose of promoting a "New Citizens' Movement," a social movement dedicated to promoting civil rights and democracy. Its members met in secrecy in a series of small semicoordinated dinners, which were particularly worrisome to the regime. Xu earned additional detentions for these efforts and was eventually tried and found guilty of "gathering crowds to disturb public order" in January 2014. He was sentenced to four years imprisonment.

In his closing statement, which was cut short by the presiding officials, Xu warned of a future reckoning for the regime. His words give a sense of his radicalization.

If the country's rulers have any intention to take citizens' constitutional rights seriously, then of course we are innocent. We had no intention to disrupt public order; our intention was to promote democracy and rule of law in China. We did nothing to disrupt public order, we were merely exercising our freedom of expression as provided for by the constitution...

The day will come when the 1.3 billion Chinese will stand up from their submissive state and grow to be proud and responsible citizens. China will become a country that enjoys a civilized political system and a happy society in which freedom, justice, and love prevail. The disempowered will be redeemed, as will you, you who sit high above with fear and shadows in your hearts. (Xu 2014)

The Importance of Selective Empathy

Xu is a fallen star in the Chinese legislative system. He fell for a very specific reason – his behavior crossed over from helpful, informational representation to subversive, destabilizing activism. Proposals about migrant education and even fair compensation schemes are somewhat sensitive, but statements about abuses in Tibet and black jails are simply out of bounds.

Recall that according to Proposition 3 of the model, the Autocrat would prefer the Deputy to share the preferences of the Citizen, but only for weak or no preference issues. I call this idea "selective empathy."

Proposition 3: Higher Deputy empathy γ has positive effects on Autocrat welfare for no preference issues, but negative effects for strong preference issues. The Autocrat prefers the Deputy to have "selective empathy" with the Citizen that varies by issue accordingly.

Observable Implication: Regimes will devise incentives to foster "selective empathy."

In the eyes of the CCP, Xu's issue might be that he cares about his countrymen too much. His closing statement above is telling in this regard. Xu works to stand up for others, and he has come to view the authoritarian system itself as the "root of so much injustice and so much pain" ("Xu Zhiyong: On the New Citizens Movement" 2013). This type of unbounded empathy is dangerous for the regime, and it must be systematically removed from the legislative system.

This chapter takes up the task of testing whether and how the CCP regime engineers selective empathy among deputies to the National People's Congress. I look for the presence of two incentive structures – a meritocratic selection process and deputy socialization/indoctrination.

Using the NPC Deputy Database described in Chapter 4, I assess whether or not deputies that are more active are more likely to be reselected into the next congress, similarly to electoral outcome analyses conducted in the U.S. setting (Tucker and Weber 1987; Abramowitz 1988; Thomas 1989; Levitt 1994; Lublin 1994; Gerber 1998; Stratmann 2013) and Blaydes's (2011, p. 62) analysis of parliamentary elections in Egypt. Both matching and standard regression analysis provide some evidence of a meritocratic career incentive. Deputies reselected into the 12th NPC have about 20–50% more proposals in the dataset. Simulations suggest that everything else being equal, an additional proposal is roughly associated with a 2% increase in the probability of reselection. We also observe historically that deputies who step out of bounds are removed from the People's Congress system, although this is more difficult to test with the data.

A qualitative analysis of training materials, as well as deputy statements, suggests the presence of socialization/indoctrination practices to instill selective empathy. Upon selection into the NPC, new deputies go through several multiday training sessions designed to teach them how to perform their duties. Deputies are told to convey public opinion through their policy proposals, but also to protect the interests of the Party. These behavioral norms complement the NPC's hard career incentives and promote representation-within-bounds behavior.

The remainder of the chapter is structured as follows. I first provide some information on China's legislative election processes, which allow the Party to tightly control who enters and exits the People's Congress system. The next sections outline the research design and the primary results for the career incentives analysis. I then test whether deputy training seems consistent with the idea of selective empathy. I close the chapter with a short discussion of alternative frameworks and the determinants of preference congruence.

Elections in the People's Congress System

Recall that the National People's Congress is the highest body of China's expansive People's Congress system. The system has five formal levels, corresponding to the five highest levels in the administrative hierarchy: township, county, prefecture (or municipality), province, and national.[2] Each unit has its own congress, and each congress has formal jurisdiction over the congresses within its geographic region in the administrative level below, creating a nested system of representative institutions. Villages, the sixth and lowest level of the hierarchy, do not have their own congresses.

The size of the congresses increases with the administrative rank ("Electoral Law" Article 9). Except in unusual circumstances, township congresses generally range from 40 to 130 deputies (depending on population); county congresses range from 120 to 450; prefectural congresses have 240 to 650; provincial congresses have 350 to 1,000; and the NPC generally has around 3,000. In total, there are over 40,000 congresses at different levels in the system, and the total number of deputies is in the hundreds of thousands.

---

[2] These labels are shorthand for a number of different units. The provincial level includes provinces, autonomous regions and municipalities directly under the central government. The prefectural level includes cities divided into districts and autonomous prefectures. The county level includes cities not divided into districts, municipal districts, counties and autonomous counties. The township level includes townships, nationality townships and towns.

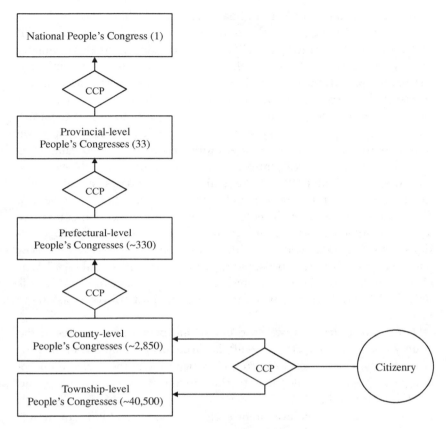

FIGURE 5.1 Elections in the People's Congress system

Selection flows upward through the People's Congress system – each unit selects a delegation to attend the congress at the next highest level. This dynamic is illustrated in Figure 5.1.

For the township- and county-level congresses, deputies are directly elected by the citizens themselves. Each township or county is subdivided into different electoral districts ("Electoral Law" Articles 24–5). The districts may be formed on the basis of residence, or often by production unit, institution, and work unit. For example, a local university may be allocated a seat in a local people's congress, and all students, faculty, and staff affiliated with that university will be assigned to that electoral unit. Each district generally elects one to three deputies. Every citizen over the age of 18 is assigned to one electoral district and is eligible to vote in this way.

Any citizen can become a candidate provided she has been nominated by ten citizens living in the electoral district. Political parties (the CCP and nominal "democratic parties") and mass organizations also nominate candidates ("Electoral Law" Article 29). If the total number of nominated candidates exceeds the permitted candidate–seat ratio for the administrative level, the election committee is supposed to submit the nomination list to "voter groups" for "discussion and consultation" to reduce the nomination list.[3] In practice, it appears that election committees reduce the nominees to the minimal level of electoral competition (two candidates for a district with one seat, three candidates for a district with two seats, and so forth) (Manion 2014). The final list of candidates is made public five days prior to the date of the election ("Electoral Law" Article 31). Candidates are then introduced live to voters by the election committee and given some opportunity to articulate their views and answer questions. This activity must cease by the day of the election, leaving at most a few days for voters to learn about the candidates ("Electoral Law" Article 33). As Manion (2000) documents, voter knowledge of candidates is quite low. Candidates only win if they earn a majority of votes cast in the district.[4]

For indirect elections, which occur within people's congresses at the county level and above, the citizenry is effectively excluded from the process entirely. County-level deputies elect deputies to the prefecture-level congresses, who elect deputies to the provincial-level congresses, who elect deputies to the NPC.

The indirect elections are run by each congress's presidium – an administrative committee selected by the full plenary session. Parties, people's organizations, and deputies themselves may nominate candidates for the congress one level above, many of which come from the pool of existing deputies at the lower administrative level. As before, the presidium narrows down the candidate list to accord with legal candidate–seat ratios, and may allow some primary elections. At the national level, the number of candidates is only 20 to 50 percent greater than the number of deputies to be elected. Deputies then vote on the full candidate list, and the deputies who have the most votes obtain seats ("Electoral Law" Articles 30, 41).

In managing the nomination process, both the election committees and the presidium must ensure that the elected congress meets certain demographic quotas mandated by the Electoral Law. Beyond geographic

---

[3] If the list cannot be reduced, the election committee may choose to allow primary elections.
[4] This leaves open the possibility that voters may derail an election by "spoiling their ballots," although these sorts of "failed elections" are quite rare (Manion 2014).

quotas,[5] there are hard rules for representation along three additional dimensions: ethnicity, gender, and party affiliation.[6] Minorities are guaranteed representation in proportion to their population. Each one of the 55 recognized minority groups receives at least one seat, which leads to a slight overrepresentation of minorities as a whole.[7] Article 6 of the Electoral Law also guarantees that there are "an appropriate number of women deputies, and the proportion thereof shall be raised gradually." The percentage of women in the 11th NPC was about 21.1% and has remained relatively static for the past thirty years (Jiang 2003). Returnees from overseas are also given special consideration.

Of course, there is very little political balance in the institution. Members of the eight nominally democratic opposition parties, as well as unaffiliated citizens, are given a portion of seats, but the CCP guarantees it holds a strong majority in every congress, usually 65–75%. Although the Electoral Law makes no mention of the Party, in practice, Party committees lead the election committees and presidia that oversee the electoral process and candidate lists. This allows the regime to ensure that only politically docile candidates are ever even placed on the ballot, giving the Party effective "veto power" at this stage of the process (Manion 2014). In local direct elections, voter-nominated candidates frequently gain office, but truly "independent candidates" without tacit Party support rarely see the ballot. Many are simply removed during the nomination process or intimidated into not running (Cabestan 2006; Manion 2014).[8] At higher levels in the system, where the citizenry have no voting rights,

---

[5] At all levels, delegations within the congresses themselves vary according to population. At the national level, the provincial delegations range from 19 representatives for Hainan to 180 representatives for Shandong. The People's Liberation Army has its own electoral rules and receives 267 seats. Hong Kong, Macao, and Taiwan are also given representation commensurate to population but operate by separate electoral rules. Seats are also allocated across urban and rural areas. Until recently, rural deputies represented four times as many constituents as their urban counterparts, but this imbalance was remedied with the 2010 amendment to the Electoral Law ("China's Parliament Adopts" 2010). As of the writing of the manuscript, each NPC deputy represents about 670,000 Chinese citizens.

[6] Other attributes are given softer protection. Deputies are also selected from different age groups, religious groups, professions, and economic sectors. This "deliberately arranges for a balance of various social sectors and interests," as Jiang (2003) describes. "The balance results from the percentages of Deputies that are elected from among various social communities." The Electoral Law similarly mandates that "areas with a relatively large number of returned overseas Chinese shall have an appropriate number of deputies who are returned overseas Chinese" ("Electoral Law" Article 6).

[7] In the 11th NPC, roughly 13.6% of deputies were non-Han, compared with only about 8.5% of the population.

[8] Cabestan (2006) documents the case of Hu Dezhai, whose candidacy was derailed when Party authorities called voters and told them to remove their signatures from his nomination petition.

TABLE 5.1 *Who's who in China's National People's Congress*

	NPCSC		NPC		China
	n	%	*n*	%	%
Basic demographics					
Female	30	17.2	638	21.1	48.7
Minority	26	14.9	404	13.6	8.5
Political experience					
CCP	122	70.1	2230	74.9	7.8
Democratic parties	41	23.6	380	12.8	0.3
Unaffiliated	11	6.3	368	12.4	91.9
In previous NPC	92	52.9	1026	34.5	~0.0
Professional experience					
Clerk	0	0.0	6	0.2	10.4
Farmer/fisherman	0	0.0	11	0.4	45.5
Government/party employee	102	58.6	1300	43.7	3.1
Manager/entrepreneur	50	28.7	793	26.6	1.1
Professional	5	2.9	363	12.2	3.6
Small business owner	0	0.0	9	0.3	7.8
Laborer	0	0.0	32	1.1	12.0
Soldier/policeman	15	8.6	300	10.1	0.4
Other	2	1.1	15	0.5	1.0

Note: NPCSC and NPC figures are drawn from the NPC Deputy Database. China statistics are drawn from the CIA World Factbook and the 2008 China Survey, a nationally representative sample. Table reproduced from Truex (2014).

CCP-dominated congresses select CCP-dominated congresses for the next level above. It is nearly impossible for a politically reformist candidate to win the support of enough deputies to gain a seat in the NPC.

The net result is a parliament that is quasi-representative in some respects, but quite unrepresentative in others. Table 5.1 compares the compositions of the NPC, NPC Standing Committee, and Chinese population using data from the NPC Deputy Database.[9] There is relatively equitable representation in terms of geography, age, and ethnicity, but certain groups are starkly overrepresented in the selection process – CCP members, men, government officials, and soldiers/policemen. Conversely, farmers and workers hold only a few token seats. According to my data,

[9] Variables in the NPC Deputy Database were coded to match those in the 2008 China Survey to facilitate this comparison.

only 11 deputies can be considered farmers in any real sense, compared with about 45% of the full population.[10]

To summarize, the tiered, indirect electoral mechanism in the People's Congress system ensures that deputies at the highest levels face no semblance of electoral accountability to the Chinese citizenry. The CCP dominates and manipulates deputy selection processes at every possible step and restricts citizen input to the lowest levels of the system. In the NPC, deputy accountability is to the regime itself.

Data and Research Design

Studying deputy selection processes can give a sense of regime priorities and allow us to evaluate the validity of the framework. If the theoretical logic is correct, we would expect to observe hard career incentives that reward deputies for good behavior. All else being equal, deputies who are more active in conveying the interests of their constituents on nonpolitical issues should be more likely to get reselected into the subsequent congress. If the regime really values the information it receives, there should be a meritocratic element to deputy selection practices. As in Chapter 4, I take the rich scholarly record on the U.S. Congress as a helpful starting point, but the research design will be adjusted to account for some of the NPC's unique features.

A number of scholars have investigated the determinants of electoral outcomes in the American political setting. The standard design is to regress a candidate's vote share in a given election on a number of attributes – incumbency status, campaign expenditures, challenger experience, previous vote share, and so forth. Unsurprisingly, a number of studies have found that campaign expenditures are strongly associated with electoral success (Tucker and Weber 1987; Abramowitz 1988; Thomas 1989; Levitt 1994; Lublin 1994; Gerber 1998; Stratmann 2013). There is also some evidence that legislative performance is correlated with reelection, although this this relationship has garnered less attention in the literature. Abramowitz (1988) constructs a measure of a senator's ideological

---

[10] This underrepresentation stems from an increasing emphasis on improving deputy quality (O'Brien and Li 1993; O'Brien 1990). Beginning in the early 1990s, there was a concerted effort to reduce the number of illiterate and semiliterate deputies, as well as inactive deputies who viewed their position as simply an honor. In the past twenty years, congresses at all levels have sought cadres, "practical intellectuals," legal and economic experts, and prominent businesspeople.

distance from her constituents. He finds that representatives who are substantially tone-deaf may lose up to 4.3% of the vote. Stratmann (2013) estimates that a \$10 million increase in secured earmarks may increase vote share by upward of 1 percent.

In the Chinese case, the task will be complicated by several factors. As before, there is a problem of data availability. There is no information available on candidate vote shares nor any real information on challengers or the nature of NPC elections. My NPC Deputy Database does contain information on deputy career paths and professional experience, including an indicator (*npc12*) for whether a deputy was reselected into the 12th Congress (2013–17). This will serve as the main career outcome of interest. About 36.7% of deputies in the 11th NPC (1,094 out of 2,978) were ultimately reselected into the 12th.[11]

Measures of legislative performance are also hard to come by. In an ideal setting, we would have a more complete registry of performance information: the deputy's attendance at training sessions and meetings; the full content and responses to all proposals, and the deputy's comments and questions at plenary sessions. These data are not available as of the writing of this manuscript. The NPC Deputy Database, described in Chapter 4, contains a variable, *prop,* with the number of publicly available opinions, motions and comments put forth from 2008 to 2012. Although this is only a small fraction of the true total, it remains the best proxy available for legislative activity.

Beyond data availability, extending a career outcomes design to China's NPC is further complicated by the presence of the legislative quota system. The major empirical concern is that candidates nominated by the provincial people's congresses are sometimes chosen because of who they are, not necessarily what they have accomplished (Personal Interview HN41113). If the quota-protected demographic variables are associated with legislative performance, as well as reselection, they could potentially obscure or augment any association. We cannot naively relate reselection and performance without accounting for these factors.

The task then, is to somehow isolate the comparison to similar individuals, deputies who would fill the same general quota needs. We want to compare younger, female, farmer, Han, CCP-member deputies from Heilongjiang with other younger, female, farmer, Han, CCP-member

---

[11] This is a relatively high level of legislative turnover. Reelection rates to the U.S. House of Representatives and Senate in 2012 were 90% and 91%, respectively ("Reelection Rates over the Years" 2012).

deputies from Heilongjiang; older, male, Tujia, unaffiliated businessmen from Hunan with other older, male, Tujia, unaffiliated businessmen from Hunan, and so forth. If we restrict our analysis to individuals with comparable profiles, we can see whether performance is really systematically related to reselection.

This thought experiment can be implemented using exact matching (Ho et al. 2007; Iacus et al. 2012), a preprocessing technique that improves covariate balance. The basic process is as follows. The analyst first identifies a set of possibly confounding covariates, which we can denote as X. An observed treated unit i with covariate values X_i is then matched with any control units j with $X_i = X_j$. These matched control units provide an estimate of the outcome variable Y for unit i in the absence of the treatment.[12] Observations without an exact match are excluded from the sample. The analyst can then compare the mean outcome across the treatment and control observations remaining in the matched sample.

To get a sense of how exactly this will look for our analysis, consider the two deputies in Figure 5.2, Zeng Qinghong and Yu Ziquan. Both men are CCP members from Guangdong who manage large SOEs. Both are CCP members who ended the 11th NPC still below retirement age. Neither served in the NPCSC nor any elite CCP institutions. On these stratifying variables X, they are an exact match.

The key difference is that Yu Ziquan was reselected into the 12th NPC, and Zeng Qinghong was not. Because they fill identical quota needs and have comparable experience, the comparison of their performance becomes more compelling. For this pair alone, the data would suggest that performance is negatively related to selection – reselected Yu had one proposal, while Zeng had six. The full analysis will employ this sort of logic, but we will pool together a much larger set of matched pairs.

Before moving on to the results, a final short technical note is in order. My main "treatment," if we could call it that, will be reselection into the 12th NPC (*npc12*). My outcome variable will be the total number of proposals (*prop*) in the 11th NPC. This is backward from a causal inference perspective, as the number of proposals is the theoretical variable of interest, hypothesized to have an effect on the career outcome of reselection. If this were a basic regression analysis, *npc12* would be the dependent variable, and *prop* would be the main independent variable.[13] Because we

---

[12] It is possible to use one-to-one exact matching, whereby each treated unit is matched with only one control unit, but this is inefficient. See Iacus et al. (2012) for a discussion.
[13] This analysis will be included as a robustness check.

Name:	Zeng Qinghong	Yu Ziquan
Delegation:	Guangdong	Guangdong
Party:	CCP	CCP
Ethnicity:	Han	Han
Gender:	Male	Male
Retirement age:	No (born 1961)	No (born 1955)
Profession:	Manager, SOE	Manager, SOE
11th NPCSC:	No	No
CCP elite:	No	No
12th NPC:	**No**	**Yes**
Proposals:	**6**	**1**

FIGURE 5.2 Sample matched pair

are using matching analysis, we need to use a binary treatment of some sort, which would preclude the use of *proposals*, a quasi-continuous count variable. Thus, the best approach is to simply conduct the difference of means in proposals on the matched sample. If the individuals in the 12th NPC had more proposals on average than their matched counterparts who were not reselected, this would suggest the presence of some sort of meritocratic career incentive.

Getting Ahead in the NPC

Figure 5.3 gives an initial glance at the key relationship of interest. The left panel shows the dependent variable, density, the total number of observed proposals (*prop*) in the 11th NPC, for individuals who did and did not get reselected into the 12th NPC. The densities are quite similar, although the average number of proposals for reselected deputies ($npc12=1$) is slightly higher. The panel on the right compares the densities for individuals who

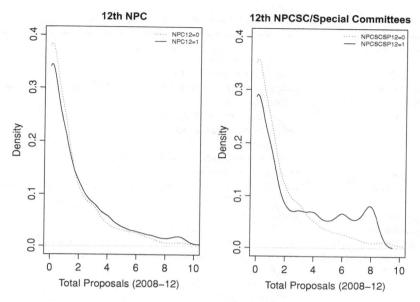

FIGURE 5.3 Proposals and career outcomes
Note: The figure shows density of *prop* for 11th NPC deputies who did and did not gain membership in the 12th NPC, and 11th NPC deputies without committee members who did and did not gain membership in the 12th NPCSC or Special Committees. All comments are drawn from the Oriprobe deputy database.

did or did not gain membership in the 12th NPCSC or a special committee. Here the difference is more pronounced, with the promoted deputies showing higher participation rates on average.

We can move to the matching analysis for a more rigorous investigation. In terms of model selection, my general approach will be to start with some basic quota-related confounders and then progress toward a richer matching model. I will present estimates from five specifications. Model M1 is the unmatched difference of means; M2 includes indicators for attributes protected by hard quotas – delegation (*del#*), ethnicity (*ethn#*) and political party (*party#*); M3 includes additional indicators for gender (*female*), being of retirement age (*retireage*), industry (*pind#*) and work unit type (*punit#*); M4 includes indicators for government rank (*govrank1:4*) and membership (including alternate) on the CCP Central Committee (*ccpcc*); and M5 includes experience indicators for being in the current or previous NPC Standing Committee (*npcsc8,...,npcsc11*), current Special Committees (*npcspec#*), or previous congresses

TABLE 5.2 *Career analysis variable definitions*

Variable	Description
npc12	Indicator for membership in 12th NPC
npcscsp12	Indicator for membership in 12th NPCSC or NPC Special Committees
prop	Total number of observed proposals (2008–12)
del#	Delegation indicators (35 in total)
ethn#	Ethnicity indicators (63 in total)
party#	Political party indicators (10 in total)
female	Indicator for female
retireage	Indicator for being of retirement age (men > 60, women> 55)
pind#	Industry indicators (18 in total)
punit#	Work unit type indicators (8 in total)
$npc8, \ldots, npc10$	Indicators for membership in 8th, 9th, and 10th NPCs
$npcsc8, \ldots, npcsc11$	Indicators for membership in 8th, 9th, 10th, and 11th NPCSCs
npcspec#	Indicators for membership in 11th NPC Special Committees (9 in total)
ccpcc	Indicator for member/alternative of 17th CCP Central Committee
govrank	Bureaucratic rank indicators (4 in total)

Note: All variables are drawn from the NPC Deputy Database, which was collected using the NPC official website, the Baidu Encyclopedia, and official membership lists.

$(npc8, \ldots, npc10)$. The definitions for key variables in this career outcomes analysis are shown in Table 5.2.

Table 5.3 shows the core empirical results. Interested readers can find balance statistics in the Technical Appendix.[14] The general findings do not appear overly sensitive to the specification of the matching model. The effect size proves relatively stable across the different covariate sets, ranging from 0.353 in M5 to 0.725 in model M3. All of the models reject the null hypothesis of no effect at conventional levels of significance. Substantively, this means that on the average, deputies who are reselected have put forth about 0.3 to 0.7 more proposals observable in my 2008–12 dataset. Recall that this is only a small fraction of the total number of proposals. This effect size translates to about a 20 to 50% difference in proposal activity between the two groups, which is substantial.

---

[14] The analysis excludes deputies from the PLA, Macao, Hong Kong, and Taiwan delegations, as their selection operates by different processes.

TABLE 5.3 *Proposals and career outcomes*

#	Variables for exact matching	12th NPC				12th NPCSC or spec. comm.			
		prop[npc12=1] − [npc12=0]				prop[npcscsp=1] − [npcscsp=0]			
		Full	CCP	Non CCP	Obs.	Full	CCP	Non CCP	Obs.
M1.	None	0.456*** (0.093)	0.645*** (0.114)	0.138 (0.153)	2,650	0.916*** (0.369)	1.128*** (0.448)	0.317 (0.614)	2,388
M2.	M1. + del1:del35 + ethn1:ethn63 + party1:party10	0.569*** (0.093)	0.699*** (0.117)	0.052 (0.129)	2,315	0.570*** (0.279)	0.605*** (0.381)	−0.442 (0.049)	1,161
M3.	M2. + female + retireage + pind1:18 + punit1:8	0.725*** (0.072)	0.759*** (0.096)	0.289*** (0.055)	1,318	0.802*** (0.058)	0.820*** (0.078)	0.100*** (0.005)	199
M4.	M3. + ccpcc + govrank1:4	0.549*** (0.066)	0.569*** (0.087)	0.349*** (0.055)	1,019	0.559*** (0.022)	0.563*** (0.029)	NA NA	61
M5.	M4. + npc8 + npc9 + npc10 + npcspec1:9 + npcsc9 + npcsc10 + npcsc11	0.353*** (0.054)	0.361*** (0.072)	0.258*** (0.044)	620	NA NA	NA NA	NA NA	

Note: The table shows results of difference of means for *proposals* comparing 11th NPC deputies who did and did not gain membership in the 12th NPC, and 11th NPC deputies without committee membership who did and did not gain membership in the 12th NPCSC or Special Committees. The data are preprocessed using exact matching to account for the influence of quotas, status, and other factors. Standard errors are shown in parentheses. * $p < 0.10$, ** $p < 0.05$, *** $p < 0.01$.

The relationship between performance and career outcomes does not seem to be conditional on party membership. The table shows the difference of means for only strata that include CCP members. The effect is slightly larger, up to a 0.759 proposal difference for reselected deputies. The estimates prove slightly smaller for non-CCP members, but they do emerge as significant for the richer models. In general it appears that the regime is able to institute meritocratic incentives for both CCP and non-CCP deputies.

Another way to see the career incentives relationship is to estimate a regression:

$$Y_i \sim \text{Bern}(\Phi(\alpha + \gamma \, prop_i + \beta X_i + \epsilon_i)). \qquad \text{(PROBIT)}$$

Here, Y signifies *npc12*, the dummy indicator for whether or not the deputy has been reselected into the 12th NPC. The indicator Y is modeled as drawn from a Bernoulli distribution with probability of success $\Phi(\alpha + \gamma \, prop_i + \beta X_i + \epsilon_i)$ – the standard probit model. The independent variable of interest is *prop*. We can also include a vector of covariates X, as was done with the matching model. The presence of some sort of meritocratic career incentive would require $\gamma > 0$.

As before, the *prop* coefficient emerges as positive and significant across the different covariate sets M1 through M5. We can simulate the predicted probability of being reselected over different values of *prop*, holding other deputy covariates constant at their median values (King, Tomz and Wittenberg, 2000).[15] For a deputy who makes no proposals, the probability of being chosen into the 12th NPC is about 35.8%. This increases to 37.5% for a deputy with one observed proposal, 45.3% for a deputy with five proposals, and 51.3% for a deputy with ten proposals. Everything else being equal, an additional proposal is associated with a roughly 2% increase in the probability of reselection.

As an additional test, we can investigate whether members of the 11th NPC are more likely to be promoted into the 12th NPC Standing Committee or its associated Special Committees. As discussed in Chapter 3, the NPCSC meets throughout the year and has effectively the same powers as the NPC. Its members serve on a full-time basis and have substantially more influence on the drafting of laws than normal NPC members. For rank-and-file members of the 11th NPC, a seat on the 12th NPCSC or

---

[15] This translates to estimating the predicted probability of being reselected for a male, 55-year-old, Han, government employee CCP member from Shandong, with no previous NPC experience, no NPCSC or Special Committee experience, no overseas experience, and no CCP leadership positions.

its special committees is a more significant promotion than simply being reselected.

We can do the same type of matching analysis, this time using the indicator for membership in the 12th NPCSC or 12th NPC special committee (*npcscsp12*) as the "treatment" of interest. I restrict the analysis to deputies who did not have committee seats in the 11th NPC, as those who did can influence policy without resorting to opinions and motions. Exactly 42 regular deputies from the 11th NPC received promotion to NPCSC or special committee status in the 12th Congress. When matching this group with comparable deputies who did not get promoted, we again observe large and significant differences in representative activity. The results are shown in the rightmost columns of Table 5.3. The estimates suggest that on the average, the promoted deputies had anywhere from 0.5 to 0.9 more publicly observable proposals in the dataset. This effect is slightly larger for CCP deputies, and difficult to estimate for non-CCP deputes, given the low number of observations.

The flip side of this meritocratic association is the relationship between political activism and punishment. When deputies step out of bounds, either with their proposals or through other channels of influence, they are punished for their transgressions. Contrary to the core predictions of cooptation theory (Gandhi and Przeworski 2007; Gandhi 2008; Malesky and Schuler 2010), the CCP regime has no interest in allowing true opposition in the parliament.[16]

It is difficult to test this with my NPC data, given that we so rarely observe out-of-bounds proposals. Anecdotally, the few deputies who do cross the CCP's red line are punished in some way, as shown in the cases of Xu Zhiyong from the beginning of the this chapter and the activist deputies from the Hundred Flowers Movement discussed in Chapter 2 and the Signature Incident discussed in the next chapter.

From a legal perspective, political purges are quite easy to achieve in the NPC system. The NPC Credentials Committee has the power to approve and dismiss deputies based on their qualifications, and it is generally composed of high-ranking regime members from the CCP Central Committee. As Hu describes, this arrangement allows the party to "ke[ep] watch for trouble-makers who had escaped detection at earlier stages in the electoral process" (Hu 1993). Incidents where multiple members are jointly

---

[16] Blaydes (2011) finds similar "performance and punishment" incentives in her study of competitive elections in the Mubarak regime. Provincial officials from areas where the Muslim Brotherhood gained representation were less likely to retain their positions.

relieved of their credentials – as in the Hundred Flowers Movement and the Signature Incident – are relatively rare, but the Committee routinely purges a few deputies each year, often for political dissent (O'Brien 1990).

Teaching Representation

Beyond hard career incentives, the theory would suggest that the regime somehow instructs deputies on how to behave. There should be processes in place that promote selective empathy with the citizenry. It is difficult to test this idea, but we can look to deputy training materials for qualitative evidence. The curriculum of these sessions gives a glimpse of regime intent.

Regimen

Deputy socialization comes about primarily through special training sessions, as well as speeches and instruction at the annual NPC plenary session in March. For the 11th NPC (2008–12), the regime provided 33 different study sessions for deputies, with a total attendance of 6,300 ("Work report of NPC Standing Committee" 2013). The training sessions covered a range of topics, some providing general instruction on deputy rights and responsibilities, others delving into specific societal issues. Table 5.4 displays a training regimen for a typical newly elected Anhui deputy for the first three years of the term, 2008–10.[17]

We see six separate sessions on the itinerary, ranging from one to six days. This actually understates the level of formal training, as there are additional workshops and meetings organized around the annual plenary sessions and lower-level training meetings also attended by the deputies.

The initial general training sessions are mandatory for all newly elected deputies and occur throughout the country just following the first plenary session. A new Anhui deputy would have attended the 2008 Third Training Session on the Performance of Duties for National People's Congress Deputies, held in Beidahe on June 30, 2008. The sessions are attended by small groups of deputies from neighboring provinces. They are designed with the purpose of instilling a commitment to representation and training deputies on how best to convey the "mass line" to the central government.

Later in the term, deputies take part in special training sessions – typically known as "Focused Study Meetings" or "Special Meetings."

---

[17] Training sessions identified from the NPC website's "Deputy Training" (*daibiao peixun*) section, http://www.npc.gov.cn/npc/xinwen/dbgz/node_12493.htm. Information on individual training sessions referenced below can be found on this site.

TABLE 5.4 *Sample deputy training regimen – Anhui deputy*

Session name	Location	Date	Attendance	Description
The 2008 Third Training Session on the Performance of Duties for National People's Congress Deputies	Beidaihe	6/30/2008–7/3/2008	180 deputies from six provinces	Teaches deputies about their responsibilities, including opinions and motions process. Features discussions on key societal issues – environmental protection, the socialist countryside, and fostering innovation.
Anhui Focused Study Meeting of the 11th National People's Congress	Hefei	2/28/2009	All Anhui deputies	Provides overview of government economic plans, constitution, and relevant laws governing the rights and responsibilities of NPC deputies.
The 2009 First Legal Studies Meeting of the 11th National People's Congress	Xiamen	5/19/2009–5/24/2009	320 deputies from 23 provinces	Training on the constitution and deputy responsibilities, as well as importance of laws and policies such as food safety, labor relations, unemployment, and stability.
Special Meeting on Researching Revisions to the Electoral Law	Hefei	1/25/10	All Anhui deputies	Provides overview of proposed amendments to the Electoral Law.
The 2010 Fourth Special Training Session of the National People's Congress	Kunming	7/9/10–7/14/10	150 deputies from 14 provinces	Additional study session on constitution and key government issues. Provides opportunities for deputies to exchange ideas and experiences.
Training Course on Implementing the Spirit of the 17th Session of the Fifth Plenary Session	Shenzhen	11/8/10–11/13/10	200 deputies from 29 provinces	Session focuses on educating the deputies about the twelfth Five-year Plan, as well as three special work reports.

For example, in June 2009, 200 deputies from 17 provinces convened the Second Legal Studies Meeting of the 11th National People's Congress in Shenzhen. The deputies spent five days studying a range of important societal issues and upcoming legislation, including food safety, labor relations, unemployment, and social stability.

In November 2010, deputies once again convened in Shenzhen, this time for the Training Course on Implementing the Spirit of the Seventeenth Session, which focused on educating deputies about the twelfth five-year plan and three other government work reports. These special sessions are designed to give deputies a general sense of major societal issues, the current government response, and how they can contribute to improving that response.

Sometimes deputies will convene just to exchange ideas and share best practices. In 2010, 160 deputies from eight provinces held a meeting in Kunming to talk about priorities for the region and best practices in gathering opinions and motions. Less experienced deputies report that these types of sessions are invaluable in learning their responsibilities to the Party and the people (Personal Interview HN42413; Personal Interview HN42313).

The regime views deputy training as vital to the institutional success of the NPC. As one official statement describes, "People's congress deputies' character, status, and function necessitates that deputies strengthen their studies, to make their training of paramount importance" (Cui 2006).

Training Content

The content of the training sessions and plenary meetings speaks to what the regime is looking for in its representatives. The need for "selective empathy" is strongly implied, if not openly stated. One set of training materials distributed in Fujian describes the role of deputies in three simple lines ("People's Congress Deputy Training Materials" 2011):

The function of people's congress deputies is to:
1. connect with the masses
2. protect the interests of the Party and the people
3. reflect public opinion

Deputies are explicitly told that they must be sensitive to public opinion and connect with common citizens, but also that they must protect the interests of the CCP.

This latter point is always heavily emphasized in the speeches at the annual plenary session in March. In his 2011 NPC Standing Committee

Work Report, Wu Bangguo touts the virtues of the one-party system, cautioning deputies against the temptations of multiparty democracy ("Work report of NPC Standing Committee" 2011):

On the basis of China's conditions, we have made a solemn declaration that we will not employ a system of multiple parties holding office in rotation; diversify our guiding thought; separate executive, legislative and judicial powers; use a bicameral or federal system; or carry out privatization. Forming a socialist system of laws with Chinese characteristics has laid a firm legal foundation for national revitalization and prosperity, and lasting peace and stability. It institutionally and legally ensures that the CCP is always the core of the leadership for the cause of socialism with Chinese characteristics.

These statements may serve to remind deputies of their commitment to CCP leadership. In other speeches, Wu has explicitly called for political loyalty among all deputies ("NPC Session Successful: Wu Bangguo" 2003).

During their training, deputies are socialized into representative norms. After attending a training session in Hunan, deputy Qi Heping describes a sense of newfound pressure, calling his time as a deputy a "glorious task" and "huge responsibility" ("Focused NPC Study Session in Hunan" 2009). The concept of responsibility is repeatedly emphasized. The training materials from Fujian remind representatives that they "should act on behalf of the will and interests of all the people . . . they are not subject to any constraints of specific citizens" ("People's Congress Deputy Training Materials" 2011). The training materials go on to describe the need for representatives to get to know their constituents and create an environment of constituent service:

Representatives should take various measures to constantly listen to the people on the performance of their duties, as well as answer constituents from their electoral units, and accept their inquiries and supervision.

Representative responsibilities are frequently couched in electoral language, even though deputies face very little in the way of voter accountability.

Often, experienced deputies will offer lessons learned from their time in office. In 2012, for example, a deputy to a county-level city in Jiangsu gave a short speech entitled "The People Elected Me to Serve as a Representative, I Serve as a Representative for the People."

The solemn commitment of "The people elected me to serve as a representative, I serve as a representative for the people" should not simply be words, but implemented in specific actions. Over the past four years, in order to better fulfill this solemn commitment, I consciously focused on the theme of happiness and the people's livelihood... I used every opportunity to visit farmers in more than 500 households, in more than twenty units, collecting the difficult, hot issues of the masses in a timely manner, resulting in more than 100 comments and suggestions to the government and relevant departments. These research visits made each motion contain valuable and high-quality recommendations, using detailed first-hand information.

This type of speech is meant to foster a sense of collective responsibility to the citizenry and model proper deputy behavior.

Beyond general norms, the sessions provide concrete information on expected performance, including detailed instructions on how to propose an effective opinion, motion, or suggestion. The materials from Fujian provide point-by-point advice for making the most of this channel and caution deputies against being too vague:

If the contents of the representative's suggestions are more abstract, general, or only talk without specific comments and requests, the implementing body will be confused as to exactly what the problem is or what is required to solve it. The proposal would not achieve the role it is supposed to play.

The session goes on to detail some more specific guidelines, instructing deputies on the different parts of a proposal, the difference between an opinion and a motion, and how proposals are handled, among other points. It holds that good opinions and motions must be focused on a single issue, contain concrete evidence and solutions, and provide assessments of feasibility. Deputies must not repeatedly advocate for the same issue over and over, must avoid getting involved in the personal legal affairs of their constituents, and should not blindly sign the motions of their colleagues ("People's Congress Deputy Training Materials" 2011).

Deputy Reactions
In their public and private statements, deputies acknowledge the importance of training to their representative performance. After attending the First Training Session on the Performance of Duties for National People's Congress Deputies in April 2008, one newly elected deputy conveyed how it was necessary to "learn representation" ("NPC Deputy Wants to 'Study Representation'" 2008):

The Central Committee has called for building a learning society, and we need to be "learning representatives" – through study and practice, to improve the performance of our duties, to adapt work of the NPC requirements for upholding and improving the people's congress system, and to play its due role.

Reporting on a similar "Focused Study" training session in Xinjiang, one article describes that attending deputies felt that "concentrated study could further unify their thinking, enhance understanding, and develop an attitude of responsibility to the people" ("Xinjiang NPC Deputies Focused Study" 2009).

Deputy statements also convey a sense of representative responsibility, mirroring the language of their training. Deputy Zhang Litong comments, "The deputies' responsibility is extremely heavy, they must convey the community's concerns and hot spots through different channels, to listen to the voice of the masses" ("Deputy Zhang Liyong" 2009).

One deputy to a county-level city in Hunan describes her sentiments upon being elected. "After I became a people's congress deputy, I realized I must pay more attention to societal problems," she said. "It is a duty, an obligation to my university and the people of this city" (Personal Interview HN42313).

The words duty, obligation, and responsibility appear consistently in personal interviews. Another deputy describes a similar realization. "As soon as I became a deputy, my sense of responsibility became much deeper. We all represent 400,000 people. I have an obligation to them," he said. The deputy was from a different province originally and felt an added obligation to learn about his constituents. "I think I feel more responsible because I am not from this city. This is not my hometown. I must do more to help" (Personal Interview HN41113).

The regime deliberately facilitates means for deputies to get to know common citizens. Deputies serve on a part-time basis – spending about 49 weeks per year in their home provinces – in order not to lose touch with their constituents. As part of its official oversight functions, the NPC also organizes special group inspections and investigations, which send small numbers of deputies to different areas to learn about specific societal issues and monitor the implementation of different laws and policies. In 2005, for example, the NPC Standing Committee organized a small team of five deputies to investigate coal mine safety throughout the country ("NPC Standing Committee to Supervise" 2005). In 2011, the NPC organized a series of inspections to monitor the protection of collective bargaining rights in labor contracts, which are guaranteed by the Labor Contract Law ("NPC's Inspections Confirm Progress" 2012). According to the NPC Standing Committee Work Report, for the eleventh NPC (2008–12), a total of "over 3,800 deputies participate[d] in inspections of law enforcement and in activities of NPC special committees . . . over 9,000 deputies to carr[ied] out investigations and studies on special issues, which resulted in more than 500 investigative reports" (Work report of NPC Standing Committee" 2013).

These statements and behaviors conform with new interview and survey evidence collected by Manion (2013, 2014) in her pathbreaking study of deputies in lower-level people's congresses. Deputies at the township, county, and municipal levels seem to be speaking a "new language" of representation and take their responsibilities quite seriously. Over 60% of delegates surveyed agree that Congress delegates "should stand with the majority of their constituents, because constituents are the best judge of their own interests." The survey results also show that for deputies at the municipal level, over half of the motions submitted (59.1%) are based on specific constituent requests.

To summarize, the deputy training regimen suggests that the regime promotes selective empathy by instilling both political loyalty and a sense of representative responsibility. Representation-within-bounds behavior is taught, and rewarded, in China's National People's Congress.

Limitations and Alternative Perspectives

The evidence can help choose between the alternate frameworks outlined in Chapter 2. If China's NPC were really a rubber stamp, or simply a conduit of power-sharing, we would not expect that deputies would be selected based on the quality of their representative activity. Nor would we expect the regime to invest as much as it does in deputy training. The selection patterns are consistent with the promotion of selective empathy, the unique prediction of the representation within bounds framework.

An important outstanding question concerns the relative influence of these different mechanisms. Which institutional structure is really doing the work, so to speak, and driving the representation within bounds pattern? Are deputies really motivated by careerist concerns, or is it just a sense of responsibility that drives their constrained representative behavior? Is there any real representation in the NPC, or is it that deputies simply look enough like the population, and this produces the congruence described in Chapter 4?

This last question is of real concern in relation to the core conclusions of the book. As Achen (1977, 1978) discusses, preference congruence can arise simply through a random selection of citizens at the voting district level. Suppose we randomly took 113 citizens from Anhui, 61 citizens from Beijing, 60 citizens from Chongqing, and on down the list, and asked them to serve as deputies in the NPC. At the end of this process, we would probably observe congruence between the deputies' proposals and the opinions of their geographic constituencies, even if the deputies acted in a purely self-interested manner. This is the nature of random sampling – the sample (Congress) preference mean is precisely the population (constituency) preference mean in expectation.

For the random selection argument to hold, we should expect the NPC to at least loosely resemble the broader population on the variables we can observe. Hard quotas do produce some balance on key demographic and geographic variables – province, gender, ethnicity – but a second glance at Table 5.1 should shed serious doubt on this alternative explanation. One of the most striking features of the People's Congress is how little it resembles the people. According to the China Survey data, roughly 10% of Chinese citizens work as clerks/retailers, 12% are laborers of some kind, and 45% are farmers and fishermen. The NPC Deputy Database estimates the relative composition of these groups in the NPC as 0.2%, 1.1%, and 0.4%, respectively. Assuming these variables are important to an individual's policy preferences – which the China Survey data suggests they are – it is unlikely that congruence arises primarily through this mechanism.

One weakness of the quantitative analysis in Table 5.3 is that it fails to fully dismiss the elite mobilization framework, which would hold that deputy promotion patterns are driven largely by favoring currying and factional ties with the political elite. We know from Shih, Adolph and Liu (2012) innovative research that factional ties are strongly associated with career outcomes in the CCP Central Committee, and more meritocratic measures have little or no influence. Perhaps deputy activism is driven by connections to Party elites, and in turn these connections drive promotion patterns in the NPC hierarchy.

Unfortunately, it is not possible to test this argument in a rigorous manner given the data constraints. The standard measure of connections in the Chinese politics literature requires detailed biographical information that can identify connected individuals via a shared workplace history (Shih, Adolph and Liu 2012). This granularity is not available in most Baidu profiles for 11th NPC deputies.

My personal sense is that while there is certainly factionalism at play in the NPC, it is unlikely that the introduction of this omitted variable would invalidate my core finding. Empirically, the link between proposals and promotion into the 12th NPC is very strong – t-statistics ranging from 5 to 10 – so it would take a very strong confounding relationship to break this association. Moreover, there is little substantive reason to believe the factional ties would be positively correlated with deputy activism in the first place. More connected deputies presumably have alternative channels to influence policy and would not need to rely on the indirect influence of the NPC's proposal process.

Finally, with respect to the relative influence of harder careerist concerns and softer representational norms, my current evidence is somewhat inconclusive. It is worth noting that in personal interviews, deputies rarely mentioned career incentives as a motivation for their representative activities. Most attributed their behavior to a sense of responsibility to their constituents and a desire to help the country and Party. Some dismissed the importance of legislative performance to the likelihood of reselection. One purged deputy explained, "Putting forth opinions/motions has nothing to do with whether you get reelected. The most important thing is whether the Party likes you" (Personal Interview BJ33113).

Before dismissing the quantitative association between performance and career outcomes, note that a similar social desirability bias may distort the interview evidence here (Arnold and Feldman 1981).[18] Deputies may be reluctant to voice more self-interested, careerist motivations for their representative activities, instead citing more altruistic reasons. In the U.S. setting, legislator behavior is frequently viewed through the lens of the "electoral connection" (Mayhew 1974). Congressmen respond to their constituents because that is what gets them reelected, and that is what they ultimately care about. Still, other scholars have identified non-careerist motivations, including prestige, personal policy preferences, and sense of civic duty (Fenno 1973; Barnett 1999). I suspect that a similar combination of incentives motivates NPC deputies. Some deputies are motivated by a sense of responsibility, but others may participate in an effort to boost their probability of reselection. Future research can focus on adjudicating between these different motivations.

This chapter has identified two mechanisms – hard career incentives and deputy training – that contribute to selective empathy. The next considers a final incentive driving deputy behavior: the returns to office associated with the institution itself. Before moving on to that analysis, I close with a short note on the NPC's role during the recent Occupy Central movement in Hong Kong, which demonstrates selective empathy in the institution.

---

[18] Studies have shown that social desirability bias causes respondents to downplay violence in their marriages (Szinovacz and Egley 1995) and inflate church attendance (Presser and Stinson 1998).

The Revolution That Wasn't

Before Hong Kong's return to mainland control in 1997, former leader Deng Xiaoping promised Hong Kong citizens that they would retain a degree of political autonomy and that the principle of "One Country, Two Systems" would govern the relationship. In advance of the 2017 election for chief executive, the NPC ratified a proposal that would allow universal suffrage but maintained the regime's right to control nomination procedures via a Party-dominated committee. This move was greeted with derision among pro-democracy forces on the island, as it would effectively ensure the election of a pro-regime candidate.

Hong Kong's so-called Umbrella Revolution began as a student-led class boycott in late September of 2014. The protestors, who at times numbered in the tens of thousands, demanded the resignation of current Chief Executive C.Y. Leung and the removal of Beijing's meddling hand from the nomination process. They peacefully occupied several prominent public spaces and government buildings, constructing barricades to block traffic and police intervention.

These moves put central Party leaders in a difficult spot. If they conceded to protestor demands, other would-be discontents might perceive this as a sign of weakness. This could then beget more protests, possibly in the mainland, that could further undermine the one-party system. On the other hand, a festering protest in Hong Kong could also foment a movement in the mainland, activating similar grievances at home and igniting an information cascade (Kuran 1991; Beissinger 2002).

Ultimately, the regime decided to play the waiting game. It allowed the protests to continue largely unfettered through mid-December, occasionally arresting and intimidating some demonstrators. This strategy yielded a decisive victory. Not only did the demonstrations peter out without the need for concessions or Tiananmen-style repression, but no similar protests emerged in the mainland. The government did not grant the students any notable concessions, nor was C.Y. Leung removed from power.

It is telling that within the NPC, there were no public statements from deputies in support of the Occupy movement, a noted departure from deputy activism during the Tiananmen Square movement twenty-five years prior. In fact, thirty-six Hong Kong deputies – tasked with representing the interests of the Hong Kong public – banned together to sign a resolution supporting the aggressive police crackdowns that occurred in the early weeks of the protest (Yin 2014).

The one notable exception was Hong Kong tycoon James Tien, who was a member of the NPC's sister consultative body, the Chinese People's Political Consultative Conference (CPPCC). A few weeks into the Occupy Movement, Mr. Tien broke ranks with colleagues and called on C.Y. Leung to consider resigning the Chief Executive post (Forsythe 2014b). This action was in direct defiance of Party leadership in Beijing, which had repeatedly voiced solidarity with Leung and praised his efforts in handling the protest movement. Formal statements in the CPPCC and NPC solidified this stance.

On October 29th, only a few days after his statement, Mr. Tien was formally relieved of his CPPCC post ("Top China Body" 2014). He refused to comment on this punishment to the media, but his brother Michael – an NPC deputy – was willing to explain the situation to the *New York Times*.

"The oath made when being appointed is that they would vow to uphold all the resolutions made by the standing committee of the CPPCC," said Michael Tien. "So they considered him as not honoring his oath."

"Whether you think this is right or wrong, this is the oath that you made" (Forsythe 2014a).

Technical Appendix

Table 5.5 illustrates the benefits of the matching approach. It shows the mean values for different covariates across reselected ($npc12 = 1$) and nonreselected deputies ($npc12 = 0$) for the unmatched and exact matched data. The table reflects output from the matching model M5. In the unmatched data, there are substantial imbalances across some of the covariates. For example, deputies in the education sector ($pind\# = 4$) compose about 17.4% of the reselected group, compared with only 11.7% among deputies not reselected. Elite Party members appear to have a better chance of getting in, as do deputies from opposition parties. Individuals past the retirement age are less likely to be reselected. Exact matching guarantees balance on these covariates, as shown in third and fourth columns. The mean values are identical across the two groups in the matched sample.

TABLE 5.5 *Results of exact matching*

	Unmatched		Exact matching	
	npc12=1	npc12=0	npc12=1	npc12=0
	μ	μ	μ	μ
del#				
1 – Anhui	0.052	0.036	0.046	0.046
2 – Beijing	0.022	0.023	0.014	0.014
3 – Chongqing	0.020	0.024	0.016	0.016
ethn#				
16 – Han	0.880	0.837	0.953	0.953
17 – Hani	0.001	0.001	0.000	0.000
18 – Hezhe	0.001	0.000	0.000	0.000
party#				
1 – CAPD	0.028	0.016	0.009	0.009
2 – CCP	0.678	0.774	0.924	0.924
3 – CDL	0.034	0.020	0.000	0.000
female	0.219	0.225	0.085	0.085
retireage	0.250	0.344	0.101	0.101
pind#				
2 – Agriculture	0.028	0.024	0.003	0.003
3 – Construction	0.014	0.014	0.000	0.000
4 – Education	0.174	0.117	0.083	0.083
punit#				
1 – Government/Party	0.415	0.523	0.727	0.727
2 – Institutional	0.227	0.173	0.090	0.090
3 – SOE	0.113	0.115	0.083	0.083
govrank#				
1 – Ministry/province	0.205	0.174	0.145	0.145
2 – Department/prefecture	0.199	0.309	0.550	0.550
3 – Bureau/county	0.022	0.043	0.003	0.003
ccpcc	0.090	0.028	0.011	0.011
npcsc11	0.065	0.056	0.000	0.000
npcsc10	0.023	0.018	0.000	0.000
npcsc9	0.003	0.001	0.000	0.000
npc10	0.347	0.308	0.106	0.106
npc9	0.104	0.098	0.016	0.016
npc8	0.045	0.033	0.003	0.003

Note: The table shows results of exact matching across 11th NPC deputies who did and did not gain membership in the 12th NPC. Only a subset of delegation, ethnicity, party, and industry indicators are shown. Special Committee indicators are excluded in the interest of space.

6

The Returns to Office

320 Bribes

Property tycoon Huang Yubiao had long wanted to be a deputy in the National People's Congress. After failing to win a seat in the Hunan delegation in 2008, Huang set his sights slightly lower the next time around, targeting a spot in the Hunan Provincial People's Congress (HPPC). Huang had heard from friends in the Shaoyang municipal congress that paying bribes would help his election chances, so he neatly packed 1,000 RMB into 320 envelopes and distributed them to sitting members (Zhang 2013).

On election day, January 2, 2013, Huang emerged disappointed once again. His 320 bribes yielded only 241 votes, well shy of the 267 needed for election. He lost despite being nominated by the Shaoyang municipal government, which engineered the election of 76 of its 97 nominated candidates.

Disgruntled and slighted, Huang approached his co-conspirators and demanded that the bribes be returned, all the while secretly filming and recording the transactions. Weeks later, he went public with his story, posting the details on numerous blogs and websites. He even mailed materials directly to Hunan provincial authorities and called for the Central Discipline Inspection Commission (CDIC), the Party's corruption watchdog organization, to intervene.

In an interview, Huang described his motivations for coming clean:

I was dismayed after losing the election as some others won by bribe ... I'm determined to sacrifice myself with real name reporting. My goal is to call for improvements for the current people's congress election system. Election organizers must make public the candidates' information and their promises made during the campaign.

Huang cited altruistic reasons for seeking a seat, stating that he wanted to be a deputy in order a make a social contribution (Zhao 2013). He also believes his acts merited affirmation from the authorities and is confident that he will not face criminal charges for his attempted bribery (Zhang 2013).[1]

Regardless of whether we believe Huang's stated motivations, his story suggests that seats may be worth something, and likely more than the proffered 320,000 RMB. Indeed, many netizens joke that Huang would have been more successful if he had properly valued the position (Li 2013). "One has to spend millions of *yuan* to be elected as a village head," one lawyer commented on his microblog. "Now this person wants to spend only hundreds of thousands to become a provincial-level congress deputy. How ridiculous is that?" (Zhai 2013).

The Importance of Loyalty

In terms of the model, recall that a key determinant of the Deputy's behavior is the rents r_D of the position, which are tied to the success of the regime. More formally:

Proposition 4: Higher Deputy rents r_D have uniformly positive effects on Autocrat welfare. The Autocrat prefers that the Deputy enjoy rents to encourage loyalty and align his incentives with the regime.

Observable Implication: Regimes will reward deputies with rents to instill loyalty.

From the perspective of the Autocrat, large rents have uniformly positive effects on Deputy behavior. On weak- or no-preference issues, rents give representatives the incentive to go out and do their jobs, to convey public grievances upward to the regime. On issues where the regime and citizenry have conflicting preferences, rents give representatives the incentive to keep their mouths shut and avoid inciting collective action. This stands in contrast to empathy, which may lead the Deputy to side with the Citizen and not with the regime.

---

[1] Legal experts are less confident. In an interview with *China Daily*, criminal law professor Han Yusheng commented, "It is good for Huang to expose the scandal himself but he should still be punished for offering bribes in the first place ... The fact that he spoke to the media or published posts on the Internet could not be deemed as a voluntary confession to law enforcement departments, and even though he voluntarily confessed to authorities, this could only be a mitigating factor rather than a reason for exoneration" (Zhao 2013).

The theory suggests that rents are key to the system of "representation within bounds" (Truex 2014).[2] Ideally, there would be reliable information on the personal assets of deputies over time, and we could see whether NPC membership was associated with an increase in income or wealth. These are the type of data used in other "returns to office" studies (Eggers and Hainmueller 2009; Lenz and Lim 2009; Querubin and Snyder 2011), but unfortunately they are not available in the Chinese case. However, recall that approximately 500 deputies in the 11th NPC (2008–12) are chairmen or CEOs of various companies. Within this group, around 50 deputies are CEOs of publicly listed firms, for which we have excellent financial data. To assess Proposition 4, the chapter will test whether having a CEO in the NPC brings financial rewards to these companies.[3] This is a second-best solution in the sense that it is difficult to generalize from CEO deputies to the full population, but I believe it is the best solution given data availability issues.

The main empirical concern is that firms that gain NPC seats may simply have better financial prospects to begin with, for any number of reasons. To make a more plausible comparison group, I use a weighting technique to construct a portfolio of Chinese companies that matches the companies with NPC representation on relevant financial characteristics just prior to the 11th NPC. The "NPC portfolio" and weighted "non-NPC portfolio" have the same operating profit margins and returns on assets over the period 2005–7, as well as identical distributions across industries and other financial metrics. Any performance differences that emerge in the 11th NPC session (2008–12) will be suggestive of an "NPC effect."

The analysis shows that a seat in the NPC may be worth an additional 1.5 percentage points in returns and an additional 3 to 4 percentage points in operating profit margin in a given year. Interviews with Chinese financial experts confirm the plausibility of these estimates, which are robust across a number of different specifications and estimation strategies.[4]

---

[2] A more detailed presentation of these findings is available in Truex, R. (2014). "The Returns to Office in a 'Rubber Stamp' Parliament." *American Political Science Review* 108(2): 235–51. Much of the text of this chapter is duplicated in that article.

[3] This design lies between two growing bodies of empirical research: one that estimates the personal financial benefits of holding political office, and another that measures the value of political connections for firms (Roberts 1990; Fisman 2001; Johnson and Mitton 2003; Faccio 2006; Jayachandran 2006; Ferguson and Voth 2008; Goldman, Rocholl and So 2009). Although I measure the performance of firms associated with the NPC, the deputies are themselves the CEOs, and presumably gain personal "returns to office" from their firms' success.

[4] See Personal Interview BJ22213; Personal Interview BJ28213a; Personal Interview BJ28213b; Personal Interview BJ28213c; Personal Interview BJ1313; Personal Interview BJ2313a; Personal Interview BJ2313b.

Additional analysis suggests that the benefits are substantial for smaller private firms and negligible for larger SOEs.

With this finding in mind, the chapter considers how NPC seats contribute to financial gain – probing the mechanisms behind the "rents" mechanism, so to speak. The primary benefit of NPC membership seems to be the reputation boost of the position. The office itself acts as a signal to outsiders, engendering positive.perceptions that foster business development and investment. Additional quantitative analysis shows that NPC firms experience a 3–4 RMB increase in stock price in the month following their membership announcements, meaning that the returns to office begin to take effect even before the deputies actually take office.[5]

The remainder of the chapter is structured as follows. The following sections summarize the data and research design. I then present different estimates for the effect of NPC representation on financial performance before evaluating the mechanisms underlying the broader rents mechanism. I conclude by discussing whether the findings extend to non-CEO deputies, how the findings relate to other theories, and the limitations of using rents as a motivating incentive.

Data and Research Design

The analysis involves the use of two datasets: the NPC Deputy Database (NPCDD), the original database described in Chapter 4, and the COMPUSTAT financial database, made available by Wharton Research Data Services.

For the analysis in this chapter, the NPCDD was helpful in identifying NPC deputies with ties to large businesses. Of the 2,987 deputies in the NPC, 503 were identified as CEOs or leaders of companies of some shape or form.[6]

Additional information was gathered on the work histories of these deputies, including any major positions held at companies over the last twenty years, as well as basic information on the companies themselves. Many are small companies or township or village enterprises (TVEs) for which there are no financial data available, but a portion are publicly listed on the Shanghai or Shenzhen exchanges. The analysis excludes companies with CEOs who held office in the 10th NPC, as we are seeking

---

[5] Interviews with market analysts confirm the importance of this signaling mechanism to company perceptions (Personal Interview BJ2313; Personal Interview BJ1313; Personal Interview BJ2313a; Personal Interview BJ1313b).

[6] Individuals who were company board chairmen, presidents, or other senior executives are included in this group and will hereafter be referred to as "CEO deputies."

to identify the effects of gaining representation. I also exclude companies with any one of the following characteristics: incomplete or incomparable financial data across the period 2005–10; headquarters located outside mainland China; not listed on the Shanghai or Shenzhen exchanges; and extreme outliers on certain financial characteristics. This leaves a total of 997 companies, 48 of which gained CEO representation in the NPC for the first time in 2008.

Once these NPC companies were identified, this NPC representation indicator was merged with the COMPUSTAT financial data from 2005 to 2010 for all publicly listed Chinese companies. The COMPUSTAT database contains reliable financial information derived from quarterly and annual accounting statements. China's domestic accounting standards, while generally less stringent than international standards, still require companies to report the core financial metrics needed for the analysis: total assets, total liabilities, net income, total revenue, the cost of goods sold, outstanding shares, and many others.

This chapter attempts to estimate the effect of gaining NPC membership on firms' financial performance, yet we know that membership might be related to other characteristics. As one NPC staffer commented, "The firms in the NPC are big and famous. They provide a lot of benefits to the local economy" (Personal Interview NH002). China scholars have also demonstrated that political connections play a role in promotion throughout the party–government hierarchy (Shih, Adolph and Liu 2012), and the NPC is no exception in this regard. A number of other firm traits – industry, state ownership, age – might also drive the relationship between NPC membership and firm performance. This dilemma poses a serious concern for the task at hand; perhaps the NPC seat is meaningless, and the NPC companies just have better growth prospects to begin with.

To address the confounding issue, I employ what is known as a "fixed effects" design that exploits within-firm variation over time. The standard fixed effects model is as follows:

$$Y_{it} = \alpha + \beta NPC_{it} + \eta_i + \theta_t + \epsilon_{it}. \tag{FE}$$

Here, i indexes each firm and t indexes each year; Y_{it} represents financial performance metrics of interest; η_i are firm indicators; θ_t are year indicators; and ϵ_{it} is the error term. The coefficient of interest is β, the effect of NPC membership on financial performance. The analysis includes yearly data from 2005 through 2010, with the "NPC treatment" taking effect for 48 companies in 2008.

Researchers employing this sort of thinking must argue for the validity of the "parallel trends assumption"; in the absence of the treatment, the average change in the outcome variable must be equal across both groups. This assumption often appears problematic, especially when the treated and control observations do not follow similar trajectories before the treatment takes effect. For this analysis, the assumption is that if the 48 NPC firms had not gained NPC membership, they would have followed the same trajectory as the other 949 firms. The raw data suggest that this assumption is suspect; the 48 firms that enter the NPC in 2008 prove to be in a more stable, profitable financial trajectory than the 949 that do not.

The task, then, as with the career analysis in the previous chapter, is to create a more comparable control group. My goal is to take the 949 non-NPC companies and somehow select a portion that resemble the "NPC portfolio" on all characteristics that are predictive of future financial performance – revenue, margins, industries, ownership structures, and so forth. If we had two portfolios of companies with the same average performance and characteristics in the pretreatment period, this would give support to the idea that differences in performance can be attributed to the NPC treatment.

To operationalize this strategy, I use a new technique called entropy balancing, which allows an analyst to weight the control group in such a way as to achieve balance on observable characteristics (Hainmueller 2012).[7] The balancing procedure guarantees that the treatment and control groups not only show parallel financial trends in the pretreatment period, but identical trends.

Note that this approach addresses several possible inferential issues. The firm indicators η_i account for any immeasurable firm characteristics that are constant over the analysis period – the business acumen of the CEO and the location of the firm, among others. The year fixed indicators θ_t remove any system-level influences that are changing over time. The effects of the global recession, fluctuations in exchange rates, and other aggregate shocks are captured in this way. The weighting technique lends more plausibility to the assumptions underlying this model, balancing the treatment and control groups on a rich set of historical financial performance indicators.

Thus far, I have been reticent about the lurking influence of political connections. If we observe a difference in performance in our NPC

---

[7] More specific details on this method are available in the Technical Appendix or in the full article associated with this analysis (Truex 2014).

portfolio and our non-NPC portfolio, it may simply be because the companies that gained NPC representation have better political connections, and these connections are responsible for their performance. Given the politicized nature of China's business environment, this alternative explanation is probably the most credible, and therefore the most pressing to address.[8]

Rather than constructing some flawed measure of connections or abandoning the inquiry entirely, I attempt to account for this confounder through the fixed effects framework. Recall that the model includes firm indicators η_i, which account for any time-invariant factors, and year indicators θ_t, which account for aggregate shocks. The remaining threat to inference is a factor that is changing over the analysis period, covarying with a firm's entry into the NPC in 2008.[9]

Political connections are not immutable, of course, but if we restrict the analysis to a short enough time period, they may be relatively constant. In other words, the benefit of a firm's stock of connections would be captured in its firm-specific indicator. To that end, I initially run the analysis over 2005–10 and then restrict the inquiry to a tight three-year window just before and after the 11th NPC took office in 2008 (2007–9). As a further test, I replicate the analysis with weekly stock data and restrict the time period to the months surrounding the change in NPC membership in 2008, as it is highly unlikely that changes in political connections could confound this relationship, given the short time window.

The Returns to Office

The analysis employs two key financial performance metrics as dependent variables: return on assets (*roa*) and operating profit margin (*margin*). The return on assets is the most basic measure of how profitable a company is relative to its invested capital. It is calculated by dividing net income by total assets, with larger values indicating that the company derives more earnings from the assets it controls. Operating profit margin, which

---

[8] Recent innovative studies in Chinese politics have attempted to quantify political connections. Shih, Adolph and Liu (2012) measure connections with rich biographical data, assuming that individuals working/studying in the same place at the same time become connected to each other. Unfortunately, the detailed biographical information necessary for this location-based approach is not available for the CEOs of the 997 firms in the analysis, nor would it really capture the complexities of firm-level connections.

[9] With respect to connections, for example, we should not be concerned about changes in connections that occur after NPC membership is gained. If the office generates new political connections, which in turn increase performance, this will be considered a mediating relationship, not a confounding relationship.

TABLE 6.1 *Rents analysis variable definitions*

Variable	Description
npc	Indicator for having representation in 11th NPC
roa	Net income divided by total assets
margin	Operating profit divided by total revenue
price	Share price (RMB)
rev	Total revenue (RMB)
firmage	Days since IPO
debtratio	Total liabilities over total assets
shares	Total shares outstanding
soportion	Percentage of shares owned by the state
taxes	Total taxes paid (millions of RMB)
ind#	Indicator for being in particular industry (65 in total)

Note: All financial variables are drawn from the COMPUSTAT database and measured on December 31 of the given year. All data are converted into RMB using exchange rates from that date. The detailed list of industry indicators is available in the COMPUSTAT variable key.

is operating profit divided by total revenue (or sales), measures the proportion of revenue left after variable costs (wages, raw materials, etc.) are accounted for. It excludes interest income and tax payments. Margins and returns are driven both by industry characteristics and by how well a firm manages its pricing and expenses.[10]

To create a more plausible control group, the NPC and non-NPC portfolios were balanced across the following financial factors for December 2007, the period directly before entry into the 11th NPC: industry (*ind#*), time since the initial public offering (*firmage*), debt ratio (*debtratio*), current shares outstanding (*shares*), share price (*price*), and the percentage of shares owned by the state (*soportion*).[11] The balancing model also includes historical values from 2005 to 2007 for our two dependent variables of interest, *roa* and *margin*, as well as for total revenue (*rev*). With these variables included, the two portfolios will have comparable financial standing directly prior to the 11th NPC, as well as identical financial trajectories over the few years prior. Table 6.1 offers more detailed descriptions of these variables, and the Technical Appendix outlines the entropy balancing technique.

[10] To fix naming conventions, the variable names will be followed by the data years. The variable *margin08* will indicate margin in 2008, *roa10* will indicate returns in 2010, and so forth.

[11] The *soportion* variable was compiled using the China Stock Market and Accounting Research (CSMAR) database, which contains information on Chinese firms. This variable was merged with the COMPUSTAT data using company stock codes.

NPC Membership and Return on Assets

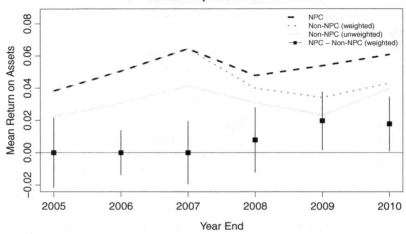

NPC Membership and Operating Profit Margin

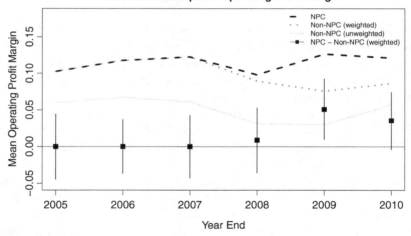

FIGURE 6.1 Effects of NPC membership on firm financial performance
Note: The figure shows changes in average *roa* and *margin* for the NPC portfolio, weighted Non-NPC portfolio, and overall unweighted set of non-NPC companies. The two portfolios are completely balanced up until the 11th NPC takes office in 2008.

With the two portfolios balanced in the pretreatment period (2005–7), we can now investigate the effects of NPC membership on firm performance. Figure 6.1 shows this visually, depicting average *roa* and *margin* for the two portfolios over the full six-year analysis period. The solid

TABLE 6.2 *Fixed-effect estimates and robustness checks*

#	Variables for entropy balancing	roa		margin	
		2005–10	2007–9	2005–10	2007–9
M1.	price + roa07 + margin07 + rev07	0.017** (0.007)	0.017* (0.009)	0.030** (0.013)	0.040*** (0.012)
M2.	M1. + roa06 + roa05 + margin06 margin05 + rev06 + rev05	0.016*** (0.005)	0.015** (0.007)	0.034*** (0.010)	0.034*** (0.011)
M3.	M2. + ind1:ind65 + soportion + debtratio07	0.014** (0.006)	0.013* (0.007)	0.031*** (0.011)	0.030** (0.012)
M4.	M3. + shares07 + taxes07 + firmage	0.015** (0.006)	0.013* (0.007)	0.031*** (0.011)	0.029** (0.013)

Note: The table shows results of entropy-weighted fixed-effect regressions of different financial indicators on the NPC representation indicator. The table explores robustness across four different balancing models and two different analysis periods. Robust standard errors clustered at the firm level are shown in parentheses. M4 is the "baseline specification" referred to throughout the chapter. $*p < 0.10$, $**p < 0.05$, $***p < 0.01$.

line depicts the entire unweighted non-NPC group as a reference point. The weighting procedure ensures that the treatment and control groups behave identically from 2005 to 2007, shown by the overlapping dashed and dotted lines. Once the 11th NPC takes office in 2008, however, the portfolios diverge substantially. The NPC portfolio maintained an *roa* of around 5% despite the global financial crisis. The weighted non-NPC portfolio plunged to almost 3% before slowly recovering. Similarly, operating profit margin remained relatively constant at around 10% to 11% for the NPC portfolio, but fell to 7% in the control portfolio. These performance differences continue through 2009 and 2010.

The figure suggests that NPC representation is associated with better performance, and this intuition is confirmed with more formal hypothesis testing. Table 6.2 presents estimates of the NPC effect for different statistical models. The table explores robustness across a narrow three-year (2007–9) time window and a wider six-year analysis period (2005–10), as well as four different balancing models that include different firm-level variables. We should have the most confidence in the specifications with the richest balancing model (M4), as these models do the most to account for possible confounding influences. Collectively, the analysis suggests that a seat in the NPC is worth an additional

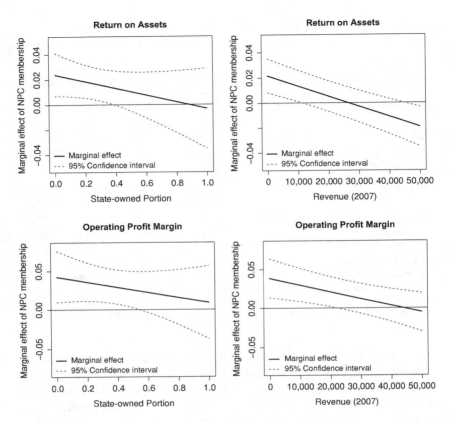

FIGURE 6.2 Conditioning effect on state ownership and revenue
Note: The figure shows the marginal effect of NPC membership on financial performance over different values of *soportion* and *rev07*. The effects reflect coefficients from an interacted model using the W4 balance specification and the five-year analysis period.

1.5 percentage points in returns and a 3 to 4 percentage point boost in operating profit margin in a given year. The estimates are relatively consistent across the different balancing models and time windows.

Certain types of firms and deputies benefit more from the office. Figure 6.2 presents estimates from models that interact the NPC indicator with firm-level covariates, state-ownership (*soportion*) and revenue (*rev07*).[12] For a firm with no shares owned by the state, the marginal effect

---

[12] The figure presents the marginal effects of NPC membership across different *soportion* values as estimated by the model:

$$Y_{it} = \alpha + \beta_1 NPC_{it} + \beta_2 NPC_{it} \cdot SOPORTION_i + \eta_i + \theta_t + \epsilon_{it}. \qquad \text{(FE)}$$

of NPC membership on *roa* is about 2.4 percentage points, and 4.3 points on *margin*. For firms with greater than 50% of shares state-owned, the effect appears negligible. We observe a similar relationship for revenue, with the benefits of membership decreasing substantially with firm size. The returns to office appear greatest for small private firms.

How Seats Matter

The purpose of this chapter is to demonstrate that deputies do reap financial benefits from their office, consistent with Observable Implication 4 of the theory. The preliminary analysis suggests an association between deputies gaining office and the performance of their firms, but we should probe the mechanisms underlying this association further. How exactly do represented companies reap financial gain?

This section provides some simple eyeball tests for two possibilities: *formal policy influence* and *positive external perceptions*. Interviews also point to two other likely mechanisms that are more difficult to test empirically: *access to information* and *preferential treatment*. The returns to office may stem in part from all of these sources, although interestingly, formal policy influence may prove the least salient.

Formal Policy Influence

The first possible mechanism is that CEO deputies use their seats to advance policies that favor their firms. Many advocacy organizations, companies, and activists now lobby NPC deputies to put forth opinions and motions on their behalf (Deng and Kennedy 2010). When prompted with the "returns to office" finding, one NPC staff member pointed to this process as the most plausible mechanism. "It isn't that having a deputy in the NPC means the company will just directly get benefits. But the deputies can help their company and industry indirectly when they give motions and opinions" (Personal Interview NH002). For the staff member to be right, and for the formal policy-influence mechanism to hold, we should observe that CEO deputies propose opinions and motions that differentially benefit their firms.

Here, the marginal effect of NPC membership is simply $\beta_1 + \beta_2 \cdot SOPORTION$. Note that this model omits the constitutive term for *soportion*, which is time-invariant and therefore falls out of the fixed-effect model (Brambor et al. 2006). This is not problematic because the fixed effects give each firm its own intercept. The equivalent model was estimated for *rev_07*.

TABLE 6.3 *Policy proposals in the 11th NPC by profession (2008–12)*

		CEOs		Non-CEOs		Total	
		n	%	*n*	%	*n*	%
1	NPC session	49	6.0	294	8.0	343	7.7
2	Legal system/lawmaking	33	4.1	138	3.8	171	3.8
3	Health care	25	3.1	163	4.4	188	4.2
4	Cultural protection/minority issues	22	2.7	164	4.5	186	4.1
5	Education	14	1.7	252	6.9	266	5.9
6	Water conservation/irrigation	8	1.0	83	2.3	91	2.0
7	Development	36	4.4	385	10.5	421	9.4
8	Energy and emissions	53	6.5	68	1.9	121	2.7
9	Taxation	38	4.7	144	3.9	182	4.1
10	Crime, order, and punishment	13	1.6	170	4.6	183	4.1
11	Housing	21	2.6	105	2.9	126	2.8
12	Economic integration	18	2.2	141	3.8	159	3.5
13	Pharmaceutical industry	34	4.2	37	1.0	71	1.6
14	Government/social stability	28	3.4	266	7.2	294	6.6
15	Coal/steel industry	73	9.0	71	1.9	144	3.2
16	Disaster prevention	11	1.4	145	4.0	156	3.5
17	Internet management	31	3.8	151	4.1	182	4.1
18	Technology/innovation	66	8.1	87	2.4	153	3.4
19	Regional development	9	1.1	142	3.9	151	3.4
20	Agriculture/food safety	46	5.7	115	3.1	161	3.6
21	Migrant workers/labor	47	5.8	108	2.9	155	3.5
22	Rural interests	37	4.6	155	4.2	192	4.3
23	Business environment	81	10.0	128	3.5	209	4.7
24	National security/interests	6	0.7	86	2.3	92	2.1
25	Environmental protection	14	1.7	71	1.9	85	1.9
	Total proposals/comments	813		3,669		4,482	

Note: The table shows the motion and opinion issues raised by CEO and non-CEO deputies. The number of issues raised exceeds the number of total motions/opinions because some motions/opinions covered multiple issues. The data are drawn from the NPC Deputy Database, which was gathered by the author using Chinese newspaper sources in summer 2011, spring 2012 and summer 2015. The topics were produced by a topic model with $K = 25$ using the STM R package (Roberts, Stewart and Tingley 2015).

No information is released at the national level on the results of different proposals, but we can observe whether CEO deputies raise opinions and motions consistent with their business interests. A close analysis of the data gives mixed evidence for the formal policy-influence mechanism. On one hand, CEO deputies do show a different set of priorities and seem to focus their energy on economic issues. Table 6.3 shows the descriptive differences between CEO and non-CEO deputy opinions and motions. Around 10.0% of all CEO deputy proposals deal with improving the business environment and regulatory conditions (Topic 23), 9.0% deal with the coal/steel industries (Topic 15), and 8.1% concern technology and innovation (Topic 18). Non-CEO deputies raise proposals primarily aimed at increasing development (10.5% of proposals, Topic 7), government efficiency and social stability (7.2% of proposals, Topic 14) and education reform (6.9% of proposals, Topic 5).

On the other hand, CEO deputies may be constrained in what they can accomplish through this channel. As discussed in Chapter 5, deputies are encouraged to be responsive to their constituents and discouraged from lobbying for their firms' narrow interests. None of the opinions and motions in the database are centered around firm-level issues. Instead, many deputies use their positions to comment on regulations for their specific industries. For example, deputy Zhong Faping, who also serves as Chairman of Hunan Corun New Energy Co. Ltd., proposed an opinion to increase financial and policy support for the production of energy-efficient vehicles. Ma Yuanzhu, president of Emei Shan Tourism Company, made several suggestions to improve policy support for the tourism industry.[13]

Financial experts are also somewhat skeptical that deputies could use their formal policy influence to get that kind of return (Personal Interview BJ22213; Personal Interview BJ1313):

> If the CEO of the company is the NPC member, he can have some say. For example, he can make a proposal to say that the government should develop the solar industry, but whether the government actually follows the idea is another thing. But at least, you have a chance to say it, and this is still important. But you can't expect too much. (Personal Interview BJ1313)

Before dismissing the formal policy-influence mechanism, we should note that while CEO proposals typically cover industrywide issues, it appears that some CEOs construct their suggestions in such a way as to differentially benefit their own firms. Deputy Zhong's proposal above calls for subsidies for energy-efficient vehicles, but he fails to mention that his company specializes in the advanced batteries used in such vehicles. In 2008, CEO deputy Sun Piaoyang called for a revision of the drug bidding system, which at the time was characterized by fierce competition among producers of low-quality generic drugs. Rather than simply choosing the

---

[13] Recall that the entropy balancing procedure includes industry indicators, so proposals that aim to benefit the entire industry cannot really account for the findings.

lowest bidder, Sun suggested that hospitals should weigh both quality and price when conducting drug procurement. In line with the ideas of this proposal, drug procurement standards have recently been revised, encouraging hospitals to purchase premium medicines. Sun's company, Jiangsu Hengrui Medicine Co., Ltd., is known for producing innovative but pricier drugs, and so it stands to gain differentially from these procurement reforms. Sun's other main proposal suggests lengthening the patent protection period for innovative drugs. This would also benefit Jiangsu Hengrui, which tends to spend more on research and development than other Chinese firms.

To summarize, there is some limited evidence that deputies attempt to use formal policy channels to benefit their own firms, but it is unlikely that these opinions and motions are wholly responsible for the returns to office, especially given the short time frame under consideration. Other mechanisms – positive external perceptions, access to information, and preferential treatment – may be more salient.

Positive External Perceptions
A second possibility is that gaining NPC membership acts as a signal to outsiders, demonstrating that a firm is well run, has achieved a certain level of status, and has connections to government officials. This signal in turns fosters investment, business relationships and general confidence in the firm.

One implication of the external perceptions mechanism is that stock prices should move in reaction to news about NPC membership. If outsiders really do take NPC membership as a positive signal, firms that gain NPC membership should experience better stock performance in the period immediately following the announcement of this information.

While the full membership of the 11th NPC was formally announced by the state-owned media in a *Xinhua* news article on February 29, 2008, the revelation of new membership occurs over a longer period of approximately six to eight weeks. Provincial-level people's congresses meet at varying times in January and February before the national-level meeting in March. Some provinces reveal their election results immediately, some delay, and occasionally candidate lists are accessible beforehand. In short, there is no one single moment which the full NPC membership list suddenly becomes known, but a longer two-month period during which the information is gradually revealed. Some traders may also seek inside information on these sorts of political matters (Personal Interview BJ28213a). Because it is unclear exactly when observers learn about

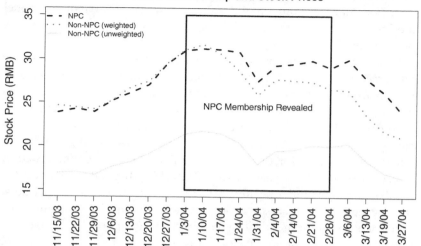

FIGURE 6.3 Testing the external perceptions mechanism
Note: The figure shows changes in average *price* for the NPC portfolio, weighted non-NPC portfolio, and overall unweighted set of non-NPC companies. The two portfolios are completely balanced up until membership begins to be revealed in January 2008. The figure illustrates a market reaction to NPC membership announcement.

NPC membership, the safest bet is to compare performance in the "no information" period– just prior to around January 4, 2008 – to the "full information" period – following February 29, 2008.

Figure 6.3 provides a visual test of the plausibility of the external perceptions mechanism. It shows the average stock prices (in RMB) for the NPC portfolio and the non-NPC portfolio over a short time window, the few weeks before and after NPC membership was revealed (shown within the dark rectangle). As before, the weighting procedure creates a more plausible counterfactual and ensures that the two groups exhibit comparable performance prior to the NPC treatment.

The figure offers some evidence in favor of the mechanism. In the period just prior to membership revelation, the NPC portfolio and non-NPC portfolio both had average stock prices of about 29.5 RMB per share. By the beginning of March, the average price dropped to 26.47 RMB per share for non-NPC firms, while the NPC firms maintained a price of 30.00 RMB. Two weeks later, the price difference neared 4.5 RMB. A formal analysis, similar to that conducted on the *margin* and *roa* measures, suggests that the NPC treatment brings about a boost in share *price* ranging from 3 to 4 RMB, depending on the balancing model and window of time included.[14] This effect is statistically significant at conventional levels.

Interviews with financial analysts confirm the intuition of the external perceptions mechanism. NPC membership is a positive signal about a company and its leadership (Personal Interview BJ2313; Personal Interview BJ1313; Personal Interview BJ2313a). "In China if you are working for the NPC, it means your company is stable and good," one financial analyst describes. "It means you have a very good background. This means good fortune for the investors, and so they will be interested in NPC companies" (Personal Interview BJ28213b). Beyond investors, NPC membership may send a positive message to potential business partners. One entrepreneur explains, "If people know you are NPC deputy, they would like to do business with you. So that's very good for business to expand...People trust you. People know you have this kind of position. So they trust you. Trust is very important for business" (Personal Interview BJ28213a).

Market analysts pay attention to NPC membership announcements, especially if a deputy and his/her company is newly selected to the congress (Personal Interview NPCBJ28213a). One analyst went so far as to claim that NPC companies always succeed, at least in the short period after announcement.

Because you know that the stock price, it has some important relationship with the political system. In China, the share index and share price is tightly related to politics. I mean, if the CEO is the NPC member, their share price will rise in the period after. At least, at least, it won't fall down. This is a guarantee. (Personal Interview BJ1313b)

Empirically, this guarantee is not strictly true, but it illustrates how NPC membership is a strong signal to would-be investors and business

---

[14] As before, I estimate an entropy-weighted fixed-effect model of the form

$$Y_{it} = \alpha + \beta \, \mathrm{NPC}_{it} + \eta_i + \theta_t + \epsilon_{it}. \tag{FE}$$

This time, Y_{it} represents the stock price of firm i in week t, and θ_t represents a vector of week fixed effects. The observations are weighted using the M1–M4 entropy balancing models shown in Table 6.4. All weeks during the information revelation period are excluded. I employ both the full analysis period (11/16/07 to 3/28/08) and a narrower two-period model (12/27/07 and 3/7/08). The estimates range from 3.00 (two-period model with M1 weights) to 4.32 (full analysis period with M4 weights). Full regression output is available from the author upon request.

partners. These impressions give further support to the plausibility of the external perceptions mechanism.

Additional Mechanisms

Beyond limited formal policy influence and reputation benefits, NPC membership may offer additional benefits in the form of *access to information* and *preferential treatment*.

NPC deputies are at the center of government policy making, and even if they cannot lobby directly for their own firms, they have an advantage in understanding government priorities and the likely direction of future policy changes. As discussed in Chapter 3, most draft laws circulate between the NPC, the State Council, and relevant government ministries for months before they are finally made publicly available. "NPC companies have the first sense and understanding of national policies' formulation and execution," explains one businessperson. "They can quickly adjust their management and business practices" (Personal Interview BJ2313a). This early access may prove less relevant as transparency improves, but NPC companies will likely always have some informational edge (Personal Interview BJ28213a).

A final advantage is that NPC companies may enjoy preferential treatment and government protection as a result of their newfound status. NPC membership signals that a firm is supported by , and many financial analysts believe that membership in the NPC makes it easier to get access to credit (Personal Interview BJ2313b; Personal Interview BJ1313; Personal Interview BJ28213b; Personal Interview BJ28213a; Personal Interview BJ22213):

> For an enterprise to be an NPC member, it means the government has supported you, and the bank will be very glad to lend money to you. If the CEO is the NPC member, it is much easier to get a loan from the national bank. If you are just a private company by yourself, it is very difficult. They will refuse you, or they will check on you all the time. (Personal Interview BJ1313)

Similarly, NPC companies may have some protection from investigations and unfavorable regulations (Personal Interview BJ1313; Personal Interview BJ2313a; Personal Interview BJ2313b; Personal Interview BJ28213b; Personal Interview BJ28213b):

> For example, if the government thinks the pollution in an area is bad, they may want some enterprise to shut down its factory, but if the CEO is NPC member, he can say that his company is important to the economy and that he is important, and he can stop this. If you don't have an NPC seat, the government will just shut it down. (Personal Interview BJ1313)

It is difficult to measure this sort of preferential treatment directly, but Hou's (2015) excellent research suggests this mechanism indeed underlies the "returns to office." She finds evidence that entrepreneurs seek out legislative offices in China because it protects them from government predation. Original survey data show that entrepreneurs with seats in the local people's congress spend less on extractive government payments. An experimental assessment reveals that officials show more responsive behavior to information requests originating from entrepreneurs with connections to the people's congress system.

*

To summarize, the analysis above suggests there are measurable returns to office for companies that gain seats in the NPC. When prompted with the idea that a seat brings as much as a two-percentage-point increase in returns, one financial analyst remarked, "I do believe that. I think it's more than two percentage points" (Personal Interview BJ28213a). Although the NPC does allow some policy influence and insider information, the status symbol of NPC membership may be more helpful for business. One local business school professor describes, "What you say in the NPC does not really matter. It matters that you are an NPC member. This is the most important" (Personal Interview BJ1313). NPC membership is a positive signal that encourages investment, fosters business relationships, and offers protection from government intervention.

Just how high are the returns to office for NPC members? Among the NPC firms, the standard deviation for *roa07* was about 0.055, and the mean was 0.064. An effect size of 0.014 to 0.017 translates to an improvement of about one-fourth to one-third of a standard deviation. The improvement in operating profit margin is roughly the same. The standard deviation for *margin07* among the 48 NPC firms is 0.123, so the effect of 0.030 to 0.040 is also about one-fourth to one-third of a standard deviation. The roughly 3 RMB difference in stock price between the two portfolios represents a 10% difference in performance over the two-month period when membership was announced, as the average price was about 30 RMB in late December 2007. It is difficult to assess whether connections to the NPC are more or less valuable than connections elsewhere, but the analysis suggests that they are certainly nontrivial.[15]

---

[15] In her study of politically connected firms across 47 countries, Faccio (2006) examines the stock returns of companies that gain a political relationship, either through a businessperson gaining office or through a politician joining the firm. She finds that new connections to MPs bring a cumulative abnormal return of 1.28% over the five-day period

Limitations and Alternative Perspectives

If the above analysis is correct, there are measurable rents to firms with CEOs in the NPC, to the tune of about a two-percentage-point increase in returns in a given year. This finding confirms the intuitions of the theory, but it suffers from two primary limitations.

The first is generalizability, specifically whether or not non-CEO deputies enjoy similar benefits. The inference above comes from data on 48 CEO deputies, and we should be careful in inferring from this small group to the rest of the NPC.

It is impossible to pin this issue down empirically, but more impressionistic evidence suggests that the benefits of NPC membership are heterogenous and likely driven by personal background. As noted above, the primary benefit of a seat seems to be positive external perceptions, the reputation boost of the position. NPC membership signals confidence, competence, and connections, and all of these things beget professional success in the Chinese context.

The heterogeneity comes from the fact that some deputies do not really need a reputation boost. According to my data on deputy backgrounds, about 51 deputies can be considered heroes, athletes, or celebrities of some kind. Another 163 are members or alternates of the CCP Central Committee, and 22 of those are Politburo members. Their social status already exceeds that of an NPC deputy. It is unlikely that the office brings them much in the way of increased positive external perceptions, in the same way that an NPC seat does not do much for larger, prominent firms.

The rest of the deputies are lower-status, scattered across an array of industries and professions. Among them are schoolteachers, farmers, migrant workers, professors, low-ranking officials, factory owners, and budding entrepreneurs. For these deputies, my working hypothesis is that NPC seats bring real advantages, perhaps exceeding those gained by the 48 CEO deputies. Many citizens hold this perception. "Ordinary people, not celebrities, that kind of ordinary people, if they can get the position, it can be a bigger difference for their lives," says one small business employee. "These kinds of people will just try to help themselves" (Personal Interview BJ28213c).

---

of the announcement. Other studies have examined the effect of key political events on stock market prices and returns (Roberts 1990; Fisman 2001; Faccio 2006; Johnson and Mitton 2003; Ferguson and Voth 2008). See Truex (2014) for more discussion of these results.

In personal interviews, some deputies hint at the reputation benefits of the position, although most are less forthright about their private "returns to office." A former deputy describes how membership is helpful in developing relationships:

> Here is why people want to be in the congress... it's like being in a big club. Professors, entrepreneurs, officials – everyone becomes good friends over these two years. It's a way to help develop connections. (Personal Interview BJ33113)

One younger deputy, a "model worker" representative in a prefectural-level congress in Hunan, believes the position has given her new status in her job at the local electric utility (Personal Interview HN42413). Other deputies comment on how gaining the position improved their standing in their local communities or their professional networks (Personal BJ32713b; Personal Interview HN42313).

We need look no farther than Shen Jilan – the longest-serving NPC deputy – to get some supporting evidence in this regard. Shen has gained notoriety for never casting a single "nay" vote during her six decades in office, citing that she does not want to "give the Party trouble." Her policy proposals also tend to adhere closely to Party doctrine and language.[16] Shen was originally selected in 1954 as an uneducated "model worker" from Shanxi, but over the course of her tenure in office, she has managed to accumulate a small fortune. She currently owns a real estate company that recently reaped 50 million RMB in seed capital ("55-year NPC Deputy Shen Jilan" 2012). These types of stories abound in the NPC, though more systematic analyses and better data will be needed to test the hypothesis more broadly.

The second criticism is that these findings do not disprove the alternative theories discussed in Chapter 2, as many of them also predict substantial "returns to office" for members of authoritarian institutions. Recall that cooptation theory states that authoritarian regimes create legislative institutions to coopt would-be opposition into the policy process (Gandhi and Przeworski 2006, 2007; Gandhi 2008; Malesky and Schuler 2010),

---

[16] In a recent interview, 84-year-old Shen offered up this amalgamation of CCP dogma in calling for greater Internet restrictions:

> I have an idea. There should be someone managing the web as well. We can't just let people do whatever they want. [The Internet] should be like the *People's Daily*. Foreigners are messing up [the Internet]. We can't be like this. We should make the Internet in accordance with our principles. We should not make a good thing turn bad and become a place where people can say whatever they want. Our country is a socialist country under the leadership of the Communist Party. ("Democracy with Chinese characteristics" 2013)

giving key actors limited policy influence and access to rents (Lust-Okar 2006). Proponents of the power-sharing view also predict rent distribution in authoritarian parliaments, which exist to help autocrats distribute resources to the rest of the ruling clique (Svolik 2009, 2012; Blaydes 2011; Boix and Svolik 2013). Blaydes (2011) notes that in Mubarak's Egypt, "parliamentary hopefuls spend millions to reap billions," a phrase that sounds applicable to the story of Huang Yubiao. Because the different frameworks all point to rent distribution, the findings can be taken as confirming evidence for each (Truex 2014).

The only way to further tease out the relative merits of the theories would be to get definitive evidence on variation in rent distribution and how that variation relates to patterns in representation. My theory implies that rents induce representation-within-bounds behavior, and so we should expect to see greater activism and loyalty from deputies who receive more rents. Interestingly, the two deputy types who would seem to benefit least from the position, celebrities and high-ranking officials, prove to be the least active in proposing opinions and motions. If data availability improves, future research can investigate whether this pattern is due to the mechanisms outlined in the theory.

Why Not More Rents?

This chapter has tested for the presence of rents in an authoritarian parliament using original data on the financial connections of NPC deputies. Although the analysis is certainly not conclusive, it suggests that there are real "returns to office" for companies whose CEOs gain membership in the body. These returns appear to come primarily through external perceptions and the "reputation boost" of the office, which suggests that non-CEO deputies may enjoy similar benefits.

Recall that the Autocrat's main problem is that representation can be beneficial at times and problematic at others. Active deputies can relay valuable information and stem citizen grievances, but they can also aggravate tensions if they fixate on the wrong issues. In Chapter 5, I showed that the CCP regime attempts to instill "selective empathy" among representatives through a combination of socialization and career incentives, but according to the model, the best route would be to raise the rents of the position r_D as high as necessary. Higher rents instill more loyalty to the regime, and if rents are high enough, they can overwhelm deputies' reformist impulses.

In the NPC, the rents of the position do seem to be substantial – a two-percentage-point increase in returns is nothing to dismiss – but they could certainly be higher. Deputies are not given much in the way of stipends or salaries or other amenities, and conceivably these types of benefits could help motivate loyalty to the regime and the appropriate kind of representation.

There are two reasons that we do not observe this in practice. First, it is likely that rents have diminishing effects in terms of incentivizing representative behavior. Numerous studies in behavioral economics and social psychology have demonstrated that external rewards can crowd out intrinsic motivations if made too salient (Titmuss 1970; Frey 1994; Frey and Oberholzer-Gee 1997; Schulze and Frank 2003), the so-called "hidden costs of reward" (Lepper and Green 1978).[17] The quality of representative activity would not necessarily be better if deputies were paid more or given additional perks.

A second and more immediate reason is that deputy rents have the potential to become a political liability. On most public opinion surveys in China, corruption and inequality consistently rank as the top two social concerns, and in recent years, deputies engaging in conspicuous consumption have come under public attack. During the 2012 annual meeting, so many deputies arrived wearing expensive designer clothing that the legislative session earned the name "Beijing Fashion Week" among skeptical netizens (Beech 2012). In late 2012, Xi Jinping ushered in a series of measures designed to curb extravagance in the bureaucracy, and the 2013 annual meeting proved noticeably more austere. There were no flowers in deputy hotel rooms, nor were there any welcoming ceremonies at airports and railway stations. Deputies refrained from partaking in the usual galas and performances, instead eating their meals at modest buffets.

To summarize, rents exist, and they matter for fostering loyalty, but the optimal solution is not for the regime simply to pay deputies as much as possible. The "returns to office" may not motivate all representatives,

---

[17] In a survey of Swiss residents, Frey and Oberholzer-Gee (1997) asked respondents whether they would be willing to allow a repository to store nuclear waste in their community. More than half of the respondents (50.8%) said they would support construction, but support dropped to only 24.6% once some compensation was offered. They conclude that "intrinsic motivation is partially destroyed when price incentives are introduced. Consequently, the price mechanism becomes less effective" (p. 746).

and rents that are too extravagant could crowd out representative norms and even engender public unrest.

To illustrate this latter possibility, I close with a few netizen comments made in response to a story about Shen Jilan's growing fortune. It is fitting that Shen, who recently demanded greater Internet censorship despite never using a computer, has become a subject of mockery on numerous blogs ("55-year NPC Deputy Shen Jilan" 2012):

Who elected her? Who does she represent? Excellent deputy? If trash could be considered excellent, then she is considered one.

You say you are a migrant worker, but you are really part of the leadership. You say you care about agriculture, but really you registered a real estate company. You say you are uncorrupted, but your son is a Party Secretary, and your daughter is a senior military official. You say you only make affirmative votes, but who would you say could be represented by this kind of representative? Shanxi Shen Jilan Trading Company. Everyone should look down upon her.

People's deputies must not become self-interested deputies.

This type of old witch. She should meet retribution some day.

Technical Appendix

In using entropy balancing, the analyst first specifies a set of moment conditions that she would like to hold across the treatment and control groups. The algorithm then searches for weights for different observations in the control group to satisfy these moment conditions (Hainmueller 2012).

The results of the full balancing procedure are shown in Table 6.4. The NPC portfolio contains 48 companies altogether. As the unbalanced data show, on the average these firms tend to have more revenue and higher returns than their 939 non-NPC counterparts, as well as more outstanding shares and a greater portion of shares owned by the state. We also observe imbalances in the industries represented. Over 12% of firms in the NPC come from the Chemicals (*ind3*) and Metals & Mining (*ind6*) industries, while the unbalanced non-NPC firms have only 9.2% and 6.5% in these industries, respectively. Similar imbalances occur across the 55 industry indicators not depicted in the table.

Despite these differences, there is considerable overlap in the covariate densities, which facilitates the balancing procedure. The Control (wt) column shows the relevant sample moments for the weighted non-NPC

The Returns to Office

TABLE 6.4 *Results of entropy balancing*

	Treatment		Control		Control (wt)	
	μ	σ^2	μ	σ^2	μ	σ^2
roa07	0.064	0.003	0.041	0.011	0.064	0.013
roa06	0.051	0.002	0.030	0.006	0.051	0.003
roa05	0.038	0.004	0.023	0.006	0.038	0.005
margin07	0.123	0.015	0.061	0.124	0.123	0.072
margin06	0.118	0.010	0.068	0.038	0.118	0.023
margin05	0.103	0.016	0.060	0.047	0.103	0.050
rev07	7976	2.1E+08	2647	3.1E+07	7976	1.9E+08
rev06	5441	7.2E+07	2081	1.8E+07	5441	1.1E+08
rev05	4463	4.5E+07	1748	1.1E+07	4463	7.4E+07
price07	29.2	1504	20.2	306	29.2	1918
soportion	0.325	0.059	0.249	0.049	0.325	0.062
debtratio07	0.500	0.024	0.507	0.068	0.500	0.034
shares07	1188	9.4E+06	424	5.0E+05	1188	4.0E+06
taxes07	39.8	5.1E+04	5.7	1.8E+04	39.8	1.6E+05
firmage	3243	3.0E+06	3185	3.3E+06	3243	2.4E+06
ind#						
1 - Energy & Eqpmnt	0.000	0.000	0.004	0.004	0.000	0.000
2 - Oil, Gas & Fuels	0.042	0.041	0.016	0.016	0.042	0.040
3 - Chemicals	0.125	0.112	0.092	0.083	0.125	0.110
4 - Construction Mat.	0.021	0.021	0.022	0.022	0.021	0.020
5 - Containers & Pckgng	0.000	0.000	0.004	0.004	0.000	0.000
6 - Metals & Mining	0.125	0.112	0.065	0.061	0.125	0.110
7 - Paper & Forest Prod.	0.021	0.021	0.019	0.019	0.021	0.020
8 - Aerospace & Defense	0.000	0.000	0.005	0.005	0.000	0.000
9 - Building Prod.	0.000	0.000	0.013	0.013	0.000	0.000
10 - Cons. & Engin.	0.021	0.021	0.024	0.024	0.021	0.020

Notes: The table shows results of entropy balancing across the NPC portfolio (Treatment) and non-NPC portfolio (Control). Industry indicators 11 through 65 are not depicted, in the interest of clarity (*ind11-ind65*). Treatment group has $n = 48$. The unweighted control group has $n = 939$, and the sum of the control weights equals 48.

portfolio. Entropy balancing has achieved the desired result. The weighted control group has identical average values across all the relevant covariates and nearly identical variances. The entropy balancing package allows the analyst to force balance on the second moment as well, but this can prove difficult when a large number of parameters are used. For the analysis here, it is preferable to have a richer set of covariates rather than balance on variance, and the current weights nearly balance the second moment anyway. The sum of the weights equals 48, the number of firms in the NPC portfolio. Different balancing models were used for different specifications, as shown in Table 6.2, but the estimates do not change appreciably.

7

The Evolution of the NPC

RWB and Institutional Change

The current version of the NPC is a "representation within bounds" parliament. Deputies convey citizen grievances but shy away from sensitive political issues, and the government in turn displays partial responsiveness to their concerns. Deputies are socialized into this behavioral pattern and are punished or rewarded depending on the quality of their representative behavior. They also enjoy substantial rents for their services.

The analysis in this book is focused on a single snapshot in time, the 11th NPC (2008–12) under the Hu-Wen administration. This decision was made largely on the basis of data availability, but it leaves open the question of how the CCP regime arrived at this equilibrium. How has representation in the NPC changed over time? How long has the representation within bounds system been in place, and what precisely spurred its creation? And importantly, can we expect it to continue in the future?

The purpose of this chapter is to explore and explain the historical evolution of the National People's Congress.[1] I will use the ideas from the formal theory in Chapter 2 to aid in the presentation and interpretation of the history. This approach has been referred to as an "analytic narrative" or a "theory guided narrative" (Bates et al. 2000; Buthe 2002; Levi 2002; Capoccia and Kelemen 2007), and it can be helpful in assessing the plausibility of a particular framework and identifying relevant actors and

---

[1] Readers with more interest in the historical development of the NPC are encouraged to read Kevin O'Brien's (1990) *Reform Without Liberalization*, which describes the early evolution of the NPC in great detail. My brief discussion of the Mao and Deng congresses is merely a summary of O'Brien's findings.

trends (Buthe 2002). In line with rational-choice institutionalism, I ascribe to the view that institutions can be manipulated to meet the ends of different political actors (Shepsle 2006; Pepinsky 2014). I will also draw on concepts developed by proponents of historical institutionalism, particularly the idea that institutional development is often the result of rapid change followed by institutional reproduction (Thelen 1999; Capoccia and Kelemen 2007).

Recall from the model in Chapter 2 that for the Autocrat, the ideal level of representation is a function of the probability of a revolution being successful, π. At extremely low values of π, the Citizen cannot credibly threaten the regime, and there is no need for policy responsiveness. The Autocrat can get away with minimal representation and prefers the Stable Nonresponsive equilibrium $E2.1$. This entails an inactive Deputy who does not convey the Citizen preference message. As the value of π rises, the Citizen threat becomes more credible, and the need for representation becomes more pressing. Here, the Autocrat prefers the Deputy to reveal the Citizen preference on any weak- or no-preference issues, in hopes of achieving the stable responsive equilibrium $E2.3$.

Of course, out-of-bounds representation on strong preference issues is always unhelpful. If the Deputy conveyed the Citizen message on something sensitive, this could potentially engender the induced unstable nonresponsive equilibrium $E2.5$. Full representation on the complete issue space is never the ideal outcome for an authoritarian regime.

The framework yields two intuitions as to when we might observe institutional change in an authoritarian parliament. First, when citizens display an enhanced capacity for revolution, we should observe efforts by the regime to improve the quality of representation and enable more responsive policy making. Second, when representatives do step out of bounds, we should observe efforts by the regime to rein them in, and to create institutions that promote loyalty and selective empathy.

Though the history is quite complex, we do observe these patterns in the institutional development of the NPC. From its inception in 1954, the NPC has been a tool of CCP leadership, and its very existence has depended on leadership support (Pepinsky 2014). When CCP leaders observed organized threats to their rule – as during the Democracy Wall and Tiananmen Square movements of the Deng era – they tended to enhance representation and information revelation in the NPC. When activist deputies proved a nuisance – as during the Hundred Flowers Movement in 1957 and again in the Tiananmen Square movement in 1989 – the NPC was marginalized or reined in. The representation within bounds system has only emerged in full in the post-Tiananmen period, after decades of this tug-of-war between openness and repression.

The NPC's evolution can be loosely divided into four periods – founding and early development (1954–7), decline and disappearance (1958–77), reestablishment (1978–89), and constrained enhancement (1990–present). The dates of these divisions are somewhat artificial, but they capture key trends in representation in the institution. The remainder of the chapter considers each phase in turn, focusing on key institutional reforms and the nature of representation in the body. I close by placing the historical development of the NPC in theoretical context.

Founding and Early Development

The first meeting of the NPC was held in Beijing in September of 1954. The 1,226 newly minted deputies formally ratified the country's new constitution, established two committees, confirmed the nomination of 227 officials, and passed laws pertaining to the institutional authority of different branches of government. The proceedings were broadcast on national radio. Mao rightly called the event a "milestone in the historical development of the People's Republic of China" (O'Brien 1990).

The PRC's 1954 constitution was based closely on the Soviet model, and it endowed the legislature with many of the formal powers it has today. The original NPC had the authority to amend the constitution, to make and amend laws, to elect the top leadership of the government, to supervise the enforcement of the constitution, and to pass state budgets (Constitution of the People's Republic of China: Article 27, 1954). Despite this nominal authority, deputies understood that the legislature would not serve as a formal check on CCP leadership. In the first meetings, deputies voted by a show of hands, and every single measure passed unanimously. The draft constitution was approved without any discussion or proposed changes (Houn 1955). Western observers dismissed the session as "hardly more than a spectacle," a "clever camouflage designed to give the regime a constitutional cloak" (Houn 1955).

The 1954 constitution introduced the indirect elections system, which was justified by Deng Xiaoping on the grounds that Chinese citizens did not understand national policies or know the names of state leaders. NPC deputies would be elected by provincial congresses, which were elected by county congresses, which were elected by "basic-level" congresses, which were directly elected by the population. Direct elections were to be instated after a period of economic development and political education (Houn 1955; O'Brien 1990).

Though only 55% of the first NPC deputies were CCP members, selection processes emphasized political loyalty. Houn (1955) describes early norms:

The 1,226 delegates elected are all unswervingly loyal to the policy and leadership of the existing regime, and some once prominent persons in the Communist regime such as Kao Kang, Li Li-shan, Ch'en Shao-Yii, Liang Shu-min, and Chang Tung-sung, who reportedly have been either unharmonious with or critical of the leadership of the regime, have failed to find their way into the new organ.

Leadership positions in the NPC were similarly dominated by Party elites. The 254-member Presidium – which controlled the agenda of the Congress – included all 26 members of the Politburo, as well as 74 members or alternate members of the CCP Central Committee (O'Brien 1990).

The first deputies tentatively embraced their representative role. Between legislative sessions, they carried out investigation tours of units of their choosing, in turn reporting back their findings and recommendations to the NPCSC (O'Brien 1990). These efforts were supported by NPC administrative staff, which had increased to 360 by 1956 (Jiang 2003). The proposal process also began to take form, with deputies offering criticism on a range of social and economic issues, though nothing of political controversy (Houn 1955). In the 1955 session, Zhou Enlai personally discussed and responded to the 39 motions submitted by deputies in the previous year (O'Brien 1990), signaling an attentiveness on behalf of Party leadership.

Despite its numerous constraints and institutional handicaps, the early years of the NPC are remembered as a time of healthy institutional development. O'Brien (1990) describes a parliament that "had elite support and was carving out a role for itself in the policy process as a forum for policy review, where deputies enunciated problems on people's minds and state officials admitted mistakes." Deputies began to display the precursors to representation within bounds behavior, albeit on a fraction of the scale we observe today.

Decline and Disappearance

This period came to an abrupt halt after the Hundred Flowers Movement in 1957, which tested and ultimately eliminated the regime's tolerance for criticism. As described in the introduction of Chapter 2, liberal-minded deputies – many of them intellectuals or members of so-called democratic parties – saw Mao's call to "let a hundred flowers bloom" as an invitation to criticize the Party and demand political reform. Deputy Zhang Bosheng, for example, proposed a bicameral democratic parliamentary system, with the NPC serving as the lower house. Deputies Wang Kunlun and Huang Shaohong criticized CCP absenteeism in the NPCSC, citing difficulties in establishing a quorum. Scholars joined the criticism and questioned the Party's respect for constitutionalism and legality (O'Brien 1990).

In the language of the theory, this was representative behavior on "strong preference issues," and it drew citizen attention to unwanted areas. On the opening day of the 1957 session, deputies were greeted with a thinly veiled threat in the form of a *People's Daily* editorial:

Some people are not prepared to extol the creative achievements of the people, and this is their freedom. But nobody has the right to obliterate objective facts. What attitude will the people's deputies take toward the fruits of the struggle of the masses of the people? We believe the overwhelming majority of the deputies will give a correct answer to the various questions. (O'Brien 1990, p. 42)

The subsequent launch of the Anti-Rightist campaign signaled the beginning of a more repressive, closed, and totalitarian turn in Mao's rule. In total, 38 deputies were branded "rightists" and removed from their positions by 1958. The message to the remaining deputies was sobering but clear: political criticism would no longer be tolerated. The relatively transparent, active legislative sessions of 1954–7 gave way to the muted, repressive sessions of 1958 and the secret, scripted sessions of 1962 and 1963.

Membership shifted away from intellectuals and former capitalists and toward CCP rank and file. The share of seats held by CCP members rose to 67% in the second NPC (1958–63) and 85% for the brief third NPC (1964). The total seats swelled to over 3,000, with many awarded to Party cadres and model peasants/workers. The annual plenary session moved to the newly constructed Great Hall of the People, an auditorium-like structure in Tiananmen Square, which could hold the oversized parliament but was completely incompatible with debate (O'Brien 1990).

Representative activity effectively disappeared during this period. Self-censorship became the new normal. The budget to cover deputy working expenses was eliminated. Deputies were relegated to a mobilization role, tasked with explaining the Party's policies to the population, not conveying the population's demands to the Party. They became socialist cheerleaders for Mao's pet campaigns. For example, in 1958, deputy statements praised the "brilliant achievements" of the Great Leap Forward, which ultimately brought about the largest manmade famine in human history (Dikotter 2010). They continued to do so long after central leadership had retreated from the campaign (O'Brien 1990).

The fate of the NPC was directly relatedly to Mao's evolving views on the role of law in society. He initially championed the rule of law and the institutionalization of the new communist state. In 1954, he declared that "an organization must have rules, and a state also must have rules; the Constitution is a set of general rules and is a fundamental charter" (Leng 1977). By the early 1960s, Mao was increasingly embracing principles of "legal nihilism" (Leng 1977; O'Brien 1990), and he grew distrustful of institutions directly copied from the Soviet model (Baum 1986).[2] He preferred the flexibility of rule by decree to the constraints of rule by law, and governed through mass-mobilization campaigns rather than the trappings of modern bureaucratic government.

Thus, the lawmaking function of the NPC became unnecessary, and the mobilization and propaganda components became cumbersome and superfluous. The NPC was informally disbanded. For the next ten years, Mao's "Great Proletarian Cultural Revolution" brought about the removal of his greatest political rivals (MacFarquhar and Schoenhals 2006). The formal authority of the NPC was rarely if ever invoked for these personnel changes (Baum 1986).

In 1975, Mao loyalists, led by the infamous Gang of Four, briefly convened the NPC to ratify a revolutionary, socialist constitution that stripped the body of its formal powers. The functions granted to the NPC dropped from fourteen to six, with much of that authority granted formally or informally to Party organs. Deputies offered no criticism at the session. This was the nadir of the parliament. It had become nothing more than a tool to institutionalize the power grab of radical anti-institutionalists (O'Brien 1990).

In terms of the theory, we can consider the years from 1958 to 1976 as the Stable Nonresponsive Equilibrium $E1.1$. There is no representation – the Deputy does not reflect the policy preferences of the Citizen – but the regime is stable and the Autocrat maintains control. Although Chinese society was anything but stable, the violence and Citizen threat were

---

[2] During the high point of the Cultural Revolution, Mao decreed, "Depend on the rule of man, not the rule of law" (Leng 1977).

directed at the perceived enemies of the regime, not the regime itself. Mao remained hugely popular and managed to maintain power despite little in the way of public good provision, meaningful political participation, or responsive governance.

Reestablishment

The NPC saw new life only with Mao's death in 1976. The more moderate Deng Xiaoping, who had been formally purged during the Cultural Revolution, used his immense personal influence throughout the Party to outmaneuver Mao loyalists, paving the way for a more pragmatic turn in Chinese policy making. Deng's pet phrase, "to seek truth from facts," signaled a willingness to elicit differing opinions and enact polices that reflected realities of the ground. Rule by law would gradually replace rule by decree, and governance through institutions would replace governance through revolution (Baum 1986; Cai 1999). Representation would reemerge in the stunted parliament.

The NPC was tasked with building a legal system from the ground up. "We are now advocating socialist democracy and socialist legal system," Deng explained in an interview in 1979. "Socialist democracy and socialist legal system are not meant to supervise the leaders and officials but also everybody has to abide by the law" (Kuan 1984). In other words, the Party would never be subservient to the law, but it would aim to develop rules and regulations (Baum 1986).

The 1982 Constitution, coupled with the 1982 Organic Law of the NPC, restored the parliament's original authority and made minor changes to the legislative system. Groups of 30 deputies or more were allowed to propose motions on amendments or new legislation. Direct elections were extended to the county level. The revised Electoral Law required the number of candidates to exceed the number of seats and allowed citizens to nominate candidates at lower levels. The NPCSC was reduced in size, which would improve legislative debates, and deputies on the committee served full time. Six permanent committees were established to aid in legislative work.

Deputies enjoyed new rights and a degree of legal protection. Article 43 of the Organic Law held that no deputy could be held legally liable for her speeches or votes at the plenary session. This protection, while relatively weak and sometimes violated in spirit, nevertheless reassured deputies against the possibility of Anti-Rightist campaign or Cultural Revolution-style ideological purges. The secret ballot was introduced (though not required for all bills) to offer deputies some semblance of anonymity (Article 18). For the first time, deputies also had the right to be informed about major agenda items in advance of the annual plenary session (Article 2).

Reformers within the Party pushed for a more representative and professional congress. The CCP's share of seats dropped to 62.5%, and the representation of various geographic constituencies (the armed forces, Beijing, Tianjin, and Shanghai) was adjusted to align more closely with the population. Educational levels among deputies began to rise, with 44.5% of deputies in the 6th NPC (1983–7) holding university degrees. The institution began to shed its reputation as a retirement home for older cadres; by the 7th NPC (1988–92), over three-fourths of deputies were under the age of 65 (O'Brien 1990).

Representative and supervisory activity rose accordingly. Deputies began registering "nay" votes and abstentions on nominations and work reports. Though no measure ever failed to pass, this represented an important departure from the Mao era. Deputies displayed similar courage in small group meetings during plenary sessions, and frequently upbraided State Council officials for incompetent policies and mistaken priorities. Inspections and other field visits were restarted in full. In 1986, the General Office of the NPCSC issued a decision giving deputies the authority to conduct unauthorized visits to various work units (O'Brien 1990).

The proposal process was also reinvigorated. Deputies to the 6th NPC submitted 14,215 suggestions, criticisms, and opinions in total during their five-year term. O'Brien (1990) summarizes the rise of "service responsiveness" and "allocation responsiveness" in this period:

Despite continued leadership hostility toward institutionalized representation and electoral sanctions, and despite Deng's belief that direct, popular elections for the NPC were at least fifty years away, activities by deputies on behalf of constituents, regions, social groups, and the whole nation appeared throughout the 1980s and had an effect on political outcomes.

Deputies touched on a broad range of social and economic issues, and often sought specific redistribution measures for their functional or geographic constituencies (O'Brien 1990).

To summarize, deputies to the rejuvenated parliament enjoyed greater influence and responsibility than ever before. The scale and scope of representation remained limited – less than one suggestion, criticism, and opinion per deputy per session – but constituted a significant improvement over the nonexistent representation of the Mao period.

Ultimately, this improvement was not enough to ensure social stability. On April 15, 1989, the death of noted reformer Hu Yaobang activated latent grievances in the population. What began with a simple commemoration and student petition lead to a full-scale revolution centered in Tiananmen Square, the hallowed ground of Party power. Within a month, over 300,000 students had converged on the center of Beijing.

Deputy activism was not the cause of the Tiananmen protest movement, but it did embolden protestors by signaling the presence of sympathetic ears within the highest institution of government. As the students began their hunger strike in May, prominent NPC deputies, including deputy Hu Jiwei, gathered outside formal NPC office space to sign a petition calling for an emergency legislative session. Three separate petitions were signed, containing 57 signatures in total, in an event that later came to be known as the "Signature Incident" (Hu 1993).

By convention, an emergency meeting of the NPCSC can be called through the adoption of a resolution at a Chairman's meeting. On May 24, 1989, five days after the imposition of martial law, and eleven days before the eventual government crackdown, deputy Hu Jiwei and his colleagues submitted the petition letters to NPCSC Chairman Wan Li and NPCSC Vice Chairman Xi Zhongxun. The very act of submitting the petition – which signaled tacit support of the student protestors – was extremely subversive. As historian Hu Shikai (1993) describes:

The "Signature Incident" was significant also because it was the first time in NPC history that so many members of the NPC leadership organ, invoking constitutional rights and acting on their own, openly sought an institutional way to challenge the control of the ruling Chinese Communist Party.

The deputy petition, and the student movement it supported, ultimately failed. At the time, NPCSC Chairman Wan Li was traveling on a diplomatic mission to the United States and China, but he returned early after viewing the escalating protest movement. Wan was widely considered a sympathizer with the student demonstrators, who planned to greet his return with a parade in Tiananmen Square. Instead of flying directly to Beijing, though, Wan was rerouted to Shanghai, reportedly for "medical treatment." Two days later, he emerged with a written statement supporting the hardliners' position, effectively quashing the possibility of an emergency NPCSC session (Hu 1993). Days later, the PLA used live ammunition to clear the square, killing hundreds of civilians.

The Party managed to survive the revolution, but the fact that it occurred at all signified that the regime had yet to create institutions that fully stabilized its rule. In the early 1980s, representation in the NPC was reactivated, but it failed to keep pace with the growing demands of the population. In 1989, a nontrivial number of deputies stepped out of bounds and actively fomented revolution, akin to the Induced Unstable Nonresponsive equilibrium E2.5. The Citizen had demonstrated the credibility of her commitment to revolution, and the Autocrat needed to do more to ensure a more responsive but bounded parliament.

Constrained Enhancement

The 1990 session was a stern affair. Days before, Hu Jiwei was removed from his NPCSC position on the grounds that he "supported and participated in the political disturbances which occurred in Beijing last spring and summer and encroached on others' rights" ("Hu Jiwei" 1990). This was part of a broader purge of leaders and officials that had deviated from "correct thought" during the 1989 protests. In his opening remarks, which lasted two and one-half hours, hardliner Premier Li Peng issued a warning to those who sought to subvert the regime:

While fostering socialist democracy and the socialist legal system, we must intensify dictatorship by the socialist state apparatus... Prosecutors and judges should fully perform their duties and be on the alert so that they can promptly crush attempts at infiltration and subversion by foreign hostile forces, and so that they can crack down on all sabotage by hostile elements at home. (Kristoff 1990)

The key legislative act of the meeting itself was the passage of a resolution calling for strengthened public security (Wilhelm 1990).

Despite the general hardline tone of the session, official statements also identified the need to strengthen lawmaking processes and enhance representation. NPCSC Chairman Wan Li, who had refused to convene an emergency session under pressure from the hardline faction, called for improved governance and public consultation. "Our party is a ruling party. It is very important for the ruling party to make correct decisions," he said. "Only when the decision is correct can the party represent the fundamental interests of the state and the people." NPCSC Vice Chairman Peng Chong echoed this sentiment, stating that it was "necessary to persist in and perfect the system of the People's Congress and do a better job in the National People's Congress" to strengthen the system of "socialist democracy" ("It is necessary" 1990).

CCP leaders appear to have internalized two core lessons from the 1989 Tiananmen protests. First, public leadership division could

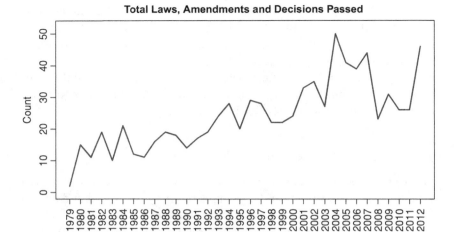

FIGURE 7.1 Legislative productivity in the NPC

embolden liberal elements in society, and political reformers must not be allowed to enter into higher echelons of government. Second, Deng's economic reforms had unleashed rising expectations within the population, and without richer "input institutions" and more responsive policy making, these grievances could easily engender another revolution (Nathan 2003). These lessons warranted reforms to enhance deputy representation in the NPC and measures to prevent troublemakers from entering the institution.

For the former, the CCP has enhanced the role of the parliament in the policy-making process. The phrase "rule of law" was added to the constitution in 1999, corresponding to the regime's increasing focus on rule-based policy making (Yin 2014). After a seven-year drafting period, the NPC's new 2000 Legislation Law established a more orderly law-making processes and carved out a greater role for the parliament (Paler 2005). The law identified ten areas exclusively under the NPC's lawmaking authority, including issues of state sovereignty, criminal offenses and punishment, and the basic systems of finance and taxation (Legislation Law of the People's Republic of China: Article 8, 2000). The law also required all draft laws to go through at least three discussions before the NPCSC, which would allow more input from deputies and topical experts (Paler 2005). Figure 7.1 shows the temporal increase the total number of laws, amendments, and decisions passed by the NPC and NPCSC, which speaks to the heightened relevance of the institution.

The Legislation Law also granted citizens the right to "participate in legislation through various channels" (Legislation Law of the People's Republic of China: Article 5, 2000), which laid the groundwork for new public participation mechanisms (Paler 2005; Horsely 2009; Truex forthcoming). Draft legislation became routinely posted for a period of public comment. Experts and common citizens were invited to legislative hearings and other policy debates to offer feedback. A new NPC website included several opinion-gathering portals, which allowed citizens to post their own motions or ask questions of senior officials (Truex forthcoming).

New policies encouraged deputies to take their responsibilities more seriously. The NPC support staff increased to 1,600 by 2000, assisting in legislative research and supervision (Jiang 2000). Training sessions improved and increased in number. Revisions to the Electoral Law (1995 and 2010) gradually improved representation for rural areas. Renewed discussions of "deputy quality" shifted selection norms and introduced more meritocratic processes (O'Brien and Li 1993; Wang 1995). The new generation of deputies were younger, more educated, and more equipped to handle the representative role. In 1993, 69% of deputies were college-educated, up from 45% in 1983 (O'Brien and Li 1993). By the 11th NPC, that figure stood at 80%.

The result of these policies was a flurry of representative activity. Each congress saw more proposals than the congress before. In the 6th NPC (1983–6), deputies raised a total of 14,215 opinions, criticisms and suggestions over their five-year term, about five per deputy. By the 10th NPC (2003–7), that figure had more than doubled, to 29,323. For the 11th, the number reached 37,527, over twelve per deputy. This was in addition to another 2,541 formal motions proposed. By all accounts, the quality of these proposals has also risen over time (Personal Interview NH002; Jiang 2000).

None of this should be taken as evidence that the CCP is losing control of the institution. The thesis of this book is precisely the opposite. In the post-Tiananmen era, the regime has relied heavily on the manipulation of personnel to rein in the parliament, as it has throughout the history of the institution. The proportion of seats going to CCP members has actually risen steadily, as shown in Figure 7.2. In the 6th NPC (1983–7), only 62.5% of deputies were CCP members. This figure increased to 68.4% in the 8th NPC (1993–7), 71.5% in the 9th NPC (1998–2002), and 73.0% in the 10th NPC (2003–7), and peaked at 74.7% in the 11th (2008–12). Those deputies not within the Party ranks have been subject to stricter

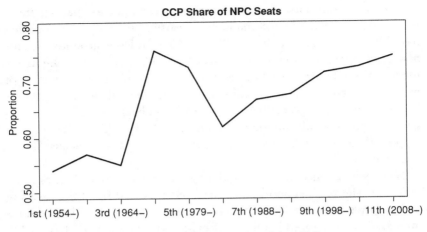

FIGURE 7.2 CCP dominance of the NPC

scrutiny, with a collective emphasis on weeding out any "unpredictable dissidents" in the indirect elections process (O'Brien and Li 1993).

The annual sessions leave little room for deputies to act out. Deputies are legally entitled to make speeches in the full chamber of the Great Hall of the People, but they rarely exercise this right. Deputy statements are usually confined to smaller delegation or subdelegation meetings, which are less public. The agenda of the full 3,000-member meeting is dominated by speeches from the leading cadres, yielding "a closely scripted and tightly controlled event" ("What Makes" 2012). In every session, the law, appointment or decision of the day is passed with little debate or discord. The entire agenda is approved in advance by senior Party leadership.

It is also telling what changes the regime has not undertaken. In a 2004 article, renowned liberal Chinese legal scholar Cai Dingjian (2004) identified several ways to reform the People's Congress system:

To reform and perfect the system of NPC, the following things should be done. The election system shall be reformed to enlarge the scope of direct elections. The chief directors of state organs shall be made through competitive election. The representatives of NPC shall be separated from the status of their enterprisers. Governmental officials should not be the representatives as well. The functions of NPC and the standing committee thereof shall be adjusted to enlarge the legislative power of the standing committee and professionalize the standing committee. The procedure and mode of deliberation of NPC shall be reformed to prolong the session period.

Effectively all of these suggestions would undermine the control of the CCP over the government, and none of them have been implemented in any real sense, other than perhaps the professionalization of the NPC Standing Committee. Direct elections have not been extended beyond the county level, despite decades of promises to do so (Cai 2004, 2010). Tweaks to the electoral law have allowed citizen nominations at lower levels and increased electoral competition slightly, but not to the point where the CCP is unable to secure seats for loyalist candidates. Deputies remain forbidden to campaign in any real sense or serve full-time (Xie 2003; Xiao 2006), as the regime does not want the representatives to develop personal bases of popular support.[3] And at nearly 3,000 deputies, the parliament remains oversized for proper legislative debate, but properly sized for a "barometer of the masses."

Though we might lament how the NPC has remained subservient to the Party, it is important to remember how far it has come. CCP leaders can manipulate the electoral process, but they cannot get away with canceling elections entirely, as they did in 1975. They can restrict media coverage, but they cannot close off the sessions completely, as was done in 1963 and 1964. They can encourage deputies to vote the Party line, but it is no longer feasible to engineer routine unanimous votes, as was the norm in the 1950s. And most importantly, they can control and manipulate NPC deputies, but they cannot dismiss them completely, as was done in the Cultural Revolution (Hu 1993). In the post-Tiananmen period, the NPC and deputies therein have generally been empowered, and the regime would face significant backlash if it attempted to reverse this trend.

Understanding Institutional Change

Throughout the duration of CCP rule, Party leaders have manipulated the NPC to fit their preferences and address the needs of the day. In the Mao era, representative dynamics began to develop, but the institution was quickly marginalized after the Hundred Flowers Movement. It reemerged again under Deng, but deputies failed to really fulfill their representative role. In the post-Tiananmen era, the representation-within-bounds system was institutionalized, complete with incentive structures that foster active representation on some issues and reticence on others. See Figure 7.3.

The evolution of the NPC can be understood through the lens of "critical junctures" – key moments where political actors face a broader range

---

[3] Deputies are also under no obligation to disclose their assets – a policy that would be hugely popular according to the CPAS data in Chapter 3 – as this could hinder rent distribution.

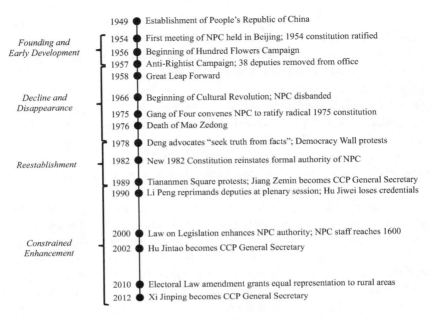

FIGURE 7.3 NPC timeline

of actions and the consequences of those actions are particularly momentous. The decisions made at these junctures can send politics down a particular path, where the institution itself is largely reproduced and changed only incrementally (Collier and Collier 1991; Thelen 1999; Capoccia and Kelemen 2007). I would argue that we have observed three such junctures in the history of the NPC: the Hundred Flowers Movement and aftermath (1957), the adoption of the 1982 Constitution (1982), and the Tiananmen Square democracy protest and aftermath (1989). These moments have also marked the beginnings of fundamental shifts in the nature of representation in the body, equilibria that were reproduced in the years following. To explain institutional change in the NPC, we can focus on the circumstances facing leaders at these junctures in time.

    In the writing of the 1954 Constitution, CCP leaders deliberately established a weak parliamentary system, but they did allow rudimentary representation dynamics to develop in the initial years. Following the 1957 Hundred Flowers Movement, Mao systematically worked to marginalize the institution, effectively turning off the "representation valve" completely. This was not the only option available at the time – Mao could have chosen to develop a system of representation within bounds similar to what we observe today. Why did he dismiss the institution rather than work to actualize its informational role?

The persuasions of individual leaders themselves play an important role in any story of institutional evolution, and certainly so in the Chinese case. We can explain the NPC's evolution through Mao's personal preferences – his general disdain for bureaucracy, his preference for "legal nihilism," or even his growing distrust of the Soviet Union. All of these factors certainly played a role in the fate of the parliament.

The key implication of the theoretical framework is that the quality of representation is linked to the revolutionary capacity of the population itself. I would argue that the NPC disappeared because it was not needed. Mao's rule witnessed some of the worst governance on record in human history, yet his numerous policy disasters had little consequence for his personal ability to maintain power. The population, weary from Japanese occupation, civil war, the Great Leap Forward and subsequent famine and the violence of the Cultural Revolution, may not have had the capacity to credibly threaten the regime itself and demand better public good provision. In terms of the model, the revolutionary constraint $\pi \geq \frac{c}{b_C}$ did not hold in this period. Mao himself enjoyed such an overpowering cult of personality that he had no need even to legitimize his rule through a parliament, let alone use one to generate information on citizen preferences. In this environment, the NPC was doomed as soon as it brought any whiff of inconvenience for the regime. The brief moment of out-of-bounds behavior in 1957 was enough to send the NPC down the path toward irrelevance.

After Mao's death in 1976, Deng worked to revive the parliament. Its core powers were reinstated and expanded with the 1982 Constitution. Deputy representation, while still quite limited by today's standards, began to emerge. The equilibrium shifted from no representation to something closer to representation within bounds, and during Tiananmen, deputies proved willing to step out of bounds. Again, the decision to rejuvenate the NPC was not the only option – Deng could have chosen to dismiss the parliament completely or eliminate its representative functions. Why was the representative valve slowly turned on during this period?

Again, Deng's personal characteristics provide numerous explanations. He had long been considered a pragmatist and moderate. His personal victimization during the Cultural Revolution may have further soured him on rule by decree and continued mass campaigns. His hands may have simply been tied, as the parliament had been called into session by Mao loyalists in 1975, and he could not consolidate power without working through formal institutions.

Beyond these factors, I would argue that citizen dissatisfaction in the post-Mao era necessitated an improvement in representation and policy making. By the end of the Cultural Revolution, a substantial portion of the population had grown disenchanted with the CCP and the up-and-down politics of continuous revolution. In 1978, citizens responded to Deng's call to "seek truth from facts" by pasting anti-Mao and anti-government slogans on a brick wall in Beijing. This "Democracy Wall Movement" originally helped Deng outmaneuver rival Hua Guofeng, but it quickly spiraled out of control. On December 5, 1978, dissident Wei Jingsheng posted an essay known entitled the "Fifth Modernization" (a play on Deng Xiaoping's own "Four Modernizations" slogan) that demanded political reform. As with the Hundred Flowers Movement two decades before, the regime was forced to crack down. Wei Jingsheng and other prominent protestors were arrested, the wall posters were removed, and discourse reverted to its usual constraints.

The net result of the movement was to demonstrate the credibility of the citizen threat. This was not a full-scale revolution, per se, but it was something close. For the first time in the history of the PRC, citizens had openly demanded democracy, and not the "democratic centralism" of the Mao years. Deng could not have safely reverted to the "no representation" of the Mao era, and he began to strengthen representation as a way to placate an increasingly demanding population. The 1982 Constitution was a reflection of that calculus.

The third critical juncture was the Tiananmen Square democracy movement, which can be interpreted as a failed revolution. As of April 1989, the regime had not done enough to placate the grievances of the population, which could credibly commit to revolution and did just that. Even worse, the revolution was actively supported by a nontrivial number of the regime's own representative agents, political liberals lurking within the highest institution of government. In the post-Tiananmen period, the regime has taken measures to fully realize the representation-within-bounds equilibrium. Enhanced deputy training, public participation mechanisms and more meritocratic selection practices combined to produce a parliament that fosters information revelation and facilitates responsiveness, while indoctrination, ample rents and the culling of reformist deputies have ensured reticence on sensitive issues. The past 25 years have seen a strengthening and reproduction of this system.

It is no coincidence that bounded representation emerged in full shortly following the regime's greatest legitimacy crisis. In the language of the theory, Tiananmen represented an Unstable Nonresponsive equilibrium E2.2 or possibly an Induced Unstable Nonresponsive equilibrium E2.5, where neither the Citizen nor the Deputy was behaving in a sustainable fashion. To survive, the Autocrat would have to improve policy making to, be more in tune with Citizen preferences, and incentivize the Deputy to aid in that task. The statements of regime leaders at the annual session in 1990 reflect these dual impulses. The regime would control "hostile elements" at home, but it was also necessary to "do a better job in the National People's Congress" ("It Is Necessary" 1990; Kristoff 1990).

Of course, it would be a mistake to attempt to attribute all shifts in the NPC to shifts in the revolutionary potential of the population. Power struggles and historical exigencies play an important role in any story of institutional evolution, and certainly so in the Chinese case. If moderates such as Liu Shaoqi and Deng Xiaoping had prevailed in the 1950s, perhaps the CCP would not have gone down the path of legal nihilism, and the NPC would not have been so easily dismissed. If reformers such as Zhao Ziyang or Hu Yaobang had been able to prevail in the late 1980s, perhaps we would observe a democratic China today, complete with unbounded representation in the NPC.

Nevertheless, even with their divergent views, China's authoritarian rulers have responded predictably to perceived threats from below and from deputies themselves. After the former, the NPC has generally been strengthened, and mechanisms have been put in place to foster deputy representation. After the latter, the NPC has been repudiated, and mechanisms have been put emplace to instill deputy loyalty. Over time, this has produced shifts in the power of the parliament, ultimately resulting in the bounded institution we observe today. To conclude, I consider whether that equilibrium is sustainable in the longer run.

8

Conclusion

Summary of Findings

This book began with a set of questions on the nature of representation and legislative institutions in authoritarian systems, and I have sought some preliminary answers through a detailed microanalysis of the Chinese case. Authoritarian parliaments, or at least the NPC, can fill an informational role by revealing citizen grievances, but they bring the risk of additional publicity on sensitive political issues. The current CCP regime is trying to engineer a system of representation within bounds using a combination of rents, socialization and career incentives. Deputies themselves are not tone-deaf and seek to convey constituent interests on a broad range of nonsensitive issues. They do so not because of electoral accountability from below, but because of top-down accountability to the regime itself. The net result is a docile but useful parliament, one that conveys public opinion but remains loyal to the CCP on policies core to the one-party state.

Much of the book is dedicated to testing the observable implications of the framework using new data on the backgrounds and behaviors of NPC deputies. Below is a summary of the core findings. Each empirical chapter roughly corresponds to one outcome measure: influence, representation, selection, and rents.

Influence (Chapter 3)

– Roughly half of randomly selected opinions from the Hainan Provincial People's Congress appear to have a tangible influence on the policy outcomes. There are no proposals in the Hainan dataset that call for political reforms. See Tables 3.1 and 3.2.

– Original public opinion data show that Chinese citizens perceive partial responsiveness in the NPC system. Highly popular policies are perceived as being more likely to be adopted, but not if they propose political reform. See Figure 3.4.

Representation (Chapter 4)

– At the provincial level, publicly available NPC deputy proposals and comments from 2008 to 2012 display congruence with constituent opinion/intensity measures constructed from the 2008 China Survey and demographic variables. See Tables 4.2 and 4.3 and Figure 4.2.
– Shocks to public opinion appear to be met with a legislative response, but not for strong preference issues. See Figures 4.3 and 4.4.

Selection (Chapter 5)

– After matching on demographic and professional characteristics, deputies who are reselected into the 12th NPC have about 20–50% more publicly available proposals than deputies who are not. An additional proposal seems to increase the probability of reselection by about 2%. See Table 5.3.

Rents (Chapter 6)

– Firms that gained NPC representation in 2008 enjoyed an additional 1.5 percentage points in returns and an additional 3–4 percentage points in operating profit margin. These firms also experience a 3–4 RMB increase in stock price following their CEO's NPC membership announcement. See Table 6.2 and Figures 6.1 and 6.3.

Collectively, these results overturn common conceptions of the National People's Congress and the quality of representation in China. The NPC should no longer be dismissed as simply a rubber stamp or political theatre. It is a representative organ of political consequence, and it has helped the CCP maintain control in the face of ever-rising popular expectations.

Conversely, we should also be skeptical when reading statements from deputies saying they are more responsive than their Western counterparts, or that China has perfected some new form of democracy. NPC deputies are more active and responsive than ever before, but they remain accountable to the Party, not the people. They are not elected in any real sense, and they most surely would be more in tune with their constituents if they were. In instances where the preferences of the citizenry conflict with those of the regime, deputies almost always side with the latter. There is a large portion of the issue space in China for which we observe practically no representation at all.

Beyond the NPC

One remaining question concerns the generalizability of the micro-level findings. This book is effectively an extended, multimethod case study of the nature of parliamentary representation in a single country at a single point in time. I believe this depth was necessary to complicate existing cross-national work on authoritarian parliaments (Gandhi and Przeworski 2007; Gandhi 2008; Wright 2008; Svolik 2012), but it remains unclear whether other regimes engineer representation in a similar way.

It is certainly not true that bounded representation can be found in all parliaments in all authoritarian regimes at all points in time. In the Chinese case alone, we have seen that a parliament may serve different roles depending on historical and political conditions. Mao's rubber stamp and nonexistent NPC gave way to Deng's rejuvenated NPC, which has given way to the mature, bounded NPC we see today.

The purpose of this book is to inspire other researches to explore the microdynamics of representation across other authoritarian systems and test for the presence of different theoretical mechanisms. In terms of scope conditions, I would expect representation-within-bounds dynamics to arise in an authoritarian regime that meets the following criteria:

1. Has a parliament
2. Does not allow true opposition parties
3. Is not resource-rich
4. Has achieved a baseline standard of welfare/education

Condition 1 is fairly straightforward; we will only observe representation in regimes that have created or inherited some representative institution. Most authoritarian countries meet this standard. According to Svolik's (2012) data, only 20% of country-years under authoritarianism since 1960 have occurred without a parliament. As of 2008, only a handful of regimes remained in this category – Myanmar, Saudi Arabia, Fiji, and the United Arab Emirates.

Condition 2 is more limiting. The intuition is that regimes that do not face organized opposition parties will be more capable of constraining the dialogue in parliament to the safe portion of the issue space. Conversely, parliaments that include oppositional parties may be more difficult control and might follow the logic of cooptation (Gandhi and Przeworski 2007; Gandhi 2008; Tzelgov et al. 2013). As of 2008, this was the modal category, with over 55% of regimes allowing opposition parties to exist (Svolik 2012). These sorts of "hegemonic party" or "competitive authoritarian" regimes likely exhibit different parliamentary dynamics than the Chinese case, which remains completely dominated by the CCP (Magaloni 2006; Gandhi and Lust-Okar 2009; Levitsky and Way 2010; Reuter and Gandhi 2010).

Conditions 3 and 4 concern the regime's need to respond to the demands of the population. Regimes that are resource-rich can use these rents to placate the population and may not need to bother with engineering constrained representation in a parliament (Ross 2001; Wright 2008). Similarly, regimes with populations that have not achieved the "social requisites of democracy" – a baseline standard of education and welfare – may not face much in the way of citizen demands (Lipset 1959). In both cases, the citizenry may not be able to commit credibly to revolution, which obviates the need for representation and responsiveness.

Using existing data on authoritarian regimes and other country characteristics (Geddes, Wright and Frantz 2012; Svolik 2012), we can identify a set of candidate regimes that appear to meet these four conditions. Table 8.1 shows several regimes as they stood in 2008 on a number of dimensions: regime type; regime duration; legislature type; whether they allow opposition parties; the percentage of the economy composed of natural resources; and the GDP per capita in constant U.S. dollars. These latter four variables loosely capture the four conditions above – regimes that meet a condition are depicted with a * symbol. Of the around 60 authoritarian regimes in existence in 2008, around four seem most comparable with the Chinese case on these four dimensions: Cuba, Swaziland, Vietnam, and Laos. They all have parliaments, do not allow formal opposition parties, are considered relatively resource-poor, and yet have achieved a baseline level of economic development (defined as GDP per capita greater than $500). Based on these characteristics alone, these countries would seem prime candidates for representation-within-bounds type dynamics in their parliamentary systems. In Gerring's (2007) terminology, these would be considered "most likely" cases for the theory.

Political scientists have already explored representation in two of these cases: Vietnam and Cuba. A closer look reveals marked similarities to the NPC.

Vietnam

The Vietnamese National Assembly has many institutional similarities to the NPC, which stems from the historical influence of the PRC over its communist neighbor. The VNA is the "highest organ of state power" and

TABLE 8.1 *Identifying similar cases*

Country	Regime type	Duration (years)	Legislature (1)	Parties (2)	Resources (3)	GDP pc (4)
Primary case						
China	Party-based	59	One party/candidate per seat*	Single*	10.42%*	$3441*
Candidate RWB parliaments						
Cuba	party-personal	49	One party/candidate per seat	Single*	5.66%*	$5382*
Swaziland	Monarchy	40	Unelected/appointed*	Banned*	3.45%*	$2616*
Vietnam	Party-based	54	One party/candidate per seat*	Single*	17.92%*	$1164*
Laos	Party-based	33	One party/candidate per seat*	Single*	16.87%*	$886*
Other cases of interest						
Singapore	Party-based	43	Largest party controls <75% seats	Multiple	0.00%*	$39722*
Saudi Arabia	Monarchy	81	None	Banned*	64.36%	$19714*
Libya	Personal	39	Unelected or appointed*	Banned*	70.35%	$14827*
Russia	Personal	15	Largest party controls <75% seats	Multiple	31.72%	$11635*
Egypt	Party-personal-military	56	Largest party controls <75% Seats	Multiple	26.47%	$2156*
Sudan	Personal	19	Unelected or appointed*	Multiple	26.89%	$1263*
Eritrea	Party-personal	15	Unelected or appointed*	Single*	4.30%*	$256
North Korea	Party-personal	60	One party/candidate per seat*	Single*	NA*	NA

Notes: Data shows authoritarian regimes of interest on several covariates drawn from the Svolik (2012), Geddes, Wright and Frantz (2012), and WBI datasets. All data drawn from 2008. Regimes that meet a condition are highlighted with a * symbol.

boasts ample legislative, budgetary and appointment powers, but remains subservient to the organs of the Vietnamese Communist Party (VCP). The roughly 500 members of the VNA meet only twice per year and are tasked with "representing the will and aspirations of the people" (1992 Constitution of the Socialist Republic of Vietnam, Article 6).

Elections to the VNA are slightly more liberal than those to the NPC, though they remain well within the control of the VCP. The delegates are directly elected by voters in 182 electoral districts across 63 provinces, but the nomination process is run by an election board controlled by a provincial VCP committee. A little fewer than one-third of delegates are directly nominated by central leadership in Hanoi, and the rest are provincial notables tasked with representing local interests (Malesky et al. 2012). The resulting parliament displays demographic diversity but political homogeneity, again similarly to the NPC. Roughly 90% of delegates are Party members, but the body increasingly includes professors, businesspeople, doctors and lawyers.

Representation and information revelation occur through public "query sessions," which allow delegates to pose pointed questions to government ministers. These queries do not have a binding influence on policy – again similarly to the NPC's proposal process – but can relay citizen grievances and put pressure on the bureaucracy. Historically, these sessions have resulted in the dismissal of ministers and adjustments to policy.

Innovative micro-level research offers some evidence in favor of representation-within-bounds dynamics. Malesky and Schuler (2010) investigate the determinants of activism in query sessions. They find that some delegates appear responsive to constituent concerns. Roughly 20% of queries to the twelfth session of the VNA directly mentioned a constituency, and 17% cited local issues. Provincially nominated candidates appear more active, and the limited electoral competition for these seats appears to provide some meritocratic incentives.

In a related study, Malesky, Schuler and Tran (2012) isolate the effect of transparency on delegate behavior. Personal websites were developed for a random subset of delegates, including detailed information and ratings on the quality of participation in the query sessions. Interestingly, delegates exposed to a high intensity of this transparency/publicity treatment display signs of conformist behavior, asking less pointed questions and self-censoring their criticisms. This suggests that delegates are accountable to regime leadership and may be worried about overstepping the boundaries of acceptable behavior.

As a whole, the VCP relies on the performance-based legitimacy characteristic of a representation-within-bounds system (Malesky and London 2014). The political system remains quite closed, with minimal room for dissent and no organized opposition, but policy making appears to be generally responsive to citizen demands. Like China, Vietnam has experienced an economic miracle in the past three decades, averaging over 7% growth. The VNA helps the regime foster legitimacy, craft reasonable policies, and respond to citizen demands.

Cuba

Cuba's National Assembly of People's Power (NAPP) is also a socialist representative organ, influenced strongly by the Soviet model. The assembly, comprising about 600 deputies, also meets twice per year for a couple of days to ratify decisions of the executive branch. As in the NPC, votes within the assembly are never contentious (and often unanimous), reflecting the control of the Communist Party of Cuba (PCC).

Although the PCC does not have formal institutional authority over the electoral process, it is nevertheless able to engineer a loyalist parliament. Deputies are "directly elected" by the population, but the elections are strictly noncompetitive – exactly one candidate per seat. Selection thus occurs in the nomination process. Half of the NAPP deputies are nominated by municipal councils, and the other half are put forth by various groups and mass organizations. Historically, anywhere from 70 to 100% of NAPP deputies are PCC members, compared with only about 15% of the population. A broad range of sectors and interests are given formal representation. The body also includes religious leaders, athletes, journalists, youth representatives, doctors, teachers, and political figures (Roman 2003, p. 134). As in the NPC, the net result is a parliament that is politically unrepresentative but linked closely demographically with the population. Castro noted the importance of maintaining strong representation in the parliament. "One of the things which most moves me regarding our electoral system is that a humble citizen can be deputy of the National Assembly," he said.

The NAPP serves a consultative role in policy making, and deputies are expected to represent the interests of their constituents. Deputies rarely initiate legislation but are expected to offer feedback on new policies throughout the drafting process. The plenary sessions themselves are too short for substantial debate (and were historically dominated by Castro himself), so much of deputy work comes through the legislature's permanent committees. Roughly 50% of deputies belong to these committees, which routinely undertake investigations of various societal issues. Roman (2003) documents several examples of information revelation through these investigations. In 1988, for example, some deputies discovered that the population of mountainous regions in Las Tunas Province had no access to milk, and dairies were later established as a result of their advocacy. In July 1998, a commission toured the country and developed a report to improve tobacco and coffee production, which had been affected by a recent drought.

There do appear to be boundaries on deputy representative activity. In descriptions of his fieldwork, Roman (2003) notes instances of intimidation, where deputies felt pressured to toe the PCC line. He describes:

> There is an underlying apprehension of contradicting, questioning, or demanding responses from Castro, or of continuing to state a point of view to which the leadership objects. During an assembly session in the late 1980s, one deputy attempted to make a minor correction to a point being made by President Castro by adding a necessary word. He was cut off and not allowed to finish, and subsequently he never spoke again in the National Assembly during his tenure (he was not renominated). (Roman 2003, p. 87)

Cuban dissidents lament the lack of meaningful representation in the NAPP system. Blogger Yaoni Sanchez describes recent parliamentary elections:

> As expected, there was not a single opponent to the government who managed to enter parliament, no one with different political ideas will become a member of the National Assembly. Not even a single deputy who doesn't possess the same ideology as the party in power. The boring homogeneity of the same thinking.

By all accounts, the NAPP is not a body with full representation and true political opposition. It is a bounded system with mechanisms and processes quite similar to what we observe in the Chinese case.

*

The table also shows other cases of interest that do not meet all four criteria. Some of them, including Russia, and Egypt, allow opposition parties to exist, which suggests a lesser degree of societal or elite control and possibly different forms of representation in parliament. Indeed, Blaydes' (2011) work on the Egyptian case suggests that the Mubarak regime used parliamentary elections primarily as a vehicle for allocating access to rent-seeking opportunities among elites, which appears consistent with the intuitions of power-sharing theory. Still, members of the Muslim Brotherhood were also allowed to play the role of a true opposition, which suggests possibly wider boundaries in the representational space. In his work on the Russian case, Noble (2015) argues in favor of a version of the power-sharing view, suggesting that the Duma allows legislative bargaining that strengthens the ruling coalition. In other contexts, the population might be too weak to credibly commit to revolution, and there is little in the way of legislative activity. North Korea's Supreme People's Assembly, for example, appears to offer minimal representation and is deserving of its rubber stamp moniker.

The next step in the research agenda on authoritarian representation is to continue to build a comparative understanding of the microdynamics of these institutions. We must map and explain variation in authoritarian elections, delegate behavioral patterns and careers, rent distribution, and policy-making processes across cases and contexts. An emerging research program has already begun to do so in China (Manion 2014, forthcoming; Truex 2014; Lu and Liu 2015), Cuba (Roman 2003), Vietnam (Malesky and Schuler 2010a, 2010b; Malesky, Schuler and Tran 2011), Russia (Noble 2015), and Egypt (Blaydes 2011; Tzelgov et al. 2013). I hope this book encourages this collective scholarly effort.

Looking Ahead

Our final outstanding question is whether or not this system is sustainable in the Chinese case. Will the constrained representation within the NPC be enough to stave off pressure for political reform? Will we observe shifts in the representational equilibrium, perhaps under the leadership of Xi Jinping?

The fashionable answer among China observers is that "the end is near," though "near" appears to be a moving target. In 2001, Gordon Chang predicted the "coming collapse of China," asserting that the fall of the CCP would occur within a decade. In a 2011 *Financial Times* editorial, Chang doubled down, wagering that the system would fall within one year's time. This prediction has also proven false. In 1996, Henry Rowen used economic data to predict that China would become democratic "around the year 2015." This forecast was recently revised, with "Free" status achieved by 2025 (Rowen, Pei and Yang 2007). In 2005's *China's Democratic Future: How It Will Happen and Where It Will Lead*, Gilley argues a transition "could be tomorrow or it could take a decade or more" (p. xi), but insists that democratization will occur sooner rather than later. In his recent 2015 editorial, David Shambaugh joined this chorus, stating that "the endgame of Chinese communist rule has now begun" (2015).

The well-established association between development and democracy lends some empirical weight to this narrative (Przeworski et al. 2000; Boix

Democracy, Development and Resources

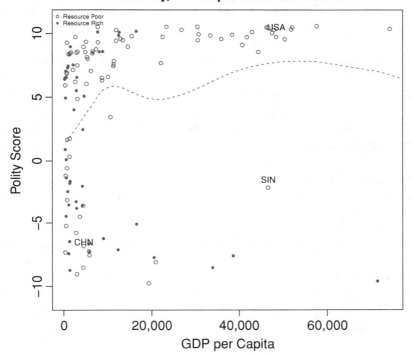

FIGURE 8.1 China's Relative Political and Economic Development
Note: The figure shows relationship between development (GDP per capita) and democracy (Polity score). Resource-rich countries (resources compose more than 25% of the economy) are shown with black points. All data are from 2008.

and Stokes 2003). Figure 8.1 is a scatterplot of countries' Polity scores against their GDP per capita, using data from 2008. Higher Polity scores indicate more democratic governance. Countries that are resource-rich, defined as having resources that compose more than 25% of the economy, are shown with black points.

As expected, China falls in the lower left corner. In 2008, its per capita income stood at $3,441, and it earned a Polity score of −7, one of the worst in the sample. By 2014, the income measure had risen to $7,593, though the Polity score had not improved.

There are very few examples of similar authoritarian regimes that have grown into middle- or high-income countries without substantial political reform. Most high-income authoritarian regimes – such as Kuwait, Oman or Saudi Arabia – are resource-rich monarchies in the Middle East. The commonly noted exception is Singapore, but it remains unclear whether a country of 1.3 billion people can follow the same political development as a city state of 5.5 million.

Still, as of 2015, the CCP regime remains alive and well at the age of 65. Purveyors of the regime change prediction may ultimately be proven right, but they have fallen flat to date, and they may be underestimating the CCP's support among the broader population. Figure 8.2 shows summary data from the fourth wave (2005–8) of the World Values Survey (WVS). Among other attitudinal questions, the WVS asks respondents to rate their level of confidence in their government on a four-point scale. The figure shows the fraction of respondents responding "a great deal" or "quite a lot." With the exception of Vietnam, Chinese citizens voice greater support of their government than citizens of any other country in the world.

This finding has been replicated in numerous public opinion surveys, drawing on a range of subpopulations, time periods, and measurement strategies.[1] In a 1999–2001 rural survey, Li (2004) asked 1,600 villagers across four counties about their levels of popular trust in different levels of government. Trust proved highest for the central government; over 80% of respondents expressed "relatively high" to "very high" levels of trust in the Central Party Committee. In my own research, I have asked Chinese netizens to directly express their levels of support for the central government and National People's Congress, as well as their agreement with statements such as "I am generally satisfied with government policies" and "The government cares what people like me think" (Truex forthcoming). The survey results, as well as those in response to identical questions on the 2008 China Survey, suggest very high levels of support (Lewis-Beck, Tang and Martini 2014). The modal rating for the central government was an 8 out of 10, and 70% of respondents expressed affirmative views.

Of course, we should be wary of taking public opinion data at face value. Cross-national surveys such as the WVS can have biases due to different cultural interpretations of question wordings, making direct country comparisons difficult.[2] Respondents living in repressive political contexts – such as China and Vietnam – may be unwilling to voice their true opinions when asked sensitive questions about government. This could

---

[1] See Chen, Zhong and Hillard (1997), Zhong, Chen and Scheb (1998), Shi (2000), Chen (2004), Li (2004), Tang (2005), Manion (2006), Chen and Dickson (2008) Lewis-Beck, Tang and Martini (2014), and Truex (2014), among others.

[2] King et al. (2004) show that response incomparability can drastically mislead researchers using cross-national survey data. While Chinese respondents report high levels of political efficacy, they also have low standards for what qualifies as having a "say in government."

Confidence in government

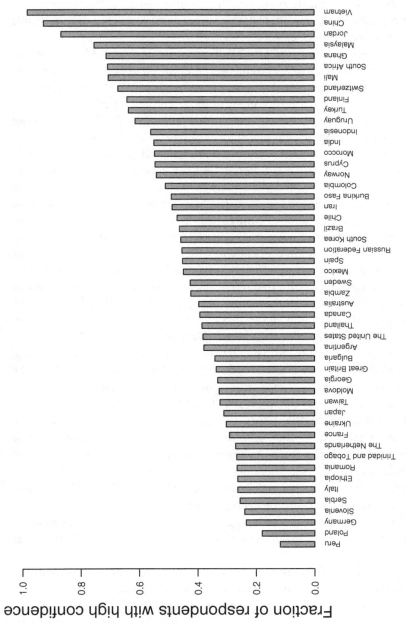

FIGURE 8.2 Confidence in government across countries (2005–8)
Note: The figure shows the proportion of respondents expressing "a great deal" or "quite a lot" of confidence in government in the World Values Survey (2005–8).

be distorting the levels of support expressed in the CPAS and other China surveys. As Huang (2013) puts it, "In a country without free speech, asking people to directly evaluate performance of leaders is like asking people to take a single-choice exam."

Thus, the evidence on "China's democratic future" is stubbornly inconclusive. Broader macro-level trends suggest imminent political change, but the Party has bucked these trends before (Nathan 2003). Central leadership seems to enjoy a reservoir of popular credibility, but it is possible that we are simply observing widespread preference falsification (Kuran 1991). Rather than attempting to place a date on the CCP's "coming collapse," I will resign myself to the more limited goal of considering the role of the NPC moving forward. I offer four predictions on the future of the parliament.

First, I expect that the regime will have to do more to contend with loyalty problems in the near future, from both NPC deputies and higher-level officials. During his first two years in power, Xi Jinping has launched a widespread corruption crackdown, which has seen the investigation of hundreds of thousands of officials at all levels of government, including dozens of Central Committee members and even one former Politburo Standing Committee member, Zhou Yongkang. As of July 2015, 39 NPC deputies to the 12th NPC have already been investigated for corruption, compared with only 19 for the entire duration of the 11th NPC.

The anti-corruption campaign has given Xi a needed legitimacy boost, but it also has the side effect of reducing rent distribution throughout the government. Rents are a key factor in inducing loyalty among representatives, and in all agents of the regime, for that matter (Bueno de Mesquita et al. 2003, 2008; Svolik 2012). If deputies have a vested interest in the success of the regime, they will be more likely to do what is asked of them – convey citizen demands but remain reticent on political reform. If rents dry up, and worse, if deputies are sacrificed on the altar of clean governance, there is a greater risk of their defection and dissent. The regime will have to compensate for decreased rents by doing more to cultivate loyalty through other channels. Indeed, it is telling that Document No. 9, which is effectively a loyalty manifesto, was issued during Xi's first year in office.

Second, the CCP will not reverse course with the NPC, nor turn off the "representation valve." Since Deng's ascension to power in 1978, we have observed China's parliament grow consistently stronger, more representative, and more responsive over time. The NPC now boasts public participation channels, a relatively transparent legislative drafting process, and deputies who annually channel thousands of citizen demands to the government. In the face of rising citizen expectations, the regime would be hard pressed to go back on the limited reforms it has already introduced.[3] A dismissal of the NPC, for example, as occurred under Mao, would be unthinkable in the contemporary environment.

We have already observed some minor improvements in the NPC under Xi Jinping, consistent with the institution's general post-Tiananmen trajectory. Historically, urban were granted four times as many deputies in proportion to population, but the 12th NPC gives equal representation to rural areas. We have also seen a slight decrease in the number of government officials in the NPC – down 6.93%, according to government statistics – and a concordant increase in deputies from migrant worker/farmer circles. The proportion of women has also increased slightly, to 23.4% of the total ("New National Legislature" 2013). These reforms were taken to ensure better descriptive representation in the body, which would likely lead to better substantive representation as well. The new deputies appear to be playing their constrained representative role with gusto. In 2014, deputies offered 8,576 opinions – the highest ever in the history of the institution – but nothing of particular political sensitivity.

Third, I would predict that in the absence of widespread citizen collective action, the regime will fail to adopt more meaningful democratic reforms in the NPC in the near future. The NPC is and always has been a distinctly authoritarian parliament, held tightly under the thumb of the CCP regime. Yet it is quite easy to envision a more democratic NPC, and the path that could be taken to get there. Direct elections could be introduced at the prefectural, provincial and national levels. Restrictions on the nomination process could be removed, allowing citizens to nominate candidates at all levels without filtering by a Party committee. The existing democratic parties could be allowed to operate with minimal CCP oversight. Candidates could be allowed to campaign for office and advertise their policy positions. A semblance of electoral accountability could prevail.

If we have learned one thing about the CCP in the post-Tiananmen era, it is that leaders with an inclination for political reform do not make it particularly far up the government hierarchy. Part of the reason the

---

[3] In 1978, at the beginning of Deng's reform period, China's per capita income was about $155. By 2010, that number had increased to $4,431. This rise in wealth has been accompanied by similar leaps in urbanization and education levels. As of 2010, roughly 50% of Chinese citizens live in urban areas, up from only 18% in 1978. Current tertiary enrollment rates stand at over 25% and continue to rise each year.

Tiananmen movement festered as long as it did was that it exposed a rift in senior leadership, with Zhao Ziyang and other liberal reformers showing some sympathy with student demands. In the post-Tiananmen era, the Party has taken stronger measures to preserve ideological cohesion on the political dimension. The third, fourth, and now fifth generations of Chinese leadership have been dominated by political hardliners of various stripes. Xi Jinping, thought to be a "Gorbachev in waiting" by some Western observers, has proven perhaps the most hardline of them all (Griffiths 2012; Lindley-French 2012; Wong and Ansfield 2012; Kristof 2013).[4] He is a reformer, but an illiberal one, and he has overseen the largest crackdown on political dissidents in the past two decades (Truex 2015). We should expect more of the same in the NPC, not some fundamental break with the authoritarian past.

Finally, I would predict that if there is indeed a popular democratic movement in China, NPC deputies will play a pivotal role. While the current NPC appears relatively docile, small shifts in deputy norms and incentives could make it the center of real political change. Deputies are socialized into their behavior of representation within bounds, but there is something inherently dangerous about instructing a group of 3,000 prominent officials to protect the interests of the common people. Twice before, we have seen numerous deputies display true courage in the face of looming political oppression, once with their activism during the Hundred Flowers Movement (O'Brien 1988, 1990) and a second time with their signatures during the Tiananmen Square protests (Hu 1993). Hundreds of deputies openly flouted CCP authority and sided with the population.

If there indeed comes a day when Chinese citizens in the mainland rise up again and demand meaningful political reform, NPC deputies will be forced to choose between the authoritarian regime that empowered them and the common people they claim to represent. Let us hope they choose the latter.

---

[4] Prior to his ascension, insiders suggested that Xi was meeting with reform-minded political theorists, and had even set up a team to research the more liberal Singapore model (Wong and Ansfield 2012). One hopeful dissident predicted that Xi would institute a popularly elected parliament within five to seven years (Simpson 2013). Selected elements of Xi's personal background, namely his father's denouncement of the Tiananmen Square Massacre, his experience living in Iowa and his willingness to send his daughter abroad to Harvard, were taken as evidence that he could be a political liberal in hiding (Griffiths 2012; Lindley-French 2012; Kristof 2012).

References

"55 Year NPC Deputy Shen Jilan" [*shen jilan 55 nian quanguorendadaibiao*]. 2012. Baidu Tieba 1447427646. http://tieba.baidu.com/p/1447427646 [in Chinese].

Abramowitz, A.I. 1988. "Explaining Senate Election Outcomes." *American Political Science Review* 82(2): 385–403.

Acemoglu, D., and J.A. Robinson. 2006. *Economic Origins of Dictatorship and Democracy*. Cambridge: Cambridge University Press.

Achen, C.H. 1977. "Measuring Representation – Perils of Correlation Coefficient." *American Journal of Political Science* 21(4): 805–15.

Achen, C.H. 1978. "Measuring Representation." *American Journal of Political Science* 22(3): 475–510.

"Advancing Rights Through Dialogue." 2014. Dui Hua. http://duihua.org/wp/wp-content/uploads/2015/05/ar/AR2014_Eng.pdf.

"[Analysis Report] Decipher the Problem of Financing" [*[fenxi baogao: pojie chouzi nanti*]. 2010. Xinhua [in Chinese].

Ansolabehere, S., J.M. Snyder, and C. Stewart. 2001. "The Effects of Party and Preferences on Congressional Roll-Call Voting." *Legislative Studies Quarterly* 26(4): 533–72.

Ardoin, P.J., and J.C. Garand. 2003. "Measuring Constituency Ideology in U.S. House Districts: A Top-Down Simulation Approach." *Journal of Politics* 65(4): 1165–89.

Arnold, H.J., and D.C. Feldman. 1981. "Social Desirability Response Bias in Self-Report Choice Situations." *Academy of Management Journal* 24(2): 377–85.

Bafumi, J., and M.C. Herron. 2010. "Leapfrog Representation and Extremism: A Study of American Voters and Their Members in Congress." *American Political Science Review* 104(3): 519–42.

Barnett, T.J. 1999. *Legislative Learning*. New York and London: Garland.

Barro, R. 1973. "The Control of Politicians: An Economic Model." *Public Choice* 14: 19–42.

Bates, R.H., A. Greif, M. Levi, J. Rosenthal, and B. Weingast. 1998. *Analytic Narratives*. Princeton, NJ: Princeton University Press.

Baum, R. 1986. "Modernization and Legal Reform in Post-Mao China: The Rebirth of Socialist Legality." *Studies of Comparative Communism* 19(2): 69–103.

Becker, G.S. 1958. "Competition and Democracy." *Journal of Law and Economics* 1: 105–9.

Beech, H. 2012. "China's National People's Congress: Bling Bling and Big Glasses." Time World Global Spin: *TIME Magazine*.

Bendor, J., and A. Meirowitz. 2004. "Spatial Models of Delegation." *American Political Science Review* 98(2): 293–310.

Berry, W.D., E.J. Ringquist, R.C. Fording, and R.L. Hanson. 1998. "Measuring Citizen and Government Ideology in the American States, 1960–93." *American Journal of Political Science* 42(1): 327–48.

Blanchard, B., and J. Ruwitch. 2013. "China Hikes Defense Budget, to Spend More On Internal Security." Reuters. http://www.reuters.com/article/2013/ 03/05/us-china-parliament-defence-idUSBRE92403620130305.

Blaydes, L. 2011. *Elections and Distributive Politics in Mubarak's Egypt*. Cambridge: Cambridge University Press.

Blaydes, L., and M.A. Kayser. 2011. "Counting Calories: Democracy and Distribution in the Developing World." *International Studies Quarterly* 55(4): 887–908.

Blei, D.M. 2012. "Probabilistic Topic Models." *Communications of the ACM* 55(4): 77-84.

Boix, C. 2003. *Democracy and Redistribution*. Cambridge Studies in Comparative Politics. Cambridge: Cambridge University Press.

Boix, C., and M. Svolik. 2013. "The Foundations of Limited Authoritarian Government: Institutions and Power-Sharing in Dictatorships." *Journal of Politics* 75(2): 300–316.

"Both Gold and Silver Mountains" [*jiyao jinshan yinshan*]. 2007. Wen Wei Po.

Brace, P., K. Sims-Butler, K. Arceneaux, and M. Johnson. 2002. "Public Opinion in the American States: New Perspectives Using National Survey Data." *American Journal of Political Science* 46(1):173–89.

Bristow, M. 2009. "Chinese Delegate Has 'No Power.'" BBC News.

Bueno de Mesquita, B., A. Smith, R.M. Silverson, and J.D. Morrow. 2003. *The Logic of Political Survival*. Cambridge, MA: MIT Press.

Bueno de Mesquita, B., A. Smith, R.M. Silverson, and J.D. Morrow. 2008. "Retesting Selectorate Theory: Separating the Effects of W from Other Elements of Democracy." *American Political Science Review* 103(3): 393–400.

Buthe, T. 2002. "Taking Temporality Seriously: Modeling History and the Use of Narratives as Evidence." *American Political Science Review* 96(3): 481–93.

Cabestan, J. 2006. "More Power to the People's Congresses? Parliaments and Parliamentarianism in the People's Republic of China." *Asien*: 42–69.

Cai, D.J. 2010. "Democracy Is Beneficial to Stability" [*minzhu shi youliyu shehui wending de zhidu*]. http://www.21ccom.net/articles/zgyj/xzmj/article_ 2010110924040.html [in Chinese].

Cai, D.J. 1999. "Development of the Chinese Legal System since 1979 and Its Current Crisis and Transformation." *Cultural Dynamics* 11(2): 8–18.

Cai, D.J. 2004. "On the Reform and Perfection of the NPC System" [*lun renmin daibiao dahuizhidu de gaige he wanshan*]. *Tribune of Political Science and Law* 22(6): 8–18. [in Chinese]

Callander, S. 2008. "A Theory of Policy Expertise." *Quarterly Journal of Political Science* 3(2): 123–40.

Canavas, S. 2009. "Beijing Frees Jailed Activist Xu Zhiyong." *The Wall Street Journal.* http://online.wsj.com/article/SB125104581176051961.html.

Canes-Wrone, B., D.W. Brady, and J.F. Cogan. 2002. "Out of Step, Out of Office: Electoral Accountability and House Members' Voting." *American Political Science Review* 96(1): 127–40.

Capoccia, G., and R. Kelemen. 2007. "The Study of Critical Junctures: Theory, Narrative, and Counterfactuals in Historical Institutionalism." *World Politics* 59(3): 341–69.

Carson, J.L., M.H. Crespin, J.A. Jenkins, and R.J. Vander Wielen. 2004. "Shirking in the Contemporary Congress: A Reappraisal." *Political Analysis* 12(2): 176–9.

Carter, L. 2013. "China's Surprising Reaction to the U.S. Government Shutdown." Tea Leaf Nation. http://www.tealeafnation.com/2013/10/chinas-surprising-reaction-to-the-u-s-government-shutdown-2/.

Carter, L. 2013. "Chinese Politician: We Must Allow the Chinese to Have a Second Child." The Atlantic. http://www.theatlantic.com/china/archive/2013/03/chinese-politician-we-must-allow-the-chinese-to-have-a-second-child/273707/.

Chang, G.C. 2001. *The Coming Collapse of China.* New York: Random House, Inc.

Chang, G.C. 2011. "The Coming Collapse of China: 2012 Edition." Financial Times.

Cheibub, J.A., J. Gandhi, and J.R. Vreeland. 2010. "Democracy and Dictatorship Revisited." *Public Choice*, 143(2–1): 67–101.

Chen, J., and B. Dickson. 2008. "Allies of the State: Democratic Support and Regime Support among China's Private Entrepreneurs." *The China Quarterly* 196: 780–804.

Chen, J., and Y. Zhong. 2002. "Why Do People Vote in Semicompetitive Elections in China?" *Journal of Politics* 64(1): 178–97.

Chen, J., Y. Zhong, and J.W. Hillard. 1997. "The Level and Sources of Popular Support for China's Current Political Regime." *Communist and Post-Communist Studies* 30(1): 45–64.

Chen, J. 2004. *Popular Political Support in Urban China.* Stanford, CA: Stanford University Press.

Chen, J., J. Pan, and Y. Xu. 2015. "Sources of Authoritarian Responsiveness: A Field Experiment in China." *American Journal of Political Science* 60(2): 383–400.

Chen, X. 2011. *Social Protest and Contentious Authoritarianism in China.* Cambridge: Cambridge University Press.

Chien-Min, C. 2005. "The National People's Congress Oversight Power and the Role of the CCP." *The Copenhagen Journal of Asian Studies* 17: 6–30.

China National People's Congress Yearbook 2009. [*zhongguo renda nianjian 2009*]. 2009. Beijing: China Made Real Press. [in Chinese]

"China Revises Individual Income Tax Law, Raising Exemption Threshold to 3,500 Yuan." 2011. Xinhua.

"China's Parliament Adopts Amendment to Electoral Law." 2010. *Xinhua Net.* http://news.xinhuanet.com/english2010/china/2010-03/14/c_13209880_2 .htm.

"China's State Organizational Structure." 2014. Congressional-Executive Commission on China. http://www.cecc.gov/chinas-state-organizational-structure.

Cho, Y.N. 2009. *Local People's Congresses in China: Development and Transition.* Cambridge/New York: Cambridge University Press.

Clinton, J.D. 2006. "Representation in Congress: Constituents and Roll Calls in the 106th House." *Journal of Politics* 68(2): 397–409.

Collier, R., and D. Collier. 1991. *Shaping the Political Arena.* Princeton, NJ: Princeton University Press.

Coppedge, M., J. Gerring, D. Altman, M. Bernhard, S. Fish, A. Hicken, M. Kroenig, S.I. Lindberg, K. McMann, P. Paxton, H.A. Semetko, S.-E. Skaaning, J. Staton, and J. Teorell. 2011. "Conceptualizing and Measuring Democracy: A New Approach." *Perspectives on Politics* 9(2): 247–67.

Crawford, V., and J. Sobel. 1982. "Strategic Information Transmission." *Econometrica* 50(6): 1431–51.

Cui, W. 2006. "Creating Studious Deputies" [*zaojiu xuexixing renda daibiao*]. Zhongguo Renda. [in Chinese]

"Democracy with Chinese Characteristics: 84 yrs Old Shen Jilan Elected Deputy to NPC for the 12th Time." 4 February 2013. Hug China.

Deng, G., and S. Kennedy. 2010. "Big Business and Industry Association Lobbying in China: The Paradox of Contrasting Styles." *The China Journal* 63: 101–25.

"Deputies' Bite Should Be Fiercer Than Their Bark." 2012. *Global Times.* http://www.globaltimes.cn/content/698847.

"Deputy Seeks Suggestions on Bill via Microblog." 2011. http://english.cri.cn/7146/2011/03/01/2021s623363.htm.

"Deputy Zhang Liyong: Deputies' Responsibility is Extremely Heavy" [*zhang liyong daibiao: daibiao zeren zhongyu taishan*]. 2009. [in Chinese]

Desposato. S.W. 2001. "Legislative Politics in Authoritarian Brazil." *Legislative Studies Quarterly* 27(2): 287–317.

Diamond, A., and J. Sekhon. 2006. "Genetic Matching for Causal Effects: A General Multivariate Matching Method for Achieving Balance in Observational Studies." Working Paper, Department of Political Science, UC Berkeley.

Dikotter, F. 2010. *Mao's Great Famine: The History of China's Most Devastating Catastrophe.* London: Walker Books.

Distelhorst, G. 2012. "Publicity-Driven Accountability in China: Qualitative and Experimental Evidence." Working Paper, MIT.

Distelhorst, G., and Y. Hou. 2014. "Ingroup Bias in Official Behavior: A National Field Experiment in China." *Quarterly Journal of Political Science* 9: 203–30.

"Document 9: A ChinaFile Translation." 2013. ChinaFile. https://www.chinafile .com/document-9-chinafile-translation.

Doolin, D. 1961. "The Revival of the 'Hundred Flowers' Campaign: 1961." *The China Quarterly* 8: 34–41.

Eggers, A.C., and J. Hainmueller. 2009. "MPs for Sale? Returns to Office in Post-war British Politics." *American Political Science Review* 103: 1–21.

"Electoral Law of the National People's Congress and Local People's Congresses of the People's Republic of China." 2011. http://www.cecc.gov/resources/ legal-provisions/electoral-law-of-the-national-peoples-congress-and-local-peoples.

Erikson, R.S. 1978. "Constituency Opinion and Congressional Behavior – Re-examination of Miller–Stokes Representation Data." *American Journal of Political Science* 22(3): 511–35.

Faccio, M. 2006. "Politically Connected Firms." *The American Economic Review* 96: 369–86.

Fehr, E., and U. Fischbacher. 2003. "The Nature of Human Altruism." *Nature* October: 785–91.

Fenno, R.F. 1973. *Congressmen in Committees*. Boston: Little, Brown.

Ferguson, T., and H. Voth. 2008. "Betting on Hitler – The Value of Political Con-nections in Nazi Germany." *Quarterly Journal of Economics* 123: 101–37.

Fiorina, M.P. 1974. "Representatives, Roll Calls, and Constituencies." Lexington, MA: Lexington Books.

Fisman, R. 2001. "Estimating the Value of Political Connections." *The American Economic Review* 91: 1095–1102.

"Focused NPC Study Session in Hunan" [*zai xiang quanguo renda daibiao jizhong xuexi*]. 2009. *Hunan Daily*. www.npc.gov.cn/npc/xinwen/dbgz/dbhd/ 2009-03/02/content_1482466.htm. [in Chinese]

Forsythe, M. 2014a. "Hong Kong Lawmaker Pays Price for Breaking Ranks with Beijing." *The New York Times*. www.nytimes.com/2014/10/29/world/asia/ james-tien-hong-kong-expulsion.

Forsythe, M. 2014b. "Pro-Beijing Lawmaker Urges Hong Kong Leader to Con-sider Quitting." *The New York Times*. www.nytimes.com/2014/10/25/world/ asia/James-Tien-says-Leung-Chun-ying-should-think-about-quitting.

Frey, B.S. 1994. "How Intrinsic Motivation Is Crowded Out and In." *Rationality and Society* 6: 334–52.

Frey, B.S. and F. Oberholzer-Gee. 1997. "The Cost of Price Incentives: An Empir-ical Analysis of Motivation Crowding-Out." *American Economic Review* 87(4): 746–55.

"From Little Things Big Things Grow." 2011. The Economic Observer. Beijing.

Gailmard, S., and J.W. Patty. 2012. "Formal Models of Bureaucracy." *Annual Review of Political Science* 15: 353–77.

Gandhi, J. 2008. *Political Institutions under Dictatorship*. New York: Cambridge University Press.

Gandhi, J., and A. Przeworski. 2007. "Authoritarian Institutions and the Survival of Autocrats." *Comparative Political Studies* 40: 1279–301.

Geddes, B., J. Wright, and E. Frantz. 2012. "New Data on Autocratic Regimes." Working Paper, Department of Political Science, Penn State University.

Gelman, A., and J. Hill. 2007. *Data Analysis Using Regression and Multi-level/Hierarchical Models*. Cambridge: Cambridge University Press.

Gerber, A. 1998 "Estimating the Effect of Campaign Spending on Senate Election Outcomes using Instrumental Variables." *American Political Science Review* 92(2): 401–11.

Gerber, E.R., and J.B. Lewis. 2004. "Beyond the Median: Voter Preferences, District Heterogeneity, and Political Representation." *Journal of Political Economy* 112(6):1364–83.

Gerring, J. 2007. "Is There a Viable Crucial-Case Method?" *Comparative Political Studies* 40(3): 231–53.

Gibson, J.L. 1992. "The Political Consequences of Intolerance: Cultural Conformity and Political Freedom." *American Political Science Review* 86: 338–56.

Gilley, B. 2005. *China's Democratic Future: How It Will Happen and Where It Will Lead*. New York: Cambridge University Press.

Gilligan, T.W., and K. Krehbiel. 1990. "Organization of Informative Committees by a Rational Legislature." *American Journal of Political Science* 34(2): 531–64.

Goldman, R. 1962. "The Rectification Campaign at Peking University: May–June 1957." *The China Quarterly* 12: 138–53.

Grimmer, J., and B.M. Stewart. 2013. "Text as Data: The Promise and Pitfalls of Automatic Content Analysis Methods for Political Texts." *Political Analysis* 21(3): 267–97.

Grossman, G., and E. Helpman. 1994. "Protection for Sale." *The American Economic Review* 84(4): 833–50.

Hainmueller, J. 2012. "Entropy Balancing for Causal Effects: A Multivariate Reweighting Method to Produce Balanced Samples in Observational Studies." *Political Analysis* 20: 25–46.

He, B., and M.E. Warren. 2011. "Authoritarian Deliberation: The Deliberative Turn in Chinese Political Development." *Perspectives on Politics* 9(2): 269–89.

"Hepatitis B Carriers Call for Equal Rights." 2012. *China Daily USA*. http://usa.chinadaily.com.cn/china/2012-07/28/content_15627950.htm.

Ho, D.E. et al. 2007. "Matching as Nonparametric Preprocessing for Reducing Model Dependence in Parametric Causal Inference." *Political Analysis* 15(3): 199–236.

Houn, F. 1955. "Communist China's New Constitution." *The Western Political Science Quarterly* 8(2): 199–233.

Hou, Y. 2015. "Private Entrepreneurs, Legislatures, and Property Protection in China." Paper Presented at the Annual Conference of the Midwest Political Science Association, Chicago.

Hu, S. 1993. "Representation without Democratization: The 'Signature Incident' and China's National People's Congress." *Journal of Contemporary China* 2(2): 3–34.

Huang, Y.S. 1995. "Administrative Monitoring in China." *The China Quarterly* 143: 828–843.

"Hu Jiwei: A Member of the Standing Committee of the National People's Congress, Is Removed." 1990. Xinhua News Agency.

Hurley, P.A., and K.Q. Hill. 2003. "Beyond the Demand-Input Model: A Theory of Representational Linkages." *Journal of Politics* 65(2): 304–26.

Iacus, S.M., G. King, and G. Porro. 2012. "Causal Inference without Balance Checking: Coarsened Exact Matching." *Political Analysis* 20(1): 1–24.

"Ice and Snow Won't Break Our Backs" [*bingxueya bukua jiliang*]. 2008. China News Service. [in Chinese]

"It Is Necessary to Persist in and Perfect the System of the People's Congress." 1990. Xinhua News Agency.

Jackson, J.E., and D.C. King. 1989. "Public–Goods, Private Interests, and Representation." *American Political Science Review* 83(4): 1143–64.

Jayachandran, S. 2006. "The Jeffords Effect." *Journal of Law and Economics* 49: 397–425.

Jiang, J.S. 2003. *The National People's Congress of China*. Beijing: Foreign Languages Press.

Jiang, T.S., Lu, X.J., Bao, T., and Y.S. Zhu 2001. "Thinking about the Role of Deputies" [*rendadaibiao fahui zuoyong wenti de diaocha yu sikao*]. *People's Congress Research* 12: 21–23. [in Chinese]

"Jiangxi High–End Talent to Play the Role of Promoting the Development of High–Tech Industries" [*jiangxisheng fahui gaoduan rencai zuoyong cujin gaoxin jishu change fazhan*]. 2008. China Economic Information Net. [in Chinese]

"Jiangxi Provincial Government and CNNC Signed a Number of Cooperation Agreements" [*jiangxi shengzhengfu yu zhonghejitua qianmeng duoxiang hezuo xieyi*]. 2009. China Economic Information Net. [in Chinese]

"Jiangxi Province Party Secretary: Worried about the Next Year to Promote Farmers' Income" [*jiangxisheng weishuji youxin mingnian nongmin zengshou wenti*]. 2008. China News Service. [in Chinese]

"Jiangxi: Strong Support for the Return of Migrant Workers" [*jiangxi dali zhichi fanxiang nongmingong chuanye*]. 2009. China Economic Information Net. [in Chinese]

Jiang, W. 2004. "Who Do People's Deputies Represent?" [*renda daibiao diabiao shei*]. People's Congress Research. [in Chinese]

Johnson, S., and T. Mitton. 2003. "Cronyism and Capital Controls: Evidence from Malaysia." *Journal of Financial Economics* 67: 351–82.

Kalt, J.P., and M.A. Zupan. 1984. "Capture and Ideology in the Economic Theory of Politics." *American Economic Review* 74(3): 279–300.

Kamo, T., and H. Takeuchi. 2013. "Representation and Local People's Congresses in China: A Case Study of the Yangzhou Municipal People's Congress." *Journal of Chinese Political Science* 18(1): 41–60.

Kennedy, S. 2008. *The Business of Lobbying In China*. Cambridge, MA: Harvard University Press.

King, G., C. Murray, J. Salomon, and A. Tandon. 2004. "Enhancing the Validity and Cross-Cultural Comparability of Measurement in Survey Research." *American Political Science Review* 98: 191–207.

King, G., J. Pan, and M. Roberts. 2013. "How Censorship in China Allows Government Criticism but Censors Collective Expression." *American Political Science Review* 107(2): 326–43.

King, G., M. Tomz, and J. Wittenberg. 2000. "Making the Most of Statistical Analysis: Improving Interpretation and Presentation." *American Journal of Political Science* 44(2): 341–55.

Krehbiel, K. 1993. "Constituency Characteristics and Legislative Preferences." *Public Choice* 76(1–2): 21–37.

Krehbiel, K. 1992. *Information and Legislative Organization.* Ann Arbor: The University of Michigan Press.

Kristoff, N. 1990. "China's Premier Urges Tighter Control." *The New York Times,* 21 March 1990.

Kuan, H. 1984. "New Departures in China's Constitution." *Studies in Comparative Communism* 17(1): 53–68.

Kuklinski, J.H. 1978. "Representativeness and Elections: A Policy Analysis." *American Political Science Review* 72: 165–77.

Kuran, T. 1991. "Now Out of Never: The Element of Surprise in the East European Revolution of 1989." *World Politics* 44(1): 7–48.

Landry, P.F. 2008. *Decentralized Authoritarianism in China: The Communist Party's Control of Local Elites in the Post-Mao Era.* Cambridge: Cambridge University Press.

Landry, P.F., D. Davis, and S. Wang. 2010. "Elections in Rural China: Competition without Parties." *Comparative Political Studies* 43(6): 763–90.

"Lawmakers Satisfying Constituencies," 2012. Xinhua. http://news.xinhuanet .com/english/china/2012-02/26/c_122756017.htm.

Lax, J.R., and J.H. Phillips. 2009a. "Gay Rights in the States: Public Opinion and Policy Responsiveness." *American Political Science Review* 103(3): 367–86.

Lax, J.R., and J.H. Phillips. 2009b. "How Should We Estimate Public Opinion in the States ?" *American Journal of Political Science* 53(1): 107–21.

Lei, C. 2012. "Opinion 2: On the Prohibition of 'Liver Disease Advertisements" [*guanyu quanmian jinzhi ganbing guanggao*]. Lei Chuang Personal Blog.

Leng, S.C. 1977. "The Role of Law in the People's Republic of China as Reflecting Mao Tse-Tung's Influence." *Journal of Criminal Law and Criminology* 68(3): 356–73.

Lepper, M.R., and D. Green (eds). 1978. *The Hidden Costs of Reward: New Perspectives on the Psychology of Human Motivation.* New York: Erlbaum.

Levi, M. 2002. "Modeling Complex Historical Processes with Analytic Narratives." In *Akteure, Mechanismen, Modelle: Zur Theoriefähigkeit Makrosozialer Analysen,* ed. Renate Mayntz, 108–27. Frankfurt/Main: Campus Verlag.

Levitsky, S., and L.A. Way. 2010. *Competitive Authoritarianism: The Origins and Evolution of Hybrid Regimes in the Post-Cold War Era.* New York: Cambridge University Press.

Levitt, S.D. 1996. "How Do Senators Vote? Disentangling the Role of Voter Preferences, Party Affiliation, and Senator Ideology." *American Economic Review* 86(3): 425–41.

Levitt, S.D. 1994. "Using Repeat Challengers to Estimate the Effect of Campaign Spending on Election Outcomes in the U.S. House." *Journal of Political Economy* 102(4): 777–98.

Lewis-Beck, M.S., W. Tang, and N.F. Martini. 2013. "A Chinese Popularity Function: Sources of Government Support." *Political Research Quarterly* 67(1): 16–25.

Li, A. 2013. "Failed Hunan People's Congress Candidate Admits to Bribing 32 Delegates." South China Morning Post. http://www.scmp.com/news/china/article/1138511/failed-hunan-peoples-congress-candidate-admits-bribing-32-delegates.

Li, J.S. 2013. "Won't Have Been Representative in Vain if Able to Solve Problems" [neng jiejue wenti jiu mei baidang daibiao]. [in Chinese]

Li, L. 2004. "Political Trust in Rural China." *Modern China* 30: 228–58.

Li, Z.R. 2015. "Listen to the 'Rubber Stamps': Legislative Cooperation in an Authoritarian Congress." Paper Presented at 2015 Meeting of the American Political Science Association.

Linz, J.J. 2000. *Totalitarian and Authoritarian Regimes*. New York: Lynne Rienner Publishers.

Liu, Y.G., and W. He. 2009. 'NPC Deputy Wang Lin: NPC Deputies Are Not Senators" [quanguo renda daibiao wanglin: daibiao bushi canyiyuan]. People's Daily. [in Chinese]

Liu, W. 2014. "Motions From the Two Sessions, How Are They Handled?" [lianghui yian, tian ruhe chuli]. Global People Editorial Email. [in Chinese]

Lorentzen, P. 2011. "Flying Blind: Authoritarian Political Cycles." Working Paper, University of California, Berkeley.

Lorentzen, P. 2014. "China's Strategic Censorship." *American Journal of Political Science* 58(2): 402–14.

Lorentzen, P. 2013a. "Designing Contentious Politics." Paper Presented at the Annual Conference of the American Political Science Association.

Lorentzen, P. 2013b. "Regularized Rioting: Permitting Public Protest in an Authoritarian Regime." *Quarterly Journal of Political Science* 8(2): 127–58.

Lublin, D.I. 1994. "Quality, Not Quantity: Strategic Politicians in U.S. Senate Elections, 1952–1990." *The Journal of Politics* 56(1): 228–41.

Lucas, C., R. Nielsen, M.E. Roberts, B.M. Stewart, A. Storer, and D. Tingley. 2015. "Computer Assisted Text Analysis for Comparative Politics." *Political Analysis* 23(2): 254–77.

Lu, J. 2006. "The Root Reason and Solutions about Discrimination against Hepatitis B in Mainland China." Beijing Yirenping.

MacFarquhar, R. 1960. *The Hundred Flowers Campaign and the Chinese Intellectuals*. New York: Praeger.

MacFarquhar, R., and M. Schoenhals. 2006. *Mao's Last Revolution*. Cambridge: Cambridge University Press.

Madison, J., A. Hamilton, and J. Jay [1788] 1987. *The Federalist Papers*, ed. I. Kramnick. New York: Penguin Books.

Magaloni, B. 2008. "Credible Power-Sharing and the Longevity of Authoritarian Rule." *Comparative Political Studies* 41(4–5): 715–41.

Malesky, E., and J. London. 2014. "The Political Economy of Development in China and Vietnam." *Annual Review of Political Science* 17: 395–419.

Malesky, E., and P. Schuler. 2010. "Nodding or Needling: Analyzing Delegate Responsiveness in an Authoritarian Parliament." *American Political Science Review* 104: 482–502.

Malesky, E., P. Schuler, and A. Tran. 2012. "The Adverse Effects of Sunshine: A Field Experiment on Legislative Transparency in an Authoritarian Assembly." *American Political Science Review* 106: 762–86.

Manin, B. 1997. *The Principles of Representative Government.* Cambridge: Cambridge University Press.

Manion, M. 2014. "Authoritarian Parochialism: Local Congressional Representation in China." *The China Quarterly* 218: 311–38.

Manion, M. 2000. "Chinese Democratization in Perspective: Electorates and Selectorates at the Township Level." *The China Quarterly* 163: 764–82.

Manion, M. 2011. "Congresses with Constituents, Constituents without Congresses: Representation for Authoritarian Rule in China." Working Paper. University of Wisconsin – Madison.

Manion, M. 2006. "Democracy, Community, Trust: The Impact of Elections in Rural China." *Comparative Political Studies* 39(3): 301–24.

Manion, M. (forthcoming) "'Good Types' in Authoritarian Elections: The Selectoral Connection in Chinese Local Congresses. *Comparative Political Studies*: DOI 0010414014537027.

Manion, M. 2008. "When Communist Party Candidates Can Lose, Who Wins? Assessing the Role of Local People's Congresses in the Selection of Leaders in China." *The China Quarterly* 195: 607–30.

Mayhew, D.R. 1974. *Congress: The Electoral Connection.* New Haven, CT: Yale University Press.

McCrone, D.J., and J. H. Kuklinski. 1979. "The Delegate Theory of Representation." *American Journal of Political Science* 23(2): 278–300.

McCrone, D.J., and W.J. Stone. 1986. "The Structure of Constituency Representation: On Theory and Method." *Journal of Politics* 48: 956–76.

McDonagh, E.L. 1993. "Constituency Influence on House Roll-Call Votes in the Progressive Era, 1913–1915." *Legislative Studies Quarterly* 18(2): 185–210.

McGeary, K. 2012. "NPC Official Runs Down Senior in Crosswalk, Flashes Government Badge Before Taking Off." 14 January 2012. https://thenanfang.com/another-official-shows-arrogance-and-inconsideration-while-driving/. In thenanfang.com.

McGuire, M.C., and M. Olson. 1996. "The Economics of Autocracy and Majority Rule: The Invisible Hand and the Use of Force." *Journal of Economic Literature* 34: 72–96.

Merli, M.G. 1998. "Underreporting of Births and Infant Deaths in Rural China: Evidence from Field Research in One County of Northern China." *The China Quarterly* 155: 637–55.

Miller, W.E., and D.E. Stokes. 1963. "Constituency Influence in Congress." *American Political Science Review* 57(1): 45–56.

Miller, G., and T.M. Moe. 1983. "Bureaucrats, Legislators, and the Size of Government." *American Political Science Review* 77(2): 297–322.

"Ministry of Railways Jiangxi Development Plans" [*tiedaobu jiangxisheng zai motilu fazhan daji*]. 2008. China News Service. [in Chinese]

Moon, B.E., and W.J. Dixon. 1985. "Politics, the State, and Basic Human Needs: A Cross-National Study." *American Journal of Political Science* 29(4): 661–94.

Mu, C.S. 2012. "China's Tone Deaf Officials." The Diplomat 24 January 2012.

Munck, G.L., and J. Verkuilen. 2002. "Conceptualizing and Measuring Democracy: Evaluating Alternative Indices." *Comparative Political Studies* 35(1): 5–34.

Myerson, R.B. 2008. "The Autocrat's Credibility Problem and Foundations of the Constitutional State." *American Political Science Review* 102: 125–39.

Nathan, A. 2003. "Authoritarian Resilience." *Journal of Democracy* 14(1): 6–17.

"The National People's Congress: What Makes a Rubber Stamp." 2012. Analects Blog: The Economist. http://www.economist.com/blogs/analects/2012/03/national-peoples-congress.

"New National Legislature Sees More Diversity." 2013. Xinhua. http://www.npc.gov.cn/englishnpc/news/Focus/2013-02/27/content_1759084.htm.

"Nine Deputies Respond to 'Anti-Hepatitis B Discrimination'" [*9 ming rendadaibiao huiying 'fanyiganqishi'*]. 2013. [in Chinese]

Niskanen, W. 1971. *Bureaucracy and Representative Government.* Chicago: Aldine Atherton.

Niu, B.L. 2011. "Hepatitis B Discrimination in China." *Atrium Magazine.* http://www.atrium-magazine.com/2011/03/hepatitis-b-discrimination-in-china/.

Noble, B. 2015. "Rethinking 'Rubber Stamps': Amending Executive Bills in the Russian State Duma, 2003–2013." Paper prepared for the 2015 annual conference of the Midwest Political Science Association, Chicago, 16–19 April.

"NPC Deputy Zhou Hongyu." 2007. CRIEnglish 10 March 2007.

"NPC Deputy Wants to 'Study Representation'" [*quanguo renda daibiao yao zuo "xuexixing daibiao*]. 2008. *The People's Daily.* http://paper.people.com.cn/rmrb/html/2008-04/18/content_48354281.htm. [in Chinese]

"NPC Session Successful: Wu Bangguo." 2003. The People's Daily 18 March 2003.

"NPC Standing Committee to Supervise Coal Mine Safety Inspections." 2005. Congressional Executive Commission on China. http://www.cecc.gov/publications/commission-analysis/npc-standing-committee-to-supervise-coal-mine-safety-inspections.

"NPC's Inspections Confirm Progress in Protecting People's Welfare." 2012. Xinhua. http://www.china.org.cn/china/NPC_CPPCC_2012/2012-03/09/content_24853245.htm.

O'Brien, K.J. 1988. China's National People's Congress: Reform and Its Limits. *The China Quarterly* 13(3): 343–74.

O'Brien, K.J. 1990. *Reform without Liberalization: China's National Congress and the Politics of Institutional Change.* New York: Cambridge University Press.

O'Brien, K.J. 1994. "Agents and Remonstrators: Role Accumulation by Chinese People's Congress Deputies." *The China Quarterly* 138: 359–80.

O'Brien, K.J., and L. Li. 1993. Chinese Political Reform and the Question of "Deputy Quality." *China Information* 8(3): 20–31.

O'Brien, K.J., and L. Li. 2006. *Rightful Resistance in Rural China.* Cambridge: Cambridge University Press.

Osnos, E. 2009. "Where Is Xu Zhiyong?" Letter from China: *The New Yorker* 31 July 2009.

Paler, L. 2005. "China's Legislation Law and the Making of a More Orderly and Representative Legislative System." *The China Quarterly* 182: 301–18.

Pan, J., and Y. Xu. 2015. "China's Ideological Spectrum." Working Paper, MIT and Stanford University.

Park, D., A. Gelman, and J. Bafumi. 2004. "Bayesian Multilevel Estimation with Poststratification: State-Level Estimates from National Polls." *Political Analysis* 12(4): 375–85.

Patty, J.W. 2009. "The Politics of Biased Information." *Journal of Politics* 71(2): 385–97.

"(Pay Attention to Snow Disaster): Jiangxi Reduce Spring Festival Visitation" [*(guanzhu xuezai): jiangxi jianjie chunjie zoufang weiwen huodong*]. 2008. Xinhua. [in Chinese]

Pei, M.X. 2010. "China's Revolutionary Hope?" The Diplomat 15 March 2010.

Peltzman, S. 1984. "Constituent Interest and Congressional Voting." *Journal of Law and Economics* 27(1): 181–210.

"People's Congress Deputy Training Materials" [*renda daibiao peixun xuexi cailiao*]. 2011. Distributed by Lufeng Township, Fujian Province. [in Chinese]

"The People Elected Me to Serve as a Representative, I Serve as a Representative for the People" [*renmin xuan wo dang daibiao, wo dang daibiao wei renmin*]. 2012. Distributed by Dafeng City, Jiangsu Province. [in Chinese]

Pepinsky, T. 2014. "The Institutional Turn in Comparative Authoritarianism." *British Journal of Political Science* 44(3): 631–53.

Percival, G.L., M. Johnson, and M. Neiman. 2009. "Representation and Local Policy Relating County-Level Public Opinion to Policy Outputs." *Political Research Quarterly* 62(1): 164–77.

Pitkin, H. 1967. *The Concept of Representation*. Berkeley: University of California Press.

Przeworski, A. (Ed.). 2000. *Democracy and Development: Political Institutions and Well-Being in the World, 1950–1990*. Cambridge: Cambridge University Press.

Pool, I.S., R.P. Abelson, and S. Popkin. 1965. *Candidates, Issues, and Strategies*. Cambridge: MIT Press.

Poole, K.T., and H. Rosenthal. 1984. "The Polarization of American Politics." *Journal of Politics* 46(4): 1061–79.

Poole, K.T., and H. Rosenthal. 1985. "A Spatial Model for Legislative Roll Call Analysis." *American Journal of Political Science* 29(2): 357–84.

Presser, S., and L. Stinson. 1998. "Data Collection Mode and Social Desirability Bias in Self-Reported Religious Attendance." *American Sociological Review* 63(1): 137–145.

"Prof a Student of Zeal." 2011. China Daily 11 March 2011.

Putnam, R.D., R. Leonardi, and R.Y. Nanetti. 1994. *Making Democracy Work: Civic Traditions in Modern Italy*. Princeton, NJ: Princeton University Press.

Querubin, P., and J.M. Snyder. 2008. "The Rents to Political Office in the U.S., 1840–1870." Massachusetts Institute of Technology. Manuscript.

Reuter, O.J., and J. Gandhi. 2010. "Economic Performance and Elite Defection from Hegemonic Parties." *British Journal of Political Science.* 41: 83–110.

Roberts, B. 1990. "A Dead Senator Tells No Lies: Seniority and the Distribution of Federal Benefits." *American Journal of Political Science* 34: 31–58.

Roberts, M.E., B.M. Stewart, and D. Tingley. 2015 "stm: R Package for Structural Topic Models." Working Manuscript. http://structuraltopicmodel.com/.

Rowen, H.S. 1996. "The Short March: China's Road to Democracy." *National Interest*: 61–70.

Rowen, H.S., M. Pei, and D. Yang. 2007. "When Will the Chinese People Be Free?" *Journal of Democracy* 18(3): 38–63.

Rui, G. 2012. "Opinion Divided on Way to Better School Bus Service." China Daily 12 March 2012.

Seawright, J., and J. Gerring. 2008. "Case Selection Techniques in Case Study Research: A Menu of Qualitative and Quantitative Options." *Political Research Quarterly* 61(2): 294–308.

Schulze, G., and B. Frank. 2003. "Deterrence Versus Intrinsic Motivation: Experimental Evidence on the Determinants of Corruptibility." *Economics of Governance* 4: 143–60.

Selb, P., and S. Munzert. 2011. "Estimating Constituency Preferences from Sparse Survey Data Using Auxiliary Geographic Information." *Political Analysis* 19(4): 455–70.

Shang, J. 2013. "On Guard Against Spillover of Irresponsible U.S. Politics." Xinhua. http://news.xinhuanet.com/english/indepth/2013-10/02/c_132768966 .htm.

Shepsle, K.A. 2006. "Rational Choice Institutionalism." In S. Binder, R. Rhodes, and B. Rockman, eds., *Oxford Handbook of Political Institutions*. Oxford: Oxford University Press, 23–39.

Shi, T. 2000. "Cultural Values and Democracy in Mainland China." *The China Quarterly* 162: 540–59.

Shi, M. 2007. "My Thoughts on Improving the Quality of People's Congress Deputies" [*tigao woguo rendadaibiao suzhi zhi wojian*]. *Journal of Heze University* 29(4): 10–16. [in Chinese]

Shi, X., and F. Kong. 2006. "Representative Democratic System and Reform the Rules and Improve the Chinese National People's Congress System [*daiyi minzhu de zhidu guize yu zhongguo quanguorenmindaibiaodaihui zhidu de gaige he wanshan*]. *Theory Monthly*: 9. [in Chinese]

Shih, V. 2008. "Nauseating Displays of Loyalty: Monitoring the Factional Bargain through Ideological Campaigns." *Journal of Politics* 70(4): 1177–92.

Shih, V., C. Adolph, and M. Liu. 2012. "Getting Ahead in the Communist Party: Explaining the Advancement of Central Committee Members in China." *American Political Science Review* 106: 166–87.

Smith, K.B. 2006. "Representational Altruism: The Wary Cooperator as Authoritative Decision Maker." *American Journal of Political Science* 50(4): 1013–22.

"State Committee on Films and Broadcast Media Halts Liver Disease Treatment and 55 Other Television Commercials" [*guangdianzongju jiaoting 'ganbing zhiliaoyi' deng 55 tiao dianshi guanggao*]. 2013. Xinhua Net. [in Chinese]

Stratmann, T. 2013. "The Effects of Earmarks on the Likelihood of Reelection." *European Journal of Political Economy* 32: 341–55.

Stockmann, D. 2012. *Media Commercialization and Authoritarian Rule in China.* Cambridge: Cambridge University Press.

"Su Rong: Accelerate Tourism Advantages into Industrial Advantages" [*jiakuai layout ziyan youshi zhuanhuawei chanye youshi*]. 2008. China News Service. [in Chinese]

"Su Rong: Play a Leading role in Supporting Science and Technology Innovation" [*surong: fahui kejide zhicheng yinling zuoyong*]. 2008. China News Service. [in Chinese]

Svolik, M.W. 2009. "Power Sharing and Leadership Dynamics in Authoritarian Regimes." *American Journal of Political Science* 53(2): 477–94.

Svolik, M.W. 2012. *The Politics of Authoritarian Rule.* New York: Cambridge University Press.

Szinovacz, M., and L.C. Egley. 1995. Comparing One-Partner and Couple Data on Sensitive Marital Behaviors: The Case of Marital Violence. *Journal of Marriage and Family* 57(4): 995–1010.

Tang, W. 2005. *Public Opinion and Political Change in China.* Stanford, CA: Stanford University Press.

Tanner, M.S. 1995. "How a Bill Becomes a Law in China: Stages and Processes in Lawmaking." *The China Quarterly* 141: 39–64.

Tanner, M.S. 1998. *The Politics of Lawmaking in Post-Mao China: Institutions, Processes, and Democratic Prospects.* Oxford: Oxford University Press.

Tanner, M.S. 2004. "China Rethinks Unrest." *The Washington Quarterly* 26(3): 138–46.

Thelen, K. 1999. "Historical Institutionalism in Comparative Politics." *Annual Review Political Science* 2: 369–404.

"This Year's Motions" [*jinnian de yian*]. 2010. Southern Weekly. http://www.infzm.com/content/42719.

Ting, M. 2003. "A Strategic Theory of Bureaucratic Redundancy." *American Journal of Political Science* 47(2): 274–92.

Titmuss, R.M. 1960. *The Gift Relationship.* London: Allen and Unwin.

"Top China Body Axes Hong Kong's James Tien for Criticism." 2014. BBC News. http://www.bbc.com/news/world-asia-china-29813847.

Truex, R. (forthcoming). "Consultative Authoritarianism and Its Limits." *Comparative Political Studies.*

Truex, R. 2014. "The Returns to Office in a 'Rubber Stamp' Parliament." *American Political Science Review* 108(2): 235–51.

Truex, R. 2015. "The Temporal Logic of Repression in China." Working Paper. Princeton University.

Tsai, L. 2007. *Accountability without Democracy: Solidary Groups and Public Goods Provision in Rural China.* New York: Cambridge University Press.

Tsai, L. 2012. "Exit as Voice: Regime-Reinforcing Noncompliance in Rural China." Working Paper. MIT.

Tucker, H.J., and Ronald E. Weber. 1987. "State Legislative Election Outcomes: Contextual Effects and Legislative Performance Effects." *Legislative Studies Quarterly* 12(4): 537–53.

Wallace, J. 2014. *Cities and Stability: Urbanization, Redistribution, and Regime Survival in China*. New York: Oxford University Press.

Wallace, J. (forthcoming). "Juking the Stats? Authoritarian Information Problems in China." *British Journal of Political Science*.

Wang, G.H. 1995. "Reflections on the Quality of China's Current People's Congress" [*dangqian woguo renda daibiao suzhi de jidian sikao*]. *Legal Research* 6: 39–42. [in Chinese]

Wang, Y. 2015. *Tying the Autocrat's Hands: The Rise of the Rule of Law in China*. Cambridge Studies in Comparative Politics. New York: Cambridge University Press.

Warshaw, C., and J. Rodden. 2012. "How Should We Measure District-Level Public Opinion on Individual Issues?" *Journal of Politics* 74(1): 203–19.

Weber, R.E., A.H. Hopkins, M.L. Mezey, and F. Munger. 1972–3. "Computer Simulation of State Electorates." *Public Opinion Quarterly* 36: 49–65.

Wilhelm, K. 1990. "Confident Premier Li Says Leadership is United, Strong." The Associated Press 5 April 1990.

Wright, G.C., R.S. Erikson, and J.P. McIver. 1985. "Measuring State Partisanship and Ideology with Survey Data." *Journal of Politics* 47: 469–89.

Wright, J. 2008. "Do Authoritarian Institutions Constrain? How Legislatures Affect Economic Growth and Investment." *American Journal of Political Science* 52(2): 322–43.

Wu, L.H. 2009. "Concentrated NPC Study Group in Anhui" [*zai wan quanguorendadaibiao jizhong xuexi*]. [in Chinese]

Wu, B. 2011. "Full Text: Work Report of the NPC Standing Committee." http://english.gov.cn/official/2011-03/18/content_1827230_5.htm.

Wu, B. 2013. "Full Text: Work Report of the NPC Standing Committee." http://news.xinhuanet.com/english/china/2013-03/20/c_132248271.htm.

Wu, J., J. Gyourko and Y.S. Deng. 2010. "Evaluating Conditions in Major Chinese Markets." NBER Working Paper Series 161–89.

Xiao, S.S. 2006. "Research on the Quality of the National People's Congress Deputies" [*renda daibiao suzhi yanjiu*]. People's Congress Research 12: 1–4. [in Chinese]

Xia, M. 2008. *The People's Congresses and Governance in China: Toward a Network Mode of Governance*. New York: Routledge.

Xie, W.Q. 2009. "NPC Deputy Zhu Guoping: Reflect the Aspirations of the Masses as Far as Possible" [*quanguo renda daibiao zhu guoping: jin keneng fanying qunzhong suqiu*]. [in Chinese]

Xie, X.W. 2003. "On Full-Time Deputies" [*lun woguo renda daibiao de zhuanzhihua*]. People's Congress Research 6: 4–7. [in Chinese]

"Xinjiang NPC Deputies Focused Study" [*xinjiang quanguo renda daibiao hui qian jizhong xuexi*]. 2009. The People's Daily. http://www.npc.gov.cn/npc/xinwen/dbgz/dbhd/2009-03/02/content_1482470.htm. [in Chinese]

Xu, Zhiyong. 2014. "For Freedom, Justice, and Love: My Closing Statement to the Court." http://chinachange.org/2014/01/23/for-freedom-justice-and-love-my-closing-statement-to-the-court/.

"Xu Zhiyong: On the New Citizens' Movement." 2013. China Digital Times. 13 May 2013.

Yin, P. 2014. "People's Democracy." *Beijing Review* 38.

Yin, S. 2014. "36 Hong Kong Deputies Issue Joint Declaration Supporting Police Action" [*xianggang 36 ming rendadaibiao fachu lianheshengming zhichi jingfang xingdong*]. People's Daily. news.qq.com/a/20141004/000994.htm.

Zhai, K. 2013. "Hunan Tycoon Discloses Attempt to Buy Seat on Provincial Congress." South China Morning Post. www.scmp.com/news/china/article/1138867/hunan-tycoon-discloses-attempt-buy-seat-provincial-congress.

Zhang, G. 2013. "Entrepreneur Bribes 320,000 Yuan to Become Provincial Deputy, Discloses Hidden Details After Losing" [*qiyejia wei dang shengrendadaibiao xinghui 32 wan, luoxuanhou jubao heimu*]. http://news.sohu.com/20130129/n364899010.shtml. [in Chinese]

Zhang, L. 2008. "Deputy Zheng Xinsui: Establishing a Unified Regulatory Body to Protect Water Quality in the South" [*zheng xinsui daibiao: baohu nanshui beidiaoshui yuanshui zhi jianli tongyi jianguan jigou*]. Beijing Times [*jinghua shibao*]. [in Chinese]

Zhang, Y.T., and Q.J. Wu. 2008. "Deputy Li Qingchang: Illuminate the Truth" [zhen qingdian liangwan jia denghuo]. [in Chinese]

Zhao, L. 2013. "Hunan Investigates Failed Election Bribery." China Daily 31 January 2013.

Zheng, C.P., and L.L. Sun. 2012. "Hepatitis B Activist Requests Attention from Deputies and Committee Members on Weibo, Multiple Respond" [*yigan doushi weiboshang xiang daibiao weiyuan qiu guanzhu, duowei weiyuan huiying*]. news.sohu.com.

Zhong, Y.J. Chen, and J. Scheb. 1998. "Mass Political Culture in Beijing: Findings from Two Public Opinion Surveys." *Asian Survey* 38(8): 763–783.

Index

Index

Cambridge Studies in Comparative Politics

Julia Lynch, *Age in the Welfare State: The Origins of Social Spending on Pensioner's Workers and Children*

Pauline Jones Luong, *Institutional Change and Political Continuity in Post-Soviet Central Asia*

Pauline Jones Luong and Erika Weinthal, *Oil is Not a Curse: Ownership Structure and Institutions in Soviet Successor States*

Doug McAdam, John McCarthy, and Mayer Zald, eds., *Comparative Perspectives on Social Movements*

Lauren M. MacLean, *Informal Institutions and Citizenship in Rural Africa: Risk and Reciprocity in Ghana and Côte d'Ivoire*

Beatriz Magaloni, *Voting for Autocracy: Hegemonic Party Survival and its Demise in Mexico*

James Mahoney, *Colonialism and Postcolonial Development: Spanish America in Comparative Perspective*

James Mahoney and Dietrich Rueschemeyer, eds., *Historical Analysis and the Social Sciences*

Scott Mainwaring and Matthew Soberg Shugart, eds., *Presidentialism and Democracy in Latin America*

Melanie Manion, *Information for Autocrats: Representation in Chinese Local Congresses*

Isabela Mares, *From Open Secrets to Secret Voting: Democratic Electoral Reforms and Voter Autonomy*

Isabela Mares, *The Politics of Social Risk: Business and Welfare State Development*

Isabela Mares, *Taxation, Wage Bargaining, and Unemployment*

Cathie Jo Martin and Duane Swank, *The Political Construction of Business Interests: Coordination, Growth, and Equality*

Anthony W. Marx, *Making Race, Making Nations: A Comparison of South Africa, the United States, and Brazil*

Bonnie M. Meguid, *Party Competition between Unequals: Strategies and Electoral Fortunes in Western Europe*

Joel S. Migdal, *State in Society: Studying How States and Societies Constitute One Another*

Joel S. Migdal, Atul Kohli, and Vivienne Shue, eds., *State Power and Social Forces: Domination and Transformation in the Third World*

Scott Morgenstern and Benito Nacif, eds., *Legislative Politics in Latin America*

Kevin M. Morrison, *Nontaxation and Representation: The Fiscal Foundations of Political Stability*

Layna Mosley, *Global Capital and National Governments*

Layna Mosley, *Labor Rights and Multinational Production*

Wolfgang C. Müller and Kaare Strøm, *Policy, Office, or Votes?*

Maria Victoria Murillo, *Political Competition, Partisanship, and Policy Making in Latin American Public Utilities*

Maria Victoria Murillo, *Labor Unions, Partisan Coalitions, and Market Reforms in Latin America*

Monika Nalepa, *Skeletons in the Closet: Transitional Justice in Post-Communist Europe*